Tom Rutherford
Sept. 1984
Madison, Wi.

HARVARD ECONOMIC STUDIES
Volume 156

The studies in this series are published under
the direction of the Department of Economics
of Harvard University. The department does not
assume responsibility for the views expressed.

# Modeling Japanese-American Trade

A Study of Asymmetric Interdependence

Peter A. Petri

HARVARD UNIVERSITY PRESS

Cambridge, Massachusetts, and London, England   1984

Library of Congress Cataloging in Publication Data

Petri, Peter A., 1946 –
    Modeling Japanese-American trade.

    (Harvard economic studies ; v. 156)
    Bibliography: p.
    Includes index.
    1. Japan — Commerce — United States — Mathematical
models.   2. United States — Commerce — Japan — Mathematical
models.   I. Title.   II. Series.
HF3828.U5P47   1984        382'.0952'0730724        83-26587
ISBN 0-674-57810-4

# Acknowledgments

Many people commented on this book in its various incarnations, and although they bear no responsibility for its weaknesses, they contributed greatly to its strengths. Particularly helpful were discussions with and suggestions by Anne Carter, H. S. Houthakker, Wassily Leontief, Ron Napier, Kazuo Sato, Masahiko Shimizu, and Jeffrey Williams. Also important was the generous, steady supply of unpublished information on the Japanese economy by Iwao Ozaki and Masahiro Kuroda. At various stages of the work, first-rate research assistance was provided by Rick Drost (who wrote the initial version of the general equilibrium solution program) and Franek Rozwadovsky. Valuable institutional support came from the Brandeis Computer Center and, for some parts of the study, from a grant by the Department of State.

# Contents

Modeling Japanese-American Trade

# 1 Objectives and Methods

Economists are not generally given to professional ebullience, but many who have studied the postwar Japanese economy have been tempted to use the term "miracle." No other major economy has demonstrated such high rates of saving, rapid technical progress, or agility in the face of external adversity as has the Japanese economy in the 1960s and 1970s. There were important virtuous circles at work: huge investments, sometimes exceeding 40 percent of national product, brought several major industries to the cutting edge of technology — and the resulting growth and productivity explosion rewarded investments with ample return. Progress was no less astonishing in Japan's external commerce, as chronic balance-of-payments problems gave way to politically embarrassing surpluses.

The core of these achievements remains mysterious; if there are simple reasons for Japanese success, they lie buried under lists of plausible, but individually less than compelling, explanations.[1] That this mystery remains is not for lack of effort: debates about the alternative causes of the miracle and about the transferability of the Japanese model to the United States have dominated recent research on Japan. The special objective of this research — to somehow differentiate Japanese experience from that of other, less successful economies — has given it a distinctly institutional, historical, and psychological flavor. In this context

it is easy to lose sight of the fact that today's Japanese economy behaves, in many important respects, like any other major industrial economy.

Whatever the organizational background of miraculous growth, the Japanese economy is now too large and too sophisticated to be thought of as "Japan, Incorporated." Japanese imports are no longer controlled by an omniscient central agency, and, as elsewhere, they respond to such determinants as prices, consumption and investment expenditure, and interindustry demand. The Japanese do protect their markets, but this too fails to distinguish them from other modern economies and can be understood in terms of conventional economic variables. And although Japanese capital accumulation and technical progress are still enviable by world standards, some of the large, unexplained residuals associated with earlier stages of Japanese growth have markedly diminished.[2]

The premise of this book is that the understanding of Japanese-American economic linkages can be significantly advanced with the tools of modern trade theory. This does not mean that the two economies are somehow treated as identical; on the contrary, some of the most interesting features of the trading relationship turn on major structural differences between the American and Japanese economies. In its general form, trade theory provides ample scope for analyzing the effects of country-to-country differences in variables such as technology, tastes, production structure, and factor endowments. One indication that this approach may be on the right track is that trade conflict between the United States and Japan turns out to make a good deal of sense in its analytical context.

This book, then, is not about the causes of the miracle but about its effects on the Japanese-American economic relationship. It examines, in rigorous, quantitative detail, the structure of interdependence, that is, how events in one economy influence the operation of the other. It looks at the evolution of interdependence over time and traces the causes of the increasing intensity of the bilateral relationship. It also looks at the sectoral dimension of interdependence — at the patterns beneath changes in the composition of trade, and at the complex

factors that determine how the individual sectors of each economy respond to economic changes in the other.

Understanding the structure of interdependence is crucial too for examining the policy conflicts that have plagued Japanese-American trade since the early 1960s. At first the crises were highly product-specific; the items involved — stainless steel flatware, women's blouses — were unimportant in the general context of the American market and mattered mainly because of their highly focused impact on specific industries.[3] But gradually the sectors in question became larger and more central to the American economy — sectors such as steel, consumer electronics, and automobiles. By the late 1970s the conflict had spread to so many products and issues that it could be understood only as conflict over bilateral trade as a whole. The structural determinants of bilateral trade and the reasons that explain its prominence in policy debate are among the issues addressed by this book.

## Bilateral Trade as an Object of Analysis

Bilateral trade is not a conventional topic of economic analysis. The major neoclassical theories of international trade do not explain bilateral trade at all (Leontief, 1973). If transport costs are small, bilateral trade patterns are indeterminate and could, for example, involve the exports of capital-intensive products from a labor-intensive to a capital-intensive economy (Baldwin, 1971). The only aspect of trade predicted by theory is the pattern of a country's overall trade, or more precisely, the net factor content embodied in this trade (Leamer, 1980). In the context of the conventional model, then, bilateral protection is likely to have no effect at all; world production and consumption can remain unchanged while trade is "rerouted" around the tariff-ridden bilateral link.

Precisely because of its inability to explain the intrasectoral and bilateral aspects of actual trade, the conventional approach has given way, in recent years, to models that treat the products of different countries as imperfect substitutes. In the context of this modern approach — the theoretical basis of this book — bi-

lateral trade does matter; indeed, bilateral intervention affects not only the countries directly involved, but to a greater or lesser extent all participants of the integrated global economy. If, say, Japanese cars are excluded from American markets, they do not simply find compensating markets in Europe, to be replaced in the United States by German cars. To be sure, all this happens, but only to a limited extent, and not without changes in exchange rates, specialization patterns, and the international distribution of income.

The structure of bilateral trade is important, then, because it affects the pattern of international adjustment and the transmission of economic disturbances from one country to another. It is also prominent as an object of policy: intervention in bilateral trade can substantially affect the distribution of the gains from trade between partner economies. The extent to which such intervention is possible or profitable depends on the volume and structure of bilateral trade. Indeed, Vernon (1981) has recently argued that, for a variety of reasons, future trade negotiations will be increasingly conducted on a discriminatory, bilateral basis.

The policy importance of Japanese-American bilateral trade needs little emphasis. For example, a balanced and analytically sophisticated congressional report starts its discussion by observing: "We went to Japan to deliver a message, as clearly as possible, that the unacceptable trade imbalance of about $12 billion in 1978 between Japan and the United States is creating pressures in the American Congress for protectionist legislation. We went as long-time supporters of free trade to report that the situation is urgent. The threat of restrictive legislation is the most serious in our experience in Congress" (Committee on Ways and Means, 1979, p. iv). There are many reasons for American concern with bilateral trade, but it is interesting to note that recent American political initiatives, including those advocated by the report just cited, have sought to increase U.S. exports to Japan rather than to limit imports. This suggests that American concern about bilateral trade is not wholly motivated by sectoral injury in the United States. The "problem" of the bilateral imbalance is, at least in part, a code name for dissatisfaction with the American terms of trade.

The fact that bilateral trade is sharply out of balance makes it a fulcrum of pressure for improving the U.S. terms of trade; Japan has far more to lose from a breakdown of trading relations than the United States. This key feature of the Japanese-American relationship—the effect of bilateral imbalance on the struggle for the gains from trade—is not widely recognized. Academic writers often dismiss the subject of imbalance in terms reminiscent of textbooks: "A bilateral imbalance of this nature reflects efficiency and patterns of comparative advantage, and [the restriction of bilateral trade] would be inconsistent with more fundamental policy priorities—controlling inflation, reducing unemployment, and maximizing economic prosperity" (Japan-United States Economic Relations Group, 1981b, p. 81). The argument is true, up to a point; efficient world specialization requires free and generally unbalanced bilateral trade. But intervention designed to appropriate the gains from trade may well be consistent with increased national prosperity. In analyzing the consequences of bilateral protection, this book seeks a clearer explanation of the economic forces behind the trade conflict.

Bilateral trade conflict does not take place in a vacuum. The political and military dimensions of the Japanese-American relationship are obviously important and doubtless cause both governments to downplay economic differences. In addition, bilateral economic policies have an international audience. A wide range of possible interventions are prohibited by international treaties, and blatant protectionism in bilateral trade would undermine American and Japanese arguments for freer world trade. Similarly, preferential bilateral access is restricted by most-favored-nation clauses; thus, even the positive actions the two governments might negotiate are limited by international law.

These broader aspects of the trade conflict—the repercussions of the resolution or intensification of the conflict on bilateral or international politics—are beyond the scope of this book. This is not because political issues are unimportant, but rather because they form a separable dimension of the problem—one that would require a wholly different methodological approach. My objective is to clarify the economic structure of the conflict

and to sketch the consequences of various types of policy actions. These purely economic questions are difficult enough and have not been adequately answered so far. But I cannot claim to contribute a complete analysis of the policy process, much less prescriptions for action on either side.


## Methodology

The main thrust of this book is substantive: to advance understanding of Japanese-American trade and the conflicts it generates. Nevertheless, this is a technical book. Its first half— and a much larger share of the research behind it — deals with the design and estimation of a multicountry, multisectoral general equilibrium model. The model does not merely illustrate general equilibrium effects with plausible parameters; it is implemented with painstaking estimates of the parameters that govern demand, production, and trade in the American and Japanese economies. In the second half of the book, the model becomes a laboratory for exploring various dimensions of interdependence and commercial policy.

A general equilibrium framework is essential for studying the determinants of trade as well as the consequences of intervention. Trade is the end product of production and consumption decisions in several economies; it reflects an interaction of technologies, consumption patterns, factor supplies, and a host of other factors and policies that affect relative prices. To understand why the structure of trade changes, or how it affects interdependence, all of these linkages must be considered. For similar reasons, general equilibrium effects are almost always important in the evaluation of trade policy, although these effects may be widely diffused over the various sectors of the economy.

The model developed for this study consists of twenty-sector, two-factor (capital and labor) general equilibrium submodels of the American and Japanese economies, solved alongside a rudimentary rest-of-the-world (ROW) "country." The core of each country's submodel is a system of input-output accounts. A good

deal of substitution is permitted in both production and consumption, and all of the consumption and input-output coefficients are determined by relative prices. Prices are endogenously calculated using the input-output dual (that is, by adding up input costs). In all but two sectors, trade is handled with Armington-type demand functions (Armington, 1969). Specifically, demand in each such sector is allocated to domestic and foreign producers in shares determined by relative product prices. In the remaining two sectors, agriculture and natural resources, prices are assumed to be determined in world markets, and each country's domestic production is specified as a function of the ratio of the world price (adjusted for protection) to average domestic production cost.

The model's relationships are intended to capture medium- to long-term responses to technical and structural change. Thus, no mechanisms are included to describe business cycles or the adjustment costs of moving from one equilibrium to another. The model has no financial sector; it is a pure trade model and explains only relative prices.

A solution of the model provides a snapshot of equilibrium at a given point in time; its main use is to show how this equilibrium responds to changes in parameters describing economic structure or policy. Most perturbations produce wide-ranging effects on U.S., Japanese, and rest-of-the-world variables; the system is highly interdependent. Many variables are computed in each solution, including output, price, and trade levels as well as indexes of real income and consumption. The model has been implemented for 1960, 1970, and 1980, permitting time-series comparisons of various simulated effects.

When this research began (Petri, 1976a, 1976b) there was little experience with comprehensive, closed general equilibrium models of this type, particularly in the area of international trade. Although a number of sophisticated models have been built since, general equilibrium modeling is still often treated as "theory with plausible numbers," and little is known about the structural features needed to represent economic behavior accurately. Some of the technical contributions of this book address the link between real behavior and model specification.

## Some Major Findings

It is difficult, in a book devoted largely to empirical results, to select "significant" findings; each estimate reported in the first half of the book and each experiment analyzed in the second half contributes its share to a general picture of Japanese-American trade. Nevertheless, it is useful to give a flavor of the analysis that follows by briefly reporting on two of the more significant results developed in subsequent chapters.

First, a variety of simulations indicate that the American and Japanese economies are a good deal more closely related than one might judge by the size of their trade. Bilateral trade, to be sure, is large; both the United States and Japan enjoy a relatively privileged access to each other's markets. Thus, U.S. shares of Japanese imports and Japanese shares of U.S. imports are about twice as high as these countries' shares in world markets. The bilateral trade imbalance, therefore, is not a result of Japanese discrimination against U.S. exports but rather a function of the overall commodity composition of U.S. and Japanese trade.

But the commodity composition of bilateral trade is even more significant than its size. An important feature of this composition was succinctly summarized by Philip Caldwell, the chairman of Ford: "Look at the types of trade between the U.S. and Japan: What is it that Japan has that we are vitally required to have? The answer is zero."[4] Since good domestic substitutes exist for most U.S. imports from Japan, this trade flow is much more price-elastic than other types of trade. It turns out, therefore, that any positive or negative adjustment of the U.S. current account is likely to cause — through exchange-rate adjustments or other means — a large opposite adjustment of the Japanese current account. The proportion of a typical U.S. adjustment that falls on Japan is, in fact, about three times as large as the share of Japanese bilateral trade in total U.S. trade.

Suppose, for example, that the U.S. current account is forced into deficit by a sharp increase in capital inflows. The structure of trade among the United States, Japan, and the rest of the world is such that a large part of the adjustment will consist of (1) increased Japanese exports to the United States and (2) losses of

third markets by U.S. producers to Japanese producers. (To a lesser extent, the same is true for Japanese adjustments.) Consequently, movements of U.S. and Japanese current accounts are unusually closely linked, especially in periods of adjustment and change. This relationship has been observed before and has generated its share of political conflict. It is now clear that it is fundamentally rooted in the structure of the two countries' trading relationship.

Another kind of finding, with equally important implications for the bilateral relationship, is that the terms-of-trade effects of intervention—particularly by the United States in bilateral trade—are surprisingly large when compared to efficiency effects. In other words, the struggle for the gains from trade is unlikely to be held in check, at least as far as the United States is concerned, by the potential loss of specialization benefits. Moreover, the terms-of-trade benefits associated with intervention seem to be growing with time. These inferences emerge from the changing commodity composition and elasticity structure of trade. If correct, they imply that the incentives for intervention are increasing, particularly for the carefully targeted and camouflaged variety that minimizes the risk of retaliation.

Several experiments were performed to assess the effects of intervention in bilateral trade. Many of these experiments generate welfare changes on a relatively significant scale. For example, U.S. protection that cuts the bilateral imbalance in half would generate U.S. gains of $2.6 billion and Japanese losses of $7.3 billion—on trade that involved (in 1980) $31.7 billion in Japanese exports and $20.8 billion in U.S. exports. In most experiments designed to reduce the bilateral imbalance, substantial gains accrue to third countries as the yen is forced to depreciate to replace export revenues lost in U.S. markets.

These experiments suggest that the stakes in intervention are large relative to the value of trade, and larger still when compared to specialization gains from trade. They also illustrate the particularly vulnerable position of bilteral trade, since the unilateral threats of intervention are of vastly unequal size. But the negative-sum nature of most protectionist options—due primarily to terms-of-trade losses to third countries, and not special-

ization effects—introduces an element of stability; it is in the mutual interest of the United States and Japan to settle trade disputes bilaterally rather than unilaterally.

The book is divided into two parts: Chapters 2–4 describe the structure and estimation of the model used, while Chapters 5–7 focus on substantive issues and present an extensive array of simulations and other related results. The appendixes provide additional information on data assembly and simulation details.

In the first part, Chapter 2 describes the basic theoretical assumptions of the model, presents its equation structure, and briefly describes its salient economic properties. Chapter 3 deals with the estimation of the market-share functions that govern the model's trade properties. The results presented in this chapter provide new, detailed trade equations for the various trading links connecting the United States, Japan, and the rest of the world. Chapter 4, which concludes the discussion of implementation, describes the algorithms used to solve the model and discusses its base solutions for 1960, 1970, and 1980.

In the second part of the book, Chapter 5 defines and analyzes interdependence, first through a statistical review of bilateral trade and then through simulations designed to measure various types of interaction. The historical evolution of interdependence is explored, with special emphasis on changes in the openness of the two economies. Chapter 6 reviews the sectoral dimensions of Japanese-American trade, starting with a time-series survey of the changing characteristics of trade over the 1960–1980 period. The chapter also presents new ideas concerning the factor content of Japanese-American trade and examines the complex sectoral linkages that connect the two economies. Chapter 7 is concerned with trade policy. Part of this analysis concentrates on the effects of present protection; another part examines a wide range of proposed alternatives. For example, the chapter reviews the results of a substantial opening of Japanese markets (negative for both Japan and the United States), as well as a range of policies that have recently been advanced to reduce the bilateral imbalance. Chapter 8 concludes by reviewing the implications of the study for model building and for the analysis and conduct of Japanese-American trade policy.

# 2 Theory and Structure

The principal tool of this book is a multisectoral, multicountry trade model. The theoretical structure of this model incorporates some major recent advances in the empirical analysis of trade and is general enough to accommodate many special features of the Japanese-American relationship. As subsequent chapters will show, the model has been carefully fitted to structural and time-series data about the two economies. But despite the flexibility of the model and its meticulous implementation, the results depend on basic theoretical assumptions. These assumptions are not picked arbitrarily or merely for theoretical elegance; they have evolved in the line of fire, so to speak, by replacing assumptions that proved unsatisfactory in past research.

The evolution of quantitative trade models is interesting in its own right. The history of trade theory is a case study in the scientific method; from its beginnings the field has witnessed a vital and productive interchange between theory and empirical analysis. Ricardo's pioneering work (1817) was based on a combination of theoretical and empirical arguments, and his numerical examples provide one of the earliest and cleverest examples of quantitative general equilibrium analysis. Trade theory continued to provide impetus for the development of general equilibrium theory, and it formed the basis for the initial applications of the empirical general equilibrium models that emerged in the 1950s and 1960s. Thus, Leontief's papers (1953, 1956) on the

factor content of U.S. trade represent one of the first substantive applications of input-output analysis, and Dorfman, Samuelson, and Solow's treatise (1958) on linear programming uses trade models extensively to demonstrate the principles of linear programming. These applications, in turn, led to significant revisions of trade theory itself.

The early programming examples of Dorfman, Samuelson, and Solow became prototypes for the first large-scale general equilibrium studies of trade in the 1960s, by Bruno (1966, 1967), Werin (1965), and others. As will be shown, models of this type had reached a high level of sophistication by the early 1970s, but their empirical performance remained unsatisfactory. Essentially, they predicted too much specialization. Ad hoc efforts to reduce specialization were not successful, and the problem eventually led to a new theoretical approach to trade modeling, generally credited to Armington's influential paper (1969) on products distinguished by place of production.

Empirical models incorporating Armington's assumption — that the products of different exporters are imperfect substitutes — followed in the mid-1970s. In this and other recent applications, Armington-type models have proved to be much more robust and reasonable than trade models constructed in the past. They are also flexible and interesting to use: results often run against intuition on the surface, only to reveal subtle but valid general equilibrium properties. These features make the model particularly attractive in analyzing policy changes that are suspected to have important second-order effects.

This chapter reviews the full mathematical specification of the model, starting with the origins of its critical assumptions. It concludes by examining the model's capabilities and limitations, and how its structure is likely to affect the results in the present substantive context. The implementation of the model is discussed in subsequent chapters.

## Empirical General Equilibrium Models of Trade

The first applications of empirical general equilibrium methods to international trade, principally by Leontief (1953, 1956), used the methodology as a way to examine observed trade patterns.

Models that actually predicted trade flows emerged in development planning. The development problem has continued to motivate the refinement of trade models to the present day, as documented by the surveys of Manne (1974), Taylor (1976), and (in a book that also contains many original contributions) Dervis, deMelo, and Robinson (1982).

Until the mid-1970s, development and trade models were typically based on an activity analysis framework. A good example of such a system is Bruno's model (1966, 1967) of the Israeli economy. Because of the openness of this economy, Bruno pays special attention to trade, although the model is mainly intended for planning. When stripped of some minor variables and relationships, the model reveals a simple structure common to a number of programming studies (see Table 2.1). For the purposes of this discussion, these models will be referred to as "first-generation" general equilibrium models of trade.

The activities of these first-generation models typically include sectoral production, export and import variables, and final con-

**Table 2.1**  Skeletal linear programming trade model

|  | max $\gamma$, subject to: |
|----|----|
| C1 | $(A - I)x + bv + c\gamma - m + x \le 0$ |
| C2 | $l'x \le L$ |
| C3 | $k'x - \theta v \le K$ |
| C4 | $p'm - p'e \le B$ |
|  | and $\quad x, v, \gamma, m, e \ge 0$ |

| Endogenous | Exogenous |
|----|----|
| $e$ = export vector | $A$ = input coefficient matrix |
| $m$ = import vector | $B$ = net external saving |
| $x$ = output vector | $b$ = investment composition |
| $v$ = investment level | $c$ = consumption composition |
| $\gamma$ = consumption level | $l$ = labor coefficients |
|  | $L$ = labor endowment |
|  | $k$ = capital coefficients |
|  | $K$ = capital endowment |
|  | $p$ = world price vector |
|  | $\theta$ = stock/flow conversion factor (approximately, number of years spanned by model) |

*Note:* Prime symbol indicates transpose.

sumption and investment. The investment activity absorbs the products of capital-good-producing sectors in proportions appropriate to new capital formation; its output is an incremental addition to the capital stock. Optimal production, trade, and investment levels are determined by maximizing the consumption activity at some future date. The constraints of the problem include sectoral supply and demand balances (C1 in Table 2.1) and limits on the overall use of labor (C2), capital (C3), and foreign exchange (C4). In an actual implementation, several types of labor may be distinguished; some products are excluded from trade while others are only available through trade.

The extent of specialization implied by this simple structure is great: domestic production is generally nonzero in only a few traded sectors — at most as many as there are primary factor constraints, as shown by McKenzie (1956). To prevent this, import and export levels are specifically limited by the constraints

$$\underline{m}_i < m_i < \overline{m}_i \quad \text{and} \quad \underline{e}_i < e_i < \overline{e}_i, \tag{2.1}$$

where  $m_i$ = imports in sector $i$,
$e_i$ = exports in sector $i$.

For each sector, the lower bound is set at the "1964 level, or some low rate of increase, and the upper bound is based on an assessment of past performance and expert advice" (Bruno, 1966, p. 334).

Werin's study (1965) of Swedish trade is similar to Bruno's, but it is specifically designed to analyze comparative advantage and therefore provides a detailed treatment of trade barriers. Transport costs are introduced as an input of international shipping services in each importing activity, and tariffs are handled by making importers buy fictitious government "services" along with each restricted foreign product. (This effectively assigns the government consumption bundle to the disposition of tariff revenue.) The careful treatment of trade barriers reduces the number of imported products but does not eliminate the problem of excessive specialization in trade. Following a strategy only slightly different from Bruno's, Werin imposes ceilings above and floors below domestic output levels. Given the rela-

tively rigid structure of demand in his model, these output constraints have roughly the same trade effects as Bruno's direct constraints on exports and imports.

Werin justifies ceilings on the assumption that the short-run nature of the model prevents the intersectoral reallocation of capital from its initial sectoral pattern. Formally,

$$\hat{k}x \leq K, \tag{2.2}$$

where  $\hat{k}$  = diagonalized vector of capital input coefficients,
$K$ = vector of sectoral capital endowments.

The floors are "intended to be approximate representations of friction and psychological barriers preventing a very rapid fall in production, of political and institutional measures having the same effect, and of the fact that the assumption of constant returns to scale in the utilization of the production process is somewhat too strict in many cases" (Werin, 1965, p. 76). Sector-specific floors and ceilings add many new constraints and reduce specialization. It is certainly true that output levels are subject to short-run capacity constraints. But can a model of this type also yield reasonable answers if its time horizon is lengthened and investment is permitted?

This question is answered negatively by the most sophisticated of the programming trade models, Evans' study (1972) of Australian commercial policy. Evans also uses sector-specific capital constraints but permits these constraints to be relaxed by capital accumulation, à la Bruno, over a ten-year period. Since the depreciation of plant and equipment is explicitly recognized, the constraints permit sectoral contraction as well as expansion. The range of output changes permitted is in fact so large that this model also needs additional constraints to keep trade in reasonable bounds. Ten years of capital formation, evidently, is sufficient to swamp the original trade pattern and to generate unacceptably specialized trade.

As experience with these first-generation trade models accumulated, it became clear that activity analysis models could not predict the magnitudes of trade flows without direct ad hoc restrictions. Proponents could and did argue that even if the

models were inaccurate, they generally gave plausible results for the direction of international specialization. But this too is doubtful: the programming framework requires hidden assumptions that largely determine the specialization patterns it generates. Essentially, it requires observations of international relative prices (for example, the price of U.S. steel relative to Japanese steel) to convert data from different countries into common international units.

Since direct information on international relative prices is not usually available,[1] they are typically estimated with an arbitrary, synthetic procedure (Evans, 1972, p. 69). All traded commodity groups are initially labeled as import or export goods. (If a country both imports and exports products of a given kind, the decision is based on the direction of net trade.) The domestic prices of exporting sectors are then set to world prices, and the prices of importing sectors to world prices plus tariffs and transport costs. The initial classification is thus quite important, because transport and tariff charges often involve markups of 25 percent or more. The estimated relative prices are then used to convert the products of different countries into "world" units. As a part of this translation, the input coefficients of importing activities are scaled up to compensate for the "small" units of the original data. When a model is set to work with such built-in cost differences, it cannot help but select imports and exports "reasonably," that is, from observed imports and exports.

By the early 1970s the shortcomings of the linear programming framework were widely recognized, and new approaches were being developed to address the specialization problem. A model built by Taylor and Black (1974) limits the extent of specialization by introducing diminishing returns in each production sector. This is accomplished by fixing sectoral capital availabilities; with labor variable, the optimal level of output and sectoral employment is determined by the sector's world price level and the wage rate. The model avoids specialized corner solutions because labor and capital are combined in flexible proportions, but in other respects it resembles Werin's model. It is essentially a short-run model, which would exhibit the specialization problems of the programming models if investment were permitted and the time horizon lengthened.

A second solution of the specialization problem, centering on the recognition that each trading sector is likely to include heterogeneous products, has led to a new generation of trade models. Actually, important features of the approach were present in a very early linear programming application but do not seem to have taken root until much later. The study, a paper by Chenery and Kretschmer (1956) on Italian reconstruction, appears to have been the first to address directly the issue of subsectoral heterogeneity.

Dealing with an economy short on capital, Chenery and Kretschmer pay special attention to intrasectoral differences in capital requirements. They assume that the commodities within each sector can be ranked by capital intensity, and that the sector's overall capital supply is allocated to commodities starting from the bottom of this scale. (All this has to be done conceptually, since no actual information is available on subsectoral detail.) These assumptions produce an unusual supply curve that traces average cost as a function of the sector's self-sufficiency ratio. Since constant returns to scale are assumed for each individual product, costs rise with market share but not with output increases that are just proportional to market growth. Quantitative guesses about the shapes of these supply curves are eventually used as nonlinear constraints in the programming problem. Thus the model avoids corner solutions, since the extremes of zero imports or zero production imply inappropriately high or low marginal capital input requirements.

This important paper left no lasting mark, probably for two reasons. First, linear programming offered a clumsy framework for solving models that typically produce interior solutions. Although activity analysis continues to be applied to nonlinear models of the same type (Ginsburgh and Waelbroeck, 1981), these applications are unnecessarily complicated to set up and solve. Second, and more important, Chenery and Kretschmer's theoretical framework was built on an intrasectoral structure that was very narrow in purpose and essentially impossible to estimate.

Operational models based on heterogeneous sectors were made practical by two subsequent developments. First, the art of designing and solving economy-wide models was sharply ad-

vanced by Johansen (1960, 1973). The novel feature of Johansen's approach, eventually widely adopted, was that it solved the primal (demand, output, trade) and dual (price) equations of equilibrium simultaneously as a single, nonlinear system. Later, an operational method for dealing with the problem of subsectoral detail was proposed by Armington (1969). Armington's key insight was to regard the products of various countries as different, imperfectly substitutable commodities. This kind of intrasectoral detail was observable (as national market shares in a particular country's demand) and ultimately could be linked to other model variables such as relative prices.

Armington himself used the assumption only in aggregated econometric analyses (Armington, 1969, 1973), and it was not until the mid-1970s that comprehensive general equilibrium models were based on this principle. The earliest models of this type (Boadway and Treddenick, 1978; Petri, 1976a) introduced substitution elasticities to determine the share of imports in demand, but otherwise they retained the first-generation structure by simply converting constraints (including dual constraints) to equations. This meant, for example, that material balances were written as if domestic and foreign products were perfect substitutes, even though the share of imports was tied to relative prices. This inconsistency was subsequently eliminated (for example, in Petri, 1976b) by using a two-level demand system. Under assumptions explained in the next section, this system separates the determination of demand for broad categories of goods (conventional sectors) from the determination of demand at the subsectoral level.

Policy issues related to international trade negotiations and world development strategy have recently led to the development of several second-generation models. The most impressive of these is a major effort by Deardorff and Stern to model the effects of the Tokyo-round agreements on thirty-four major trading countries (1981). The model has twenty-nine producing sectors, uses either Leontief or Cobb-Douglas production specifications, and can be run in both short-term (fixed sectoral capital stocks) and long-term modes. More aggregated models addressing commercial policy and the resource shocks of the 1970s were developed for the World Bank by Gunning et al. (1982), and

most recently by Whalley (forthcoming). Still other models address the trade relations of individual countries; a survey of these and other related efforts has been recently compiled by Shoven and Whalley (1983).

Most second-generation models share important structural characteristics along the lines indicated below. They differ chiefly in the degree of detail (number of distinct agents) specified in production, trade, and consumption, and in the empirical specification of the elasticities that guide adjustment in these areas. Generally, ranges of plausible elasticities are used since actual estimates are not available. In a few studies more direct efforts are made to collect elasticities through a search of the empirical literature. Since this literature often applies different models and assumptions, the results are seldom directly applicable to the simulation systems that are constructed. For example, except for the work of Almon (1974) and Nyhus (1975), no direct empirical studies exist of the trade/domestic requirement shares commonly used in general equilibrium modeling. Thus a major difference between this book and other similar studies is that the second-generation methodology is applied with parameters that accurately reflect the model's conceptual requirements. In this process, new insights emerge regarding the strengths and liabilities of the modeling strategy.

A skeletal version of the second-generation approach — the basis for the present model — is presented in Table 2.2. In each sector the model determines two kinds of prices: the prices of products ($p$), and the prices of consumption bundles, which include several products ($q$). Producers' prices describe the prices received by domestic producers, and consumers' prices the prices paid by consumers for bundles that include both domestic and foreign products. (Thus, $p = q$ only in the absence of trade.) These two sets of prices correspond to two quantity concepts: output ($x$) and demand ($d$). Demand measures the number of consumption bundles purchased. Output, which would equal demand in the absence of trade, is determined by market share equations that allocate demand in each market to producers at home and abroad.

Market share equations play a double role in the model as the link between demand and output and between producers' prices

**Table 2.2**  Skeletal second-generation trade model

| | |
|---|---|
| R1 | $p = A'q + lw + k\pi$ |
| R2 | $q = \hat{s}_d p + \hat{s}_m p^*$ |
| R3 | $s_d = s_d(p, p^*)$ |
| R4 | $s_m = s_m(p, p^*)$ |
| R5 | $d = Ax + bv + c\gamma$ |
| R6 | $x = \hat{s}_d d + \hat{s}_m^* d^*$ |
| R7 | $l'x = L$ |
| R8 | $k'x - \theta v = K$ |
| R9 | $p'\hat{s}_m^* d^* - p^{*'}\hat{s}_m d = B$ |

|  Endogenous | Exogenous |
|---|---|
| $d$ = demand vector | $A$ = input coefficient matrix |
| $p$ = producers' price vector | $B$ = net external saving |
| $q$ = consumers' price vector | $b$ = investment composition |
| $\pi$ = return on capital | $c$ = consumption composition |
| $s_d$ = home share of home market | $l$ = labor coefficients |
| $s_m$ = foreign share of home market | $L$ = labor endowment |
| $v$ = investment level | $k$ = capital coefficients |
| $w$ = wage rate | $K$ = capital endowment |
| $x$ = output vector | $p$ = world price vector |
| $\gamma$ = consumption level | $\theta$ = stock/flow conversion factor (approximately, number of years spanned by model) |

*Note:* Foreign variables are indicated by an asterisk; hat symbol indicates diagonalized vector, prime symbol indicates transpose.

and consumers' prices. Formally, market shares specify the composition of a demand bundle in terms of the products of different countries. Since the bundle is essentially a composite good (it simply guarantees a utility state, reachable by many different combinations of goods), the measurement unit of demand is not related in any special way to the "sum" of its component products. Thus, market shares are not shares in the conventional sense — they need not sum to one. (Of course, the value of demand must equal the sum of component values.) At the same time, it is useful to choose demand and product units so that all prices equal one dollar in the base period. With these units, base-year market shares do sum to one, and base-year real demand equals output plus imports minus exports, just as in the conventional homogeneous-product accounting system.

The first relationships of Table 2.2 (R1 and R2) define the price system of the model. R1 calculates producers' prices with the dual of the production function, that is, by adding intermediate input and primary factor costs. R2 calculates consumers' prices as product prices weighted by market shares. The market shares themselves are calculated in R3 and R4, based on the producers' prices of competing producers. R5 and R6 describe the quantity side of the economy: R5 calculates demand as a sum of intermediate and final demands, and R6 then uses trade shares to allocate demand to producers in different countries. The system is completed by two types of equilibrium conditions. National factor market equilibrium requires the full employment of each domestic factor (R7 and R8). International payments equilibrium requires that the trade balance equal an exogenously given surplus or deficit (R9). Through a series of substitutions, this trade imbalance can be shown to equal domestic factor income less expenditure, that is, the nation's net external saving.

This system has been solved for single economies as well as for several economies engaged in trade. In single-country solutions, factor endowments, the desired trade balance, and foreign product prices and demands are usually treated as given. If $N$ is the number of product catagories, this leaves the remaining the $6N + 3$ variables ($p$, $q$, $x$, $d$, $s$, $s^*$, and the scalars $\gamma$, $w$, and $\pi$) to be determined by an equal number of available equations.

If the demand relationships represented by the market share equations are homogeneous in prices (a reasonable theoretical requirement), the system determines only relative prices, and the burden of setting the price level falls on exogenous variables. For example, in single-country applications the price level is implicitly determined by the exogenously specified foreign price vector and by the value of $B$. Doubling these variables would double all domestic prices without affecting real quantities.

A fully closed world system — a system consisting of countries that trade only among themselves — would have a redundant trade balance equation; by Say's law, income has to equal expenditure for the world as a whole. In practice, this means that an external saving level cannot be specified for the "last" country; the world as a whole cannot save or dissave. In general, the price

level of the world system would continue to depend on the values specified for $B$. But if all countries engage in balanced trade ($B_i = 0$ for all $i$), the price homogeneity of the model implies indeterminacy, and an additional price-normalization equation is needed to anchor the relative price system.[2]

## Theoretical Foundations

The principal difficulty faced by second-generation trade models is the integration of the "invisible" (subsectoral) and "visible" (sectoral) details of economic structure. This task is dramatically simplified by the assumption of the block-independence of sectoral and subsectoral demand. Block-independence means that the demand for a product within a particular group of products depends only on expenditures and relative prices within the group. Prices and expenditures outside the group affect intragroup demand only indirectly through group expenditures.

In the present context, block-independence separates the analysis of intrasectoral choices (the import decision) from the analysis of intersectoral choices (substitution in production and consumption). This means, for example, that U.S. imports of Japanese steel depend only on total U.S. steel demand and Japanese prices relative to other steel prices in the American market. Such potentially relevant variables as the American demand for automobiles or the Japanese price of textiles affect U.S. steel imports only through their impact on relative prices and total steel demand.

The formal representation of this assumption is similar for both final and intermediate consumers. Both are assumed to maximize a transformation function by choosing appropriate inputs — yielding welfare in the case of consumers and tangible output in the case of intermediate users. In either case, the transformation function relates an output $x$ to a set of inputs $u$:

$$x(u_1, u_2, \ldots, u_n) \quad \text{such that } \partial x/\partial u_i \geq 0. \quad (2.3)$$

Associated ("income-compensated") demand functions can be derived by minimizing the function (2.3) while holding output (or utility) constant. Block-independence assures that the im-

plied demand functions include only a small number of variables and are thus easy to estimate.

If the demand system is block-independent, one can define a series of lower-level transformation functions that are related to the overall function by the structure

$$x(y_1, y_2, \ldots, y_m), \qquad (2.4)$$

where $y_j = y_j(u_{j1}, u_{j2}, \ldots, u_{j,n_j})$.

In the present case, the $y$ functions define relationships among products distinguished by origin, the $x$ functions among sectoral aggregates. The conditions under which the special structure of Eq. (2.4) is equivalent to the general function (2.3) were identified by Leontief (1947) and later applied to production and demand theory by Solow (1956) and Strotz (1957), respectively. They are

$$\frac{\partial}{\partial u_{mn}} \left( \frac{\partial x / \partial u_{ij}}{\partial x / \partial u_{ik}} \right) = 0 \quad \begin{array}{l} \text{for all } i, j, k, m, n, \\ \text{such that } m \neq i. \end{array} \qquad (2.5)$$

In words, the marginal rate of substitution among products in the same class must not depend on the purchases of products outside the class.

Armington (1969) initially argued that block-independence could be achieved by appropriately grouping commodities; if so, it would not constitute much of a restriction. But convenience in demand analysis is not the only criterion imposed on the sectoral classification of an empirical study. If the model includes production functions, for example, it is also important to group products according to similarities in production structure. And in practice, the sectoral specification is likely to be dictated by data availability.

Assuming that sectoral and subsectoral issues can be segregated with block-independence, Armington's contribution is a workable strategy for handling international competition at a subsectoral level. The identification of trade determination with conventional demand analysis is a breakthrough because it associates invisible subsectoral detail with a visible variable, trade. Unlike Chenery and Kretschmer's intrasectoral capital require-

ment function, Armington's system can be readily estimated and implemented with conventional data.

Although it is easy to see why Armington's formulation became so popular, it is not without conceptual difficulties. The identification of each national producer with a different product requires stringent hidden assumptions. Specifically, the approach presumes that each nation continues to make the same differentiated product (or products) over time. In other words, the international specialization pattern is frozen at the subsectoral level.

To see the problem with this assumption, consider the detailed effects of, say, a real devaluation by country $A$. $A$'s products will gain market shares in various markets because $A$'s prices improve relative to other producers. But this is not the only source of $A$'s gain: the devaluation may also enable $A$ to market products that it has never sold before. In fact, changes in subsectoral specialization patterns may be just as important as shifts of demand among differentiated products.

A model formalizing intrasectoral specialization shifts has been analyzed in Petri (1980) to see whether an Armington-type approach is still feasible if both types of change occur. A model of specialization change is constructed on the assumption that each sector contains many finely defined commodities in which different countries enjoy Ricardian production advantages — special technical efficiencies unrelated to other country characteristics. Such Ricardian differences lead to a distribution of intrasectoral relative prices across countries: a specific commodity $X$ may be relatively cheap in country $A$, while $Y$ is cheap in country $B$. If the commodities within the sector share similar production functions (perhaps because of appropriate grouping),[3] the country's production costs for both $X$ and $Y$ will tend to move together in response to changes in costs or exchange rates. Thus, when cost conditions improve in country $A$ relative to country $B$, a larger portion of $A$'s finely defined commodities will enjoy a price advantage over their competitors from $B$.

A two-country illustration of this approach is given in Figure 2.1. The axes measure the amount of input required in each of the two countries to produce a particular finely defined com-

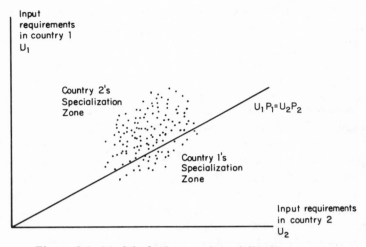

**Figure 2.1**  Model of subsectoral specialization patterns

modity. The many specific products contained in the sector are represented by dots in the figure. Commodities in the southeast quadrant, for example, are made more efficiently in country 1 (low $u_1$) than in country 2 (high $u_2$). Given input prices in the two countries ($p_1$ and $p_2$), the sector's products can be partitioned into those cheaper in country 1 and those cheaper in country 2. The dividing line itself cuts across products for which inter-country differences in input costs exactly offset differences in efficiency. The actual specialization pattern depends on the slope of this line, that is, on the intercountry relative price of inputs.

Mathematical analysis of the "Ricardian" model yields strong restrictions on the shape of the derived trade relationships. Surprisingly, however, the market share equations generated by this model must meet the same conditions of homogeneity and symmetry that are implied by demand theory. Thus, Armington's demand system and the alternative Ricardian approach lead to the same kind of trade share equations, right down to parameter restrictions. Consequently, there is no need to choose one or the other system in empirical estimation. Neither is it possible, for that matter, to determine which theory is supported by the data. Subsectoral trade probably reflects both Ricardian

and Armingtonian determinants, and it is safest to interpret estimated coefficients as weighted averages of parameters emerging from both processes.

## Details of the Model

The broad outlines of the present model have been established in Table 2.2 and in the assumptions described in the previous section. This section turns to the details of these relationships, ranging from substitution structures to the treatment of trade barriers. Many features of the model reflect a compromise between the goal of transparency and the need to capture essential features of real economic behavior. Inevitably, the model is less elegant than others with more modest substantive goals, and it is also less closely tied to institutional detail than, say, a sophisticated econometric forecasting model. Applied general equilibrium analysis is still experimental, and each study must seek its own balance of realism, empirical feasibility, and theoretical polish.

To provide a central reference to the detailed structure of the model, its main relationships are grouped in Table 2.3. The discussion that follows is keyed to equation numbers within the table. Equations R1 – R17 are country-specific and are implemented for both the United States and Japan. Equation R18 deals with world markets for homogeneous products. This equation and other aspects of the treatment of the rest of the world are discussed separately near the end of this section.

### Production Structure

Assumptions about the structure of production affect both price formation and the determination of demand. Accurate price simulation is obviously important in analyzing international competition. In many cases the accurate representation of intersectoral demand is equally important, since some sectors (especially the large service sectors) are only indirectly linked to the world economy through consumption effects and transactions with sectors involved in trade. Significantly, total sectoral de-

mand also turns out to be the single most important variable for explaining long-term changes in trade (see Chapter 6).

The substitution mechanisms commonly used in second-generation trade models tend to be too simple and do not provide reasonable predictions of consumption or demand changes. For example, many investigators describe commodity demand with fixed input-output relationships (Whalley, forthcoming; Gunning et al., 1982; deMelo and Dervis, 1977). This specification would miss, for example, the crux of the adjustments witnessed in the late 1970s — a systematic shift away from demand categories with increased relative prices. At the same time, a uniformly flexible specification, such as the Cobb-Douglas input-output system (Johansen, 1960, 1973; Deardorff and Stern, 1981), may be equally appropriate; with unit elasticities of demand in the energy sectors of the economy, for example, the crises of the 1970s would never have happened.

There has been substantial recent progress in developing and estimating new functional forms for multisector production functions. Much of this work is based on the elegant translog system developed by Christensen, Jorgenson, and Lau (1975) and first implemented in a modeling context by Hudson and Jorgenson (1974). The advantage of the translog system is great parametric flexibility. Thus, for example, the system provides opportunities for testing the validity of various theoretical restrictions (such as homogeneity, homotheticity, and symmetry) that are implicitly assumed in other functional forms (Nadiri, 1982).

But the real problem in developing multisectoral production functions is that very large numbers of parameters are needed to fully specify such systems.[4] Even with all theoretically justified restrictions in force, only small multisectoral models can be estimated in general form. Most translog applications, for example, involve only four inputs: capital, labor, energy, and materials. Because the focus of this study is trade, it is desirable to estimate price elasticities for all traded goods. At the same time, the generally smaller cross-price elasticities of the multisector system are of less immediate concern. What the present model needs is a simple framework that provides price responsiveness

**Table 2.3.A**  Equations of the model

| R1 | Production costs | $c_i = (1 + \hat{u}_i)\{A_i' q_i + l_i' w_i + k_i'(\pi_i + \delta_i q_i^v)\}$ |
|---|---|---|
| R2 | | $p_i = (1 + \hat{r}_i)c_i$ (heterogeneous) |
| R3 | Producers' prices | $p_i = \sigma_i(1 + \hat{r}_i)c_i + (1 - \sigma_i)(1 + \hat{t}_{3i})(p_3 + f_{3i}q_i^{20})$ (homogeneous import) |
| R4 | | $p_i = \sigma_i(1 + \hat{r}_i)c_i + (1 - \sigma_i)p_3$ (homogeneous export) |
| R5 | Rent index | $\rho_i = p_i / c_i - 1$ (homogeneous) |
| R6 | Consumers' prices | $q_i = \Sigma_j \hat{s}_{ji}(1 + \hat{t}_{ji})[(1 + \hat{h}_{ji})p_j + f_{ji}q_i^{20}]$ |
| R7 | Trade shares | $s_{ij} = s_{ij}\{((1 + \hat{t}_{kj})[(1 + \hat{h}_{kj})p_i + f_{kj}q_j^{20}]\}, \quad k = 1, 2, 3$ |
| R8 | Investment | $v_i = \psi_i^v \gamma_i n_i$ |
| R9 | External saving | $B_i = \psi_i^B \gamma_i n_i$ |
| R10 | Demand | $d_i = A_i x_i + e_i \gamma_i n_i + b_i v_i + F_i \Sigma_j f_{ji}' \hat{s}_{ji} d_i + \Sigma_j (z_{ij} - z_{ji})$ |
| R11 | Output | $x_i = \Sigma_j \hat{s}_{ij} d_j$ (heterogeneous) |
| R12 | | $x_i = x_i^0 + \sigma_i d_i + \mu_i \rho_i$ (homogeneous) |
| R13 | Labor | $l_i' x_i + \Sigma_j (z_{ij} - z_{ji}) = L_i$ |
| R14 | Capital | $k_i' x_i + \Sigma_j (z_{ij} - z_{ji}) = K_i$ |
| R15 | External saving | $B_i q^3 = \Sigma_j \{p_i'(1 + \hat{h}_{ij})(\hat{s}_{ij}d_j + z_{ij}) - p_j'(1 + \hat{h}_{ji})(\hat{s}_{ji}d_i + z_{ji})\}$ |
| R16 | Foreign purchasing power index | $q^3 = p_3' d_3 / p_3^0{}' d_3$ |
| R17 | National income | $y_i = w_i L_i + \pi_i K_i + q_i^v(\delta_i k_i)' x_i + (\rho_i c_i)' x_i$ $+ (\hat{r}_i c_i)' x_i + (\hat{u}_i(1 + \hat{u}_i)^{-1} c_i)' x$ $+ \Sigma_j [\hat{t}_{ji}((1 + \hat{h}_{ji})p_j + f_{ji}q_i)]' \hat{s}_{ji} d_i$ $+ \Sigma_j \{\hat{h}_{ij} p_i\}' \hat{s}_{ij} d_j$ |
| R18 | World demand | $p_3 = \xi_a + \xi_b \Sigma_i(x_i - d_i)$ (homogeneous only) |

in intermediate and consumption demand and that can be implemented with modest information. With suitable restrictions the translog system could serve this purpose, but an appealing simpler alternative is also available.

**Table 2.3.B**  Explanation of the notation

| Endogenous | Exogenous |
|---|---|
| $A$ = input-output coefficients | $f_{ij}$ = freight to ship from $i$ to $j$ |
| $b$ = investment composition | $F$ = composition of freight service |
| $B$ = next external saving | $h_{ij}$ = taxes applied to export $i$ to $j$ |
| $c$ = production cost vector | $K$ = capital endowment |
| $d$ = demand vector | $L$ = labor endowment |
| $e$ = consumption composition | $n$ = population |
| $l$ = labor coefficients | $t_{ij}$ = taxes applied at sale of $i$ in $j$ |
| $k$ = capital coefficients | $u$ = taxes applied at production |
| $p$ = producers' prices | $z_{ij}$ = exogenous trade from $i$ to $j$ |
| $q$ = consumers' prices | $\delta$ = depreciation coefficients |
| $q^{20}$ = price of freight | $\sigma$ = share of "homogeneous" sector that is |
| $q^3$ = foreign purchasing power | not traded |
| $q^v$ = capital goods deflator | $\xi$ = parameters of world demand for |
| $r$ = rents (market power, etc.) | homogeneous products |
| $s_{ij}$ = shares of $i$ in market $j$ | $\psi$ = parameters of macro demand system; |
| $v$ = investment level | superscript indicates type of demand |
| $w$ = wage rate | $\rho$ = rents (natural resources) |
| $x$ = output levels | $\pi$ = return on capital |
| $Y$ = gross national income | $\mu$ = parameter of homogeneous output |
| $\gamma$ = consumption levels | equation |

*Note:* The demand structure variables $A$, $b$, $e$, $l$, $k$ are determined by equations described in Chapter 2; the determination of the variable $s$ is described in Chapter 3. Subscript $i$ refers to country; 1 = United States, 2 = Japan, 3 = rest of the world. A hat symbol indicates diagonalized vector; a prime symbol indicates transpose.

Each sector's production function is defined in terms of the input demand functions:

$$a_i = a_i^o \left( \frac{q_i}{\prod_j q_j^{\beta_j a_j^o / \Sigma \beta_k a_k^o}} \right)^{\beta_i}, \tag{2.6}$$

where  $a_i$ = input $i$ used per unit of output,
$a_i^o$ = base period value of $a$,
$q_i$ = price of input $i$ (base period = 1),
$\beta_i$ = elasticity-like parameter for input $i$.

A sectoral cost function can be readily calculated from these demand functions by summing the values of inputs: $\Sigma_j q_j a_{ji}$. An explicit production function, however, cannot be derived. The cost function is zero-degree homogeneous in prices (prices enter

only as a ratio) and, near base-period prices, it satisfies the Slutsky symmetry requirement (Nadiri, 1982). To see this, differentiate Eq. (2.6):

$$\partial a_i / \partial q_j = -\frac{\beta_i a_i^o \beta_j a_j^o}{(\Sigma \beta_k a_k^o) q_i} \quad \text{for } i \neq j. \tag{2.7}$$

Given base-period prices ($q_i = 1$), Eq. (2.7) is clearly symmetric in $i$ and $j$. But it is also clear that the system is not symmetric at other prices. Thus, Eq. (2.6) is not associated with a "true" maximizing production system; it merely approximates such systems in the neighborhood of base-period prices. (The approximation can be recalibrated, of course, if the model strays too far from initial relative prices.) Universally symmetric functions (for example, an appropriately constrained translog system) could represent a true production system, but in practice, of course, they are also likely to act as approximations.

The only parameters required by this input demand system are the $\beta$'s. These parameters are related to sectoral own-price elasticities[5] by the equation

$$\epsilon_i = \beta_i \{1 - \beta_i a_i^o / \Sigma_j \beta_j a_j^o\}, \tag{2.8}$$

where   $\epsilon_i$ = own-price elasticity of input $i$.

For small inputs, then, the $\beta$'s are essentially equal to own-price elasticities. It is worth noting that the system is equivalent to a fixed-coefficient specification with $\beta_i = 0$, and to a Cobb-Douglas specification with $\beta_i = 1$. It also provides a close approximation to the constant elasticity of substitution (CES) function with $\beta_i = k$. But the main advantage of the system over the Cobb-Douglas and CES alternatives is that it readily absorbs input-specific demand elasticities; it can be "told," for example, that energy inputs are much less price-elastic than, say, labor inputs.

The empirical implementation of this input demand system is discussed in Chapter 4. The model applies the system in a straightforward way: given a vector of input prices, the input demand system is solved for each column of the input-output table. The complete table is then used to determine both product prices and intermediate demand. This represents a simultaneous problem because product prices have feedback effects on input

prices; in practice, as described in Chater 4, iterative methods are used to achieve a solution.

## Costs and Prices

A first step in calculating producers' prices is to add up production costs and taxes paid by producers (Table 2.3, R1). Significant discrepancies may then exist between costs and actual prices. These differences may reflect noncompetitive behavior (profits from the exercise of market power) or disequilibrium (rents earned on temporarily fixed factors of production). To allow for such discrepancies—which are important in the model's base-year data—prices are determined as costs plus rents (R2). Since the model is usually applied in a long-run equilibrium setting, in most simulations rents are set to either base-period levels (a treatment consistent with the market power hypothesis) or zero. Algebraically, rents are expressed as percentages of production cost.

An important distinction between the present model and most other second-generation trade models is that the products of agriculture and natural resources are treated as homogeneous (as distinct from differentiated) products. Because of the importance of major homogeneous commodities in these sectors (wheat, oil), it would have made little sense to estimate Armington-type substitution elasticities based on price changes at home and abroad. At the same time, movements in the domestic prices of agricultural and natural resource products only partially reflect price developments in world markets.

Aside from protection, the discrepancy between domestic and foreign price changes is probably due to aggregation; activities like sand mining or egg production are obviously isolated from trade by high transport costs. In addition, processing activities like oil refining and food processing are also included in the relevant aggregates. The prices of processing services (as distinct from the prices of the raw materials processed) are also more closely tied to domestic demand and cost conditions than to world markets. The solution adopted was to treat parts of these sectors as homogeneous world-market goods and the balance as domestic nontraded goods.

Equations R3 and R4 show the price implications of the mixed approach. The first terms of these equations replicate Eq. R2, the usual cost-based approach to price formation. The second terms reflect price formation based on world market prices. The sector's overall price is computed as a weighted average of these methods. The "law of one price" is applied to the homogeneous component as in the linear programming studies surveyed earlier. Three of the four cases at hand (U.S. and Japanese trade in agriculture and natural resources) involve importing relationships; only U.S. agriculture involves net exports. A net importer's domestic price is assumed to exceed the world price by the tariff equivalent of protection and by international transport costs (R3). A net exporter's domestic price, adjusted for export taxes, is assumed to equal the world price (R4).[6]

The agriculture and natural resource sectors also differ from other branches of the economy by virtue of fixed, sector-specific factors of production — land and resource reserves. The supplies and prices of these factors are not easily measured, especially on an economy-wide basis. In most statistical sources the relevant factor returns appear (or more accurately, disappear) as returns to capital. In the present model, resource rents are automatically generated by the homogeneous price formation system described above. Essentially, resource rents explain the difference between the prices calculated in relationships R3 and R4 and conventional input cost. Based on this comparison, a measure of resource rents (expressed as a fraction of conventional cost) is explicitly calculated in R5. This measure is subsequently used (see the discussion of R12 later) to determine the rate of exploitation of the resource base, that is, the level of domestic output.

*Consumers' Prices*

Intermediate and final consumers are assumed to buy the same bundle of domestic and imported goods. This is an unwelcome simplification, made necessary by the absence of data on sectoral imports distinguished by place of production. The price of the bundle — conveniently, but somewhat inaccurately, labeled the

"consumer's price"[7] — is calculated as a market-share-weighted average of the prices of the bundle's component products (R6). Before weighting, the price of each component is adjusted to include, as applicable, (1) international transport costs, (2) domestic tariffs and tariff equivalents (in the case of quantitative restrictions), (3) domestic sales taxes, and (4) foreign export taxes and subsidies.

The quantities of individual goods needed to obtain a unit of the composite good are given by an extensive system of share functions (R7). The principal determinants of shares include the prices of competing producers, appropriately adjusted for trade barriers. The functional forms and empirical estimates of these relationships are described in Chapter 3.

*Demand*

The model provides for three types of final expenditures from national income: consumption, investment, and external saving (net capital outflows). Once the overall levels of these expenditure types are established, the commodity composition of consumption and investment is determined by additional relationships, described below. In most simulations the levels of real investment and real external saving are tied to the consumption level with fixed coefficients (R8, R9). (These relationships can be seen as a primitive Leontief-type demand system for goods, domestic assets, and foreign assets.) The real consumption level itself is not explicitly specified; it is determined, in effect, as a residual by the various equilibrium requirements of the system, including especially the full employment conditions.

Several alternative specifications of the investment and external saving conditions are possible. For example, the external saving equations can be dropped in favor of constraints on national price levels. Experiments of this type are really "fixed-exchange-rate" simulations: by fixing the domestic price levels of each economy, one can impose disequilibria on international relative prices, and hence on current account balances. Without the saving equation, capital flows are endogenously determined as the balancing complement of the (imbalanced) current ac-

count. (In the real world, central banks are charged with carrying out these capital transactions in order to defend fixed exchange rates.)

In a series of experiments not reported here, investment is also made endogenous. The distinguishing feature of these experiments is the introduction of a link between capital stocks and investment, along lines described in the capital constraints of the skeletal diagrams (for example, Table 2.2, R8). With this link in place, the investment equation can be dropped, say, in favor of a fixed, externally determined rate of return to capital. Indeed, with a more ambitious treatment of the allocation of expenditures among goods and assets of various nationalities, the model could provide a sophisticated picture of real national saving and investment, international capital flows, and world capital market equilibrium. However, because capital market linkages have not, so far, played an important role in the Japanese-American economic relationship, these theoretically interesting extensions are not pursued in this book.

Following the conventional input-output format, the domestic demand for products (that is, for composite goods made up of foreign and domestic products) is calculated as the sum of intermediate plus final demands (R10). Specifically, the five terms of the demand equation reflect intermediate demand, consumption demand, investment demand, the demand for international transportation services, and certain exogenous demands. The composition of these vectors is examined in sequence below.

Intermediate demand (first term, R10) is obtained as the product of the input-output matrix and output. The calculation of input-output coefficients has already been described in the context of the production system.

Consumption demand (second term, R10) is distributed across sectors with a linear expenditure system (LES; see Stone, 1954; Barten and Bohm, 1982). Formally, per capita consumption expenditures in a given country are given by

$$y_i = q_i \alpha_i - \beta_i (Y / n - \Sigma_k q_k \alpha_k), \qquad (2.9)$$

where   $n$ = population,

        $y_i$ = per capita consumption expenditure on $i$,

$q_i$ = consumers' price of $i$,
$Y$ = total consumption expenditure,
$\alpha_i$ = "subsistence" consumption parameter of the LES function for good $i$,
$\beta_i$ = marginal expenditure parameter for good $i$.

Since the LES system is associated with an explicit welfare function, real consumption can be conveniently measured by the welfare index associated with any particular level of per capita consumption expenditure. Formally, real consumption is defined as the level of income needed, at base-period prices, to achieve the level of welfare provided by $Y/n$ at current (for example, simulated) prices. The equivalent base-period income is given by

$$\gamma = \Sigma_i q_i \alpha_i + (Y/n - \Sigma_k q_k \alpha_k)/\Pi_k q_k^{\beta_k}, \qquad (2.10)$$

where $\gamma$ = real consumption level.

Equation (2.10) can best be interpreted by viewing the LES consumption bundle as the sum of a fixed subsistence bundle and a bundle generated by discretionary income. The discretionary component is allocated by a Cobb-Douglas demand system. The first term of Eq. (2.10), then, is the base-period value of the subsistence bundle. The second term is discretionary income deflated by the ideal Cobb-Douglas price index. For national consistency, LES results are entered in the main demand equation of the model (R10) not as expenditures but as input-output type real demand coefficients. These coefficients are calculated from the LES expenditure results by

$$e_i(\gamma,q) = (y_i/q_i)/\gamma. \qquad (2.11)$$

Investment demand (third term, R10) is distributed across individual investment goods with the same demand system that is used to represent production input decisions. This investment bundle generates demand primarily for three sectors: construction (structures), machinery, and transport equipment.

Demand for international freight services (fourth term, R10)

is tied to imports. Although not all imports are shipped by domestic carriers, transport demand, by convention, "registers" in the importing country. Thus, the shipment of imports by foreign carriers constitutes an import of transport services. The interindustry composition of this demand ($F$) consists of a single entry: sector 20, the international freight sector.

Finally, demand includes exogenous vectors (last term, R10) to account for international transactions that, for various reasons, are not predicted within the model. These include automobile trade between the United States and Canada and service trade, including trade in factor services. The vectors are needed to complete the model's national accounting identities and are generally held fixed across simulations.

*Output*

For heterogeneous commodities — the Armington case — output levels are found by adding the demands implied by a country's shares in its own and foreign markets (R11). The long-term nature of the model figures importantly in this operation, since the equation implicitly assumes that each industry — except for the agriculture and natural resource sectors — can expand at close to constant cost. (Each sector's production function is assumed to have constant returns to scale, but prices may change slightly if the industry's derived input demands exert pressure on the markets of an important primary input.) In the short run, the existence of durable, industry-specific capital goods would impede entry and exit, and the constant-returns assumption used here would be inappropriate even if technology itself had that characteristic.

The treatment of the agriculture and natural resource sectors follows the textbook diagram of the firm (see Figure 2.2). Here the diagram refers to an industry rather than a firm, and the fixed factor is not capacity but the country's resource base. In particular, the diagram identifies a direct relationship between output and the ratio of unit rent to average cost ($\rho$ from Eq. R5). The determination of output is based on an economic estimate of this output/rent relationship (R12). A second term in Eq. R12,

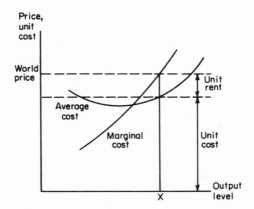

**Figure 2.2** Output determination in homogeneous product industries

linking production to domestic demand, is included to deter-mine the output levels of the sector's nonhomogeneous compo-nents. (As argued earlier, both the agriculture and natural re-source sectors contain substantial nontraded activities.) The estimation of these rent and domestic demand effects is de-scribed in Chapter 4.

*Factor Markets*

Domestic factor markets are in equilibrium when total factor demands are equal to exogenously specified factor supplies (R13, R14). These relationships further emphasize the long-term na-ture of the system. A single capital constraint makes sense only under the assumption that equilibrium exists (or is projected to exist) for a sufficiently long time for capacities to adjust to market requirements. This does mean that the model cannot be used to study short-term adjustment patterns, as is possible, for example, in models with sector-specific labor and capital. At the same time, more complicated formulations would be of little value in long-run analysis, since it would be difficult to imagine long-run solutions predicated on anything but fully adjusted factor mar-kets.

*External Balance*

The net external savings determined in R9 represent the capital transactions of the balance-of-payments accounts. External balance (R15) requires that these net savings equal the surplus on current account. Because the external accounts must balance in nominal terms, the left-hand side is written as the value of external saving — the product of real saving and an index of foreign prices. In turn, the right-hand side shows the value of exports minus imports, in f.o.b. terms. The prices used to value trade are adjusted for taxes (and the tax equivalent of quantitative restrictions) applied to exports. In addition to endogenous merchandise trade, the right-hand side also includes the exogenous trade components already described in Eq. R10.

An alternative way to introduce the net saving constraint would be to set the difference between national income and national expenditure equal to nominal external saving. In other words, external balance could be guaranteed just as well by restrictions on absorption as by the balance of payments. This fundamental economic law could be rigorously demonstrated by establishing the equivalence of the right-hand side of R15 to national income less expenditure. National expenditure, in the present case, is the sum of consumption and investment. National income, shown in R17, is the sum of: (1) wages, (2) returns to capital, (3) depreciation, (4) resource rents, (5) rents due to market power or fixed capacity, (6) indirect producers' taxes, (7) tariffs and the tariff equivalent of quotas, and (8) export taxes and the tax equivalent of export restraints. The algebraic demonstration of the equivalence is too cumbersome to include here, but a direct quantitative demonstration is provided by the model's income and product accounts presented in Table 4.5.

## Properties of the Model

The behavior of the model will be scrutinized continuously throughout this book, because the final empirical conclusions of the book depend on estimates developed with the model in subsequent chapters. It is therefore useful to review here the

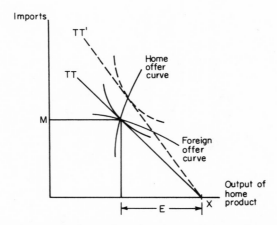

**Figure 2.3**  Single-product Armington-type trade model

main features of the theoretical framework and its likely impact on the results generated by the model.

Figure 2.3 illustrates an Armington-type system in which each national economy produces only one commodity. The output of the domestic commodity appears on the horizontal axis; imports of the foreign commodity appear on the vertical axis. (With more than two countries, the diagram would need additional dimensions.) The domestic equilibrium conditions of the model assure that production takes place at a point $(X)$ where all factors are fully utilized. The home good can be traded for imports at the prevailing terms of trade — the line $p/p^*$. The Armington demand system appears as an indifference map drawn in the space of domestic and imported commodities. At any given terms of trade, the highest indifference curve defines the nation's consumption and trade position. A locus of such trade positions, traced by varying the terms of trade, defines the nation's offer curve. In turn, international equilibrium is established by the intersection of the home offer curve with a similarly derived foreign offer curve.

The representation becomes slightly more complicated for a multisectoral economy. In Figure 2.4, the right-hand panel illustrates both the production and consumption choices of the economy, while the left-hand panel shows how exports are "trans-

MODELING JAPANESE-AMERICAN TRADE

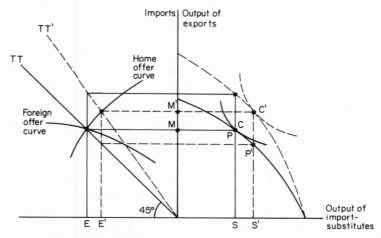

**Figure 2.4** Multiproduct Armington-type trade model

formed" into imports in international markets. The figure shows equilibrium in the domestic economy at two different terms of trade, represented by solid and dashed lines.

In the multisectoral context, exports are not necessarily the same goods as those required for home consumption. In general most goods are both exported and consumed, but usually in quite different proportions. To make this distinction clear, a transformation frontier is drawn between exports that are never consumed at home and import-substitutes that are never exported. Changes in the terms of trade now affect not only consumption but also the allocation of resources between the export and import-substitute industries.

Assume initially that the export/import exchange ratio (the terms of trade) is one-for-one. This means that the terms-of-trade line in the left-hand panel (*TT*) is drawn with a 45-degree angle. Because of this special price relationship between exports and imports, the consumption possibilities available to this economy are very much like the production possibilities defined by the export/import-substitute transformation curve. It is best to picture this equivalence in terms of two overlaid frontiers: a production frontier drawn in the export/import-substitute

space, and a consumption frontier drawn in the import/import-substitute space. Equilibrium consumption is at $C$, and equilibrium production is at $P$. The economy produces $S$ import-substitutes and $E$ exports, and exchanges the latter for $M$ imports.

Suppose now that the terms of trade improve to the steeper, dashed line, causing a given quantity of exports to be exchanged for more imports. The previous $E$ exports, for example, could now buy $M^*$ imports. This point can be found by moving horizontally from the production point in the right panel to the 45-degree line in the left panel, and then moving vertically to the new terms of trade. Thus, while the production locus remains unchanged, the consumption locus shifts out, as shown by the dashed curve. Consumption equilibrium shifts to $C'$, and production equilibrium directly below it to $P'$. The economy now produces $S'$ import-substitutes and $E'$ exports, and receives $M'$ imports. Successive shifts of the terms of trade generate an offer curve in the left panel, and equilibrium is again determined by the intersection of this curve with a similar foreign offer curve.

These diagrams highlight several important features of the model. The diagrams clearly show that changes in a country's offer (and hence in its terms of trade) can substantially increase or decrease welfare. They also show that offer curve elasticities are closely related to the substitutability of domestic and imported products. Specifically, if the price elasticities in a country's home market are low, the country will present inelastic offer curves to its trading partners. If the price elasticities of a country's export markets are low, the country faces an inelastic offer curve.

In a multisector model, terms-of-trade changes involve not only changes in consumption but also changes in production and in the domestic relative prices of exports and import-substitutes. The elasticity of the offer curve presented by a country to the rest of the world now depends on both substitution in demand and the elasticity of the transformation frontier. Thus, a trade model with an inelastic transformation frontier — say, because of sector-specific resources — will generate much larger changes in the terms of trade than a model with mobile resources. The present model with its long-run factor specification is at the high

end of the spectrum of transformation elasticities, and it is therefore likely to produce modest terms-of-trade changes relative to models with shorter time horizons. This is a significant point, because one of the striking findings of this book is the importance of terms-of-trade effects in Japanese-American trade.

The long-term orientation of the book has repeatedly surfaced in this chapter as an influence on the specification of the model. It is useful to conclude by summarizing how this objective has affected the overall specification strategy. First, the model has concentrated on the real side of the economy. The system is homogeneous in prices; it determines only relative prices in terms of a single common currency. In the real world, of course, the price level is not neutral; many contracts — explicit or implied — are denominated in money. But most of these contracts have limited lives, and very little is known about the effects of price-level changes on real variables in, say, a ten-year context. To predict price-level changes over this kind of horizon seems unwise. The capital side of the balance of payments falls into the same category. It is well known that capital flows triggered by portfolio shifts have an important influence on exchange-rate changes in the short run, and it is even possible to model such shifts in special circumstances. But we cannot yet tie such behavior in any reliable way to long-term structural change.

On the real side, the model has selectively emphasized features with a sustained impact on production and trade (technology, price and income elasticities in production, consumption, and trade) and avoided others that primarily affect adjustment and disequilibrium behavior (sector-specific capacities, price rigidities, and financing constraints). As shown in the brief survey of general equilibrium models earlier in the chapter, the problems of short-term adjustment are quite different from those of long-term specialization, and most models that do a good job of tracking adjustment are not well suited for analyzing structural change. In principle one could build models that answer both types of questions, but this would spread research resources thinly over two relatively disjoint problem areas.

In short, the present model has been specially fitted to analyze structural change and is probably better equipped for this pur-

pose than others of its type. But the long-term forces analyzed by the model will undoubtedly be overwhelmed, from time to time, by the effects of sharp, short-term adjustments in financial or real variables. At best, a long-term model defines the central axis of a highly variable prediction cone. In some cases, differences between alternative simulations of the model may be small relative to the standard error of the cone. But this is not an argument against long-term models; no matter how wide the cone, it is important to know why it moves and how it may be manipulated by policy into a slightly more advantageous position.

# 3 The Trade Share Functions

The share functions (Table 2.3, R4) allocate composite demand in a particular market (for example, steel in the United States) to different suppliers (the United States, Japan, and the rest of the world). Along with the determination of market demand, these functions crucially affect the model's ability to simulate trade. Thus the estimates of the trade share functions had to be robust and accurate. Fortunately, an extensive theoretical literature and three decades of related empirical research (see, for example, the survey by Leamer and Stern, 1970) provided support for this task; the estimation of price-sensitive international trade functions has obviously advanced beyond the stage of hypothesis testing. This backdrop is vigorously exploited in the present estimates by means of explicit theoretical and quantitative priors.

The main theoretical restrictions applied require that the share functions satisfy the symmetry and homogeneity constraints of demand theory. As argued in the previous chapter, the validity of these constraints is not limited to circumstances that strictly conform to the Armington assumptions. Demand-theoretic restrictions also apply when price changes induce shifts in specialization patterns, rather than substitution in consumption. The main empirical priors of the study consist of subjective distributions of the own-price elasticities of each trade flow. These priors were pooled with a good deal of sample information to generate the posterior estimates used in the model.

Of the study's 20 production sectors, 13 consist of regularly traded goods (see Table 3.1). Consequently, some 117 different trade shares (3 markets × 3 suppliers × 13 tradeables) are ultimately calculated in a solution. Since one share in each market can be analytically derived from the other two, no statistical estimates are made for the shares of suppliers in their home markets (for example, U.S. sales of steel in the U.S. market). In addition, trade shares are not statistically estimated in the international freight sector, and, as described in Chapter 4, trade is estimated by different methods in the "homogeneous" sectors of agriculture and natural resources. This leaves 60 trade share equations to be estimated by econometric methods.

The balance of this chapter describes the logic, functional form, and technical details of the estimated relationships. It concludes with a review of the estimates and their implications for the substantive questions addressed by the study.

**Table 3.1** Composition of traded sectors

| No. | Sector | Standard international trade classification, pre-1978 version | Standard international trade classification, current version |
|-----|--------|------------------------------------------------------------|------------------------------------------------------------|
| 1 | Agriculture, food | 0, 1, 2 n.e.s.,[a] 4 | 0, 1, 2 n.e.s., 4 |
| 2 | Natural resources | 27, 28, 3, 68 | 27, 28, 3, 68 |
| 3 | Textiles, apparel | 61, 65, 83–85 | 61, 65, 83–85 |
| 4 | Wood products, paper | 243, 251, 63–64, 82 | 248, 25, 63–64, 82 |
| 5 | Chemicals | 231, 266, 5, 62 | 23, 266, 5, 62 |
| 6 | Stone, clay, and glass | 66 | 66 |
| 7 | Iron and steel | 67 | 67 |
| 8 | Metal products | 69, 81 | 69, 81 |
| 9 | Machinery, instruments | 71 n.e.s., 86 | 71–74, 87–88 |
| 10 | Electrical machinery | 714, 72 | 75–77 n.e.s. |
| 11 | Transport equipment | 73 | 78–79 |
| 12 | Miscellaneous manufactures | 89 | 763, 89 |
| 20 | International freight services | No SITC Category | |

a. Not elsewhere specified.

## Identification of Share Functions

Since the market share functions are demand relationships, their estimation may be subject to simultaneous equation bias.[1] The concern is that "errors" in demand (due to factors omitted from the estimating equation) will cause movements along the implicitly simultaneous supply curve, generating a positive correlation between prices and demand. Thus the estimated price elasticity may partially reflect the positive elasticity of the supply curve rather than the negative elasticity of the demand curve. The bias is minimized when (1) the demand curve is accurately specified, (2) the elasticity of supply is high, and (3) shifts in the supply curve are frequent and large. There is reason to believe that all three of these factors operate to reduce estimator bias in the present case.

First, demand shifts are more accurately identified here than in most other studies. An explanation for this can be seen in Richardson's critique (1976) of the empirical trade literature: most other studies are highly aggregated and do not pay close attention to the role of domestic import substitutes. In the present case, the domestic activity variable driving each trade flow — market demand — is not general domestic activity (such as consumption or GNP) but the overall sector-specific demand for the import and its domestic substitutes throughout the economy. Although this reduces the potential estimation problem, it does so by shifting the burden of predicting trade to the simulation of sector demand — a luxury not usually open to builders of smaller econometric trade models.

Second, the supply elasticity of imports is likely to be large because the relevant supply curve is actually the excess supply curve of the exporting economy. This point is illustrated in Figure 3.1, where the left panel illustrates the home market of the exporter and the right panel the export market itself. The export supply curve seen by the trading partner is elastic because it reflects the relatively massive reactions of both consumers and producers to a change in its prices. Formally:

$$\xi_e = \left(\frac{1-e}{e}\right)\xi_d + \left(\frac{1}{e}\right)\xi_s, \tag{3.1}$$

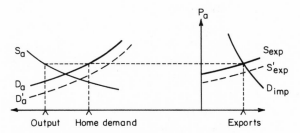

**Figure 3.1** Cause of high export supply variance

where  $e$  = percentage of output exported,

$\xi_e$  = export supply elasticity,

$\xi_s$  = overall supply elasticity of export producer,

$\xi_d$  = demand elasticity in exporter's home market.

In the case of exports of Japanese transport equipment to the American market — an example of an unusually outward-oriented industry — $e$ was about 0.11 in 1980, yielding an export supply elasticity of roughly 17, assuming that Japanese domestic demand and supply are both unit-elastic.

Finally, because the export supply curve is an excess supply curve, it shifts more frequently and more dramatically than a usual single-country supply curve. Normally, supply curves shift in response to additions of capacity, changes in technology, and changes in input prices. In addition to these factors, an excess supply curve also responds to various systematic and random changes in the exporter's domestic demand. The export supply shift caused by a small domestic demand change is illustrated in Figure 3.1 by dashed curves in both the domestic and foreign markets.

These arguments notwithstanding, econometric tests were performed to assure the absence of bias from the estimates. Following Hausman (1978), instrumental price variables were added to all of the basic estimating equations (in addition to the actual price variables normally included), and tests were performed to ascertain whether their coefficients differed from zero. In most equations they did not. Hausman argues that in the absence of clear bias, single-equation estimators should be used to minimize estimator variance. This suggestion has been

adopted here, but, in any case, Appendix A shows that instrumental variable estimators of the share functions yield very similar results. As one might expect, simultaneous techniques produce somewhat larger (about 15 percent on average) and less accurate elasticities. Some findings in Chapter 6 suggest that the estimated price elasticities may understate actual long-term price responsiveness. Several possible reasons for this will be considered, but simultaneity bias does not appear to contribute significantly to the problem.

## Functional Form

For each commodity group in each market (for example, steel in the United States) the two import share equations were estimated with the functional form

$$\log s_i = a_i + \Sigma_j b_{ij} \log p_j + c_i T, \tag{3.2}$$

where   $s_i$ = demand for supplier $i$'s product per unit of composite demand,

$p_j$ = price of supplier $j$ including transport cost and trade barrier adjustments,

$T$ = trend ($t = 1, 2, 3, \ldots$),

$a_i$ = constant,

$b_{ij}$ = elasticity of supplier $i$'s share with respect to supplier $j$'s price,

$c_i$ = non-price-related rate of change of shares.

Theoretical considerations lead to two types of restrictions on the parameters of this demand system. First, shares are required to be homogeneous of degree zero in prices:

$$\Sigma_j \partial s_i / \partial p_j = s_i \Sigma_j b_{ij} = 0, \tag{3.3}$$

which implies

$$\Sigma_j b_{ij} = 0. \tag{3.4}$$

Second, the matrix of the price derivatives of the share equations—the income-compensated price derivatives of the demand system—is required to be symmetric:

$$\partial s_i / \partial p_j = \partial s_j / \partial p_i, \tag{3.5}$$

which implies

$$b_{ij}s_i = b_{ji}s_j. \tag{3.6}$$

The homogeneity constraint can be implemented directly by replacing the individual price terms of Eq. (3.2) with relative prices:

$$\log s_i = a_i + \Sigma_{j \neq k} b_{ij}^* \log (p_j/p_k) + c_i T, \tag{3.7}$$

where $k$ = index of home producer,

and in terms of the previous definitions:

$$b_{ij}^* = b_{ij} \quad \text{for } j \neq k,$$

and $$b_{ik}^* = -\Sigma_{j \neq k} b_{ij}^*. \tag{3.8}$$

The symmetry constraint, however, cannot be imposed strictly in the context of function (3.2)—or equivalently, (3.7). To retain the double logarithmic form, which is attractive from the viewpoint of estimation, symmetry is imposed only approximately by the linear restriction

$$\bar{s}_i b_{ij} = b_{ji}\bar{s}_j, \tag{3.9}$$

where $\bar{s}_i = (\Pi_t s_{i,t})^{1/t}$, the geometric mean of $s$.

As already mentioned, the home producer's market share, $s_k$, can be derived analytically from the market's two import equations. The point of the derivation is to keep the overall "utility" of the composite bundle constant: changes in the home producer's share must exactly offset the utility impact of changes in the two import shares. Since the marginal utility of a product is proportional to its price in equilibrium, the overall utility of the bundle is constant if:

$$\Sigma_i p_i ds_i = 0. \tag{3.10}$$

Solving for changes in the home ($k$) producer's share:

$$ds_k = -\Sigma_{i \neq k}(p_i/p_k)ds_i. \tag{3.11}$$

But Eq. (3.11) holds only for small changes in shares and prices; with larger shifts, account must be taken of changes in marginal utility, that is, in the relative price ratios in the equation.

The obvious solution is to integrate Eq. (3.11) over the path traced out by prices as they move from an initial equilibrium, say, the base-period price vector $(1,1,1)$, to some new values $(p_1^*, p_2^*, p_3^*)$. Unfortunately, there are many ways to do this, depending on the exact path traced by the price vector, and each gives a slightly different answer.[2] For practical reasons a particularly simple path was used:

$$\Delta s_k = -\Sigma_{i \neq k} \, \Sigma_{j \neq k} \int_1^{\rho_j^*} \rho_i \frac{\partial s_i(\rho_i, \rho_j)}{\partial \rho_j} \, d\rho_j, \qquad (3.12)$$

where $\rho_i = p_i / p_k$.

This expression yields:

$$\Delta s_k = -\Sigma_{i \neq k} \left( \frac{b_{ii}}{1 + b_{ii}} \right) \{ s_i(\rho_i^*, \bar{\rho}_j) - s_i(1, \bar{\rho}_j) \} \qquad (3.13)$$

$$-\Sigma_{j \neq i, j \neq k} \, \rho_i \{ s_i(\bar{\rho}_i, \rho_j^*) - s_i(\bar{\rho}_i, 1) \}.$$

This formulation evaluates the impact of changes in the relative prices $p_i / p_k$ one at a time by holding the other relative price at its geometric mean value during the change.[3]

One thing the share functions do not have is a variable to capture the *income* elasticity of imported products. While the economy's overall income elasticity for imports can still differ from one — U.S. imports from Japan, for example, are predominantly in sectors with high income elasticities (see Chapter 6) — the elasticity of imports with respect to demand within a sector is constrained to one. This formulation represents a departure from usual econometric practice. Nevertheless, income terms are excluded because they are not meaningful in the case of intermediate goods, and because income variables often "pick up" the effects of other relatively smoothly growing variables.

Most traded sectors of the present study include intermediate products, and some, like steel and chemicals, consist almost exclusively of such goods. Unlike consumption demand, the composition of intermediate demand does not systematically change when its level changes; indeed, the same intermediate demand change may be associated with different users of the intermediate input at different times.[4] Thus, a correlation be-

tween the volume of demand for intermediate goods and its import content is more likely to reflect short-term forces such as industrial bottlenecks than a systematic income-related relationship.

Estimating equations which include income terms often generate implausible results. For example, high income elasticities are typically estimated for the imports of low-quality products. Although one could theoretically explain this finding with income distribution arguments, it is probably spurious, and is explained by the rapid growth and rising market shares of developing countries which produce low-quality goods. Unfortunately, these extraneous trends are highly correlated with income, and their effects cannot be estimated separately. With additional information—say, from cross-section consumption data—proper estimates of both income-associated and trend-associated effects might be developed. But without embarking on this effort, the safest course is to associate unexplained trade share changes with time rather than an important endogenous variable.[5]

## Estimating the Share Functions: Technical Details

The share system described in the previous section was estimated with annual time-series data for 1960–1980. Before the results are presented, some technical aspects of estimation, including variable definitions, estimating techniques, and estimating statistics, will be briefly reviewed. The data sources and adjustments will be described in Appendix C.

*Variables.* The dependent variable, the import market share, is constructed by dividing constant-price trade flows with a measure of real composite demand in the importing market. This procedure is complicated by the fact that the composite demand measure cannot be constructed, strictly speaking, without the parameters of the demand system (the share functions). In principle, the parameters of the share system and composite demand could be estimated simultaneously. But since total demand is usually dominated by domestic demand, the estimate of total demand is only marginally affected by changes in the ratios used to convert imports and domestic demand into common units. A

simple alternative to simultaneous estimation, therefore, is to approximate composite demand by using prior, rather than posterior, estimates of share system parameters. The priors are given below.

The price variables used in this study are producers' price indexes for the exporting economy. The producers' price index for the rest of the world is constructed as a weighted average of the producers' price indexes of major exporting countries other than the United States and Japan. This also differs from the usual practice of using unit-value indexes derived from trade values and quantities. Producers' price indexes are preferable to unit-value indexes because they (1) attempt to distinguish quality improvements from price increases, and (2) are less vulnerable to the effects of arbitrary trade composition changes. Prices are adjusted for trade barriers by adding tariffs and the tariff equivalents of quotas. Fortunately, extensive estimates of the price effects of quantitative restrictions in Japanese-American trade are available from the work of Turner (1981).

Prices enter the estimating equations with built-in distributed lags, that is, as moving averages. Three alternative lag forms are tested, and the equation with the best fit is used. This method amounts to introducing a nonlinear three-valued choice variable into the analysis and presumably reduces the remaining degrees of freedom, as does any additional variable. When tried, the lag shapes postulate the following weights:

| Year | Lag A | Lag B | Lag C |
|------|-------|-------|-------|
| $t$ | 1.00 | 0.60 | 0.30 |
| $t-1$ | 0.00 | 0.30 | 0.40 |
| $t-2$ | 0.00 | 0.10 | 0.30 |

The procedure is admittedly crude, but lag patterns are of little direct interest and are included mainly to improve the efficiency of the long-run elasticity estimates. In any case, the lag alternatives do provide a range of plausible adjustment patterns and the estimates distribute themselves reasonably across the three shapes, with the median equation falling in column $B$.

*Estimation techniques.* Because the symmetry constraints imposed on a demand system involve parameters in both import

equations, and because errors in the two imports serving a given market are likely to correlate, the pair of import share functions of each market is jointly estimated. Zellner's "seemingly unrelated regression equations" method (1962, 1964), modified to handle linear restrictions and prior information, is used. This method involves a three-step procedure. First, separate regressions are run on the two import functions. Second, the covariance of errors between equations is estimated from the first-stage error sequences. Finally, the two import equations are reestimated using generalized least squares and the interequation error covariance matrix estimated in the second step. The symmetry constraint is in force throughout the procedure.

Prior information on the own-price elasticity of each import share is introduced as a subjective distribution with given mean and variance. The mean of the prior distribution is constructed by averaging the somewhat more detailed elasticities published by Cline et al. (1978). Additional information on sectoral import elasticities is available for Japan from a study by Kawanabe (1978), and for the United States, Japan, and other major industrial countries from Stone (1979). These elasticities, although drawn from essentially the same "real" experiment as the sample of the present study, are based on quite different observations (quarterly rather than annual data, often covering a different, shorter time period), conceptual models, independent variables, equation forms, and estimation methods. Thus, it can be argued that they constitute a different source of information. The several elasticity estimates, including the Cline estimates that are ultimately used as the priors of this study, are compared in Table 3.2. The data also give an impression of the variability of elasticity estimates. Without formal estimation, the standard deviations of the subjective distributions were set at 1.0 for elasticities smaller than 2.0 in absolute value, and at one-half of the value of the elasticity for elasticities larger than 2.0 in absolute value.

Prior information was pooled with sample information following a method proposed by Theil and Goldberger (1961), Theil (1963), and Christ (1966). In practice, the approach works much as if extra "observations" were being added to the regression. The covariance terms associated with these new observations reflect the variance of the subjective distribution. In the present

**Table 3.2** Alternative estimates of trade price elasticities

| No. | Sector | U.S. imports | | Japanese imports | | | ROW imports[a] |
|-----|--------|-------|-------|-------|----------|-------|-------|
| | | Cline | Stone | Cline | Kawanabe | Stone | Cline |
| 3 | Textiles, apparel | 2.16 | 0.99 | 1.56 | 1.33 | 1.20 | 1.23 |
| 4 | Wood products, paper | 1.30 | 0.44 | 1.43 | 1.77 | 2.48 | 1.39 |
| 5 | Chemicals | 1.36 | 1.78 | 1.42 | 1.65 | 1.54 | 0.99 |
| 6 | Stone, clay, and glass | 2.51 | 1.72 | 1.13 | — | 1.22 | 1.23 |
| 7 | Iron and steel | 1.99 | 1.67 | 2.36 | 5.20 | 2.43 | 1.23 |
| 8 | Metal products | 1.99 | 1.75 | 2.36 | 5.30 | 0.91 | 1.23 |
| 9 | Machinery, instruments | 1.04 | 0.99 | 1.89 | 2.07 | 1.08 | 1.23 |
| 10 | Electrical machinery | 0.87 | 0.69 | 1.78 | 2.51 | 1.11 | 1.23 |
| 11 | Transport equipment | 2.53 | 2.66 | 1.87 | 2.02 | — | 1.15 |
| 12 | Miscellaneous manufactures | 4.44 | 1.47 | 1.42 | 2.96 | 1.10 | 1.23 |

*Sources:* Aggregated from tables in Cline et al. (1978), p. 58; Kawanabe (1978), pp. 260–263; Stone (1979), pp. 308–309.

a. ROW = rest of the world.

case, with only the own-price elasticity subject to prior information, the estimator proposed by Theil is

$$b = (X'X/s^2 + \delta_i/z_i^2)^{-1}(X'y/s^2 + \delta_i b_i^*/z_i^2), \qquad (3.14)$$

where  $b$ = vector of posterior parameter estimates,
$X$ = matrix of exogenous variable values,
$y$ = vector of endogeneous variable values,
$s$ = estimated standard error of regression,
$b_i^*$ = mean of prior distribution for parameter $i$,
$z_i^2$ = variance of prior distribution for $i$,
$\delta_i$ = diagonal equals 1 for parameter with prior, 0 otherwise.

The properties of the posterior estimates can be analyzed with two intuitive statistics. The first, which Theil terms a "compatibility statistic," evaluates the significance of the difference between the posterior and prior values of an estimated parameter:

$$T1 = \frac{(b_i^* - b_i)^2}{s^2(X'X)_{ii}^{-1} + z_i^2}. \qquad (3.15)$$

The statistic has an $F$ distribution with one degree of freedom in the numerator (in the present case of a single prior), and

$n - r - 1$ degrees of freedom in the denominator ($n$ is the number of observations and $r$ the number of exogenous variables net of restrictions). Theil's second statistic quantifies the share of posterior knowledge — essentially, the share of the variance of the posterior estimator — attributable to information from prior and data, respectively. The statistic for the share of the prior is

$$T2 = \frac{z_i^2}{(X'X/s^2 + \delta_i/z_i^2)_{ii}^{-1}}. \qquad (3.16)$$

The derivation of $T2$ ensures that the expression $1.0 - T2$ provides a similar measure for the contribution of the sample. The $T1$ and $T2$ statistics are presented below, together with the usual estimation results.

Finally, also for reasons of efficiency, steps were taken to eliminate serial correlation. Specifically, equations with suspicious Durbin-Watson statistics were reestimated with several different discrete values of the autocorrelation coefficient $\rho$. This technique was devised by Hildreth and Lu (1960). As a consequence of its application, the number of degrees of freedom is further reduced. In general, the estimated residuals usually have 12 to 13 degrees of freedom, based on twenty observations, five independent variables, two parameters estimated by equation selection, and one linear restriction (shared by two equations).

Given the various special estimation features required, the analysis of such a large number of share functions would not have been practical if only a standard regression package had been available. A special computer program was therefore developed, based on a general regression package in use at Brandeis University, to extract the relevant data from a large data base, to prepare it for estimation, and to implement the combination of techniques described above.

### Results

The sixty estimated import share functions are presented in Tables 3.3 through 3.5. The columns of Tables 3.3 – 3.5 show

**Table 3.3** Market share functions of the U.S. market

| Sector | $R^2$ | SE | DW | Rho | L | Theil's statistics | | Own-price elasticities | | Cross-price elasticity | Trend | |
|---|---|---|---|---|---|---|---|---|---|---|---|---|
| | | | | | | T1 | T2 | Prior | Post | | 1971− | 1971+ |
| **Textiles** | | | | | | | | | | | | |
| Japan | .96 | .088 | 2.28 | 0 | C | 0.5 | .16 | −2.3 | −2.9 (8.0) | — | .050 (6.0) | −.003 (0.2) |
| ROW | .98 | .067 | 1.62 | 0 | C | 1.4 | .13 | −2.2 | −1.2 (3.7) | — | .085 (16.7) | .104 (6.7) |
| **Wood, paper, and related products** | | | | | | | | | | | | |
| Japan | .92 | .136 | 1.37 | .25 | C | 4.9 | .55 | −1.4 | −2.1 (5.3) | — | −.012 (0.8) | −.056 (2.5) |
| ROW | .58 | .055 | 1.94 | .25 | C | .0 | .27 | −1.3 | −1.4 (5.1) | — | .009 (1.4) | .032 (3.1) |
| **Chemicals and rubber** | | | | | | | | | | | | |
| Japan | .93 | .129 | 2.48 | .25 | A | .0 | .70 | −1.4 | −1.5 (3.3) | 1.5 (2.2) | .135 (7.5) | .021 (1.0) |
| ROW | .93 | .054 | 2.53 | .25 | A | 1.5 | .19 | −1.4 | −0.8 (3.3) | 0.3 (2.2) | .045 (6.8) | .054 (6.0) |
| **Stone, clay, and glass** | | | | | | | | | | | | |
| Japan | .23 | .099 | 1.83 | .50 | A | 3.4 | .05 | −2.6 | −1.0 (4.1) | — | .011 (0.6) | .023 (1.2) |
| ROW | .75 | .079 | 1.69 | .50 | A | 2.4 | .10 | −2.5 | −0.8 (2.5) | — | .048 (3.5) | .049 (3.5) |
| **Iron and steel** | | | | | | | | | | | | |
| Japan | .89 | .187 | 1.30 | .25 | B | 2.0 | .45 | −2.1 | −3.1 (5.7) | 0.8 (1.7) | .156 (7.4) | .019 (0.8) |

| | | | | | | | | | | | |
|---|---|---|---|---|---|---|---|---|---|---|---|
| ROW | .83 | .138 | 2.86 | .25 | B | 0.2 | .24 | −2.1 | −1.6 (3.8) | 0.8 (1.7) | .118 (7.2) | .006 (0.4) |
| **Metal products** | | | | | | | | | | | |
| Japan | .77 | .107 | 2.51 | .50 | B | 0.9 | .24 | −2.0 | −1.4 (3.5) | 1.4 (4.1) | .091 (4.7) | −.005 (0.2) |
| ROW | .91 | .058 | 2.49 | .50 | B | 1.3 | .09 | −2.0 | −1.1 (4.6) | 1.0 (4.1) | .070 (6.5) | .059 (4.2) |
| **Machinery, instruments** | | | | | | | | | | | |
| Japan | 1.00 | .054 | 2.15 | 0 | C | 1.6 | .20 | −1.1 | −1.7 (7.6) | — | .126 (28.0) | .135 (18.6) |
| ROW | .96 | .072 | 1.27 | 0 | C | .0 | .26 | −1.1 | 0.9 (3.7) | — | .097 (14.8) | .057 (3.9) |
| **Electrical machinery** | | | | | | | | | | | |
| Japan | .93 | .108 | 1.95 | .50 | C | 2.9 | .63 | −0.9 | −1.6 (4.0) | 0.6 (1.4) | .170 (8.6) | .029 (1.3) |
| ROW | .94 | .084 | 1.41 | .50 | C | 0.6 | .55 | −0.9 | −0.6 (1.3) | 0.6 (1.4) | .159 (9.5) | .074 (4.1) |
| **Transportation equipment** | | | | | | | | | | | |
| Japan | .98 | .208 | 1.82 | .25 | C | 0.3 | .60 | −2.6 | −2.4 (3.0) | 1.1 (1.6) | .369 (10.6) | .126 (2.9) |
| ROW | .81 | .126 | 1.49 | .25 | C | 0.2 | .52 | −2.6 | −2.5 (3.4) | 1.4 (1.6) | .134 (6.4) | .082 (2.4) |
| **Miscellaneous manufactures** | | | | | | | | | | | |
| Japan | .98 | .063 | 1.47 | 0 | C | 1.4 | .02 | −4.6 | −2.5 (8.7) | — | .125 (26.6) | .087 (4.8) |
| ROW | .98 | .066 | 2.44 | 0 | C | 4.2 | .03 | −4.5 | −0.8 (2.7) | — | .081 (16.4) | .076 (5.2) |

**Table 3.4** Market share functions of the Japanese market

| Sector | $R^2$ | SE | DW | Rho | L | Theil's statistics | | Own-price elasticities | | Cross-price elasticity | Trend | |
|---|---|---|---|---|---|---|---|---|---|---|---|---|
| | | | | | | T1 | T2 | Prior | Post | | 1971− | 1971+ |
| **Textiles** | | | | | | | | | | | | |
| U.S. | .73 | .265 | 1.70 | .50 | A | .0 | .60 | −1.6 | −1.3 (2.7) | 0.3 (0.4) | .067 (1.4) | .106 (2.3) |
| ROW | .92 | .179 | 1.48 | .50 | A | .0 | .19 | −1.6 | −1.4 (5.0) | 0.1 (0.4) | .206 (6.3) | .148 (5.1) |
| **Wood, paper, and related products** | | | | | | | | | | | | |
| U.S. | .66 | .187 | 2.01 | .25 | B | 0.8 | .56 | −1.5 | −1.6 (3.6) | .0 (0.0) | .029 (1.4) | −.019 (0.6) |
| ROW | .86 | .193 | 1.79 | .25 | B | 3.3 | .70 | −1.5 | −2.2 (4.5) | .0 (0.0) | .123 (5.9) | .024 (0.7) |
| **Chemicals and rubber** | | | | | | | | | | | | |
| U.S. | .79 | .117 | 1.90 | 0 | C | .0 | .31 | −1.5 | −1.2 (3.5) | — | −.041 (4.4) | .040 (2.2) |
| ROW | .66 | .106 | 1.68 | 0 | C | 0.9 | .57 | −1.5 | −1.5 (3.3) | — | −.011 (1.0) | .037 (4.0) |
| **Stone, clay, and glass** | | | | | | | | | | | | |
| U.S. | .59 | .125 | 1.99 | .25 | C | 0.1 | .62 | −1.2 | −1.0 (2.6) | — | .041 (2.9) | −.053 (1.9) |
| ROW | .72 | .164 | 1.50 | .25 | C | 6.9 | .80 | −1.1 | −0.5 (1.1) | — | .063 (4.0) | .029 (1.3) |
| **Iron and steel** | | | | | | | | | | | | |
| U.S. | .36 | .393 | 1.77 | .50 | B | 0.3 | .77 | −2.4 | −2.5 (3.1) | — | −.131 (1.9) | .009 (0.1) |

|  |  |  |  |  |  |  |  |  |  |  |  |  |
|---|---|---|---|---|---|---|---|---|---|---|---|---|
| ROW | .54 | .352 | 2.13 | .50 | B | 3.6 | .79 | −2.4 | −3.2 (3.8) | — | −.137 (2.3) | .004 (0.1) |
| **Metal products** | | | | | | | | | | | | |
| U.S. | .46 | .208 | 1.81 | 0 | C | 0.7 | .48 | −2.4 | −2.2 (3.4) | — | .039 (2.7) | −.030 (0.9) |
| ROW | .63 | .275 | 2.10 | 0 | C | 0.1 | .60 | −2.4 | −2.1 (2.9) | — | .045 (1.9) | .095 (3.8) |
| **Machinery, instruments** | | | | | | | | | | | | |
| U.S. | .72 | .094 | 1.07 | .25 | B | 1.4 | .16 | −1.9 | −1.0 (3.4) | — | −.056 (5.2) | .003 (0.2) |
| ROW | .88 | .073 | 2.26 | .25 | B | 0.1 | .36 | −1.9 | −1.9 (4.1) | — | −.016 (1.1) | .037 (2.7) |
| **Electrical machinery** | | | | | | | | | | | | |
| U.S. | .00 | .110 | 2.03 | .50 | B | 2.6 | .32 | −1.8 | −0.9 (2.2) | — | −.001 (0.0) | −.009 (0.5) |
| ROW | −.07 | .137 | 1.64 | .50 | B | 9.8 | .53 | −1.8 | −0.3 (0.6) | — | .009 (0.3) | .017 (0.8) |
| **Transportation equipment** | | | | | | | | | | | | |
| U.S. | −.01 | .313 | 1.69 | .25 | B | 0.8 | .75 | −1.9 | −1.5 (2.4) | 0.3 (0.3) | .021 (0.5) | −.055 (1.1) |
| ROW | .54 | .242 | 2.51 | .25 | B | 0.6 | .89 | −1.9 | −1.7 (2.4) | 0.3 (0.3) | −.085 (2.7) | .125 (3.1) |
| **Miscellaneous manufactures** | | | | | | | | | | | | |
| U.S. | .74 | .163 | 2.04 | .25 | B | 1.4 | .47 | −1.4 | −0.7 (1.8) | — | .098 (5.2) | −.061 (0.4) |
| ROW | .88 | .144 | 1.32 | .25 | B | 0.5 | .73 | −1.4 | −1.4 (2.8) | — | .125 (7.7) | .006 (0.4) |

**Table 3.5** Market share functions of the rest-of-the-world market

| Sector | $R^2$ | SE | DW | Rho | L | Theil's statistics | | Own-price elasticities | | Cross-price elasticity | Trend | |
|---|---|---|---|---|---|---|---|---|---|---|---|---|
| | | | | | | T1 | T2 | Prior | Post | | 1971− | 1971+ |
| **Textiles** | | | | | | | | | | | | |
| U.S. | .95 | .052 | 1.45 | 0 | B | 0.1 | .15 | −1.3 | −1.6 (7.6) | 0.2 (0.9) | −.057 (12.9) | .003 (0.3) |
| Japan | .94 | .065 | 2.02 | 0 | B | 0.5 | .22 | −1.3 | −1.6 (6.4) | 0.2 (0.9) | −.005 (0.9) | −.037 (3.8) |
| **Wood, paper, and related products** | | | | | | | | | | | | |
| U.S. | .59 | .052 | 1.16 | .25 | A | 0.6 | .13 | −1.4 | −1.0 (4.9) | — | −.018 (3.0) | −.028 (3.3) |
| Japan | .70 | .101 | 2.43 | .25 | A | 0.1 | .24 | −1.6 | −1.4 (4.5) | — | .010 (0.9) | −.028 (2.1) |
| **Chemicals and rubber** | | | | | | | | | | | | |
| U.S. | .70 | .044 | 2.32 | .50 | B | 1.9 | .23 | −1.1 | −0.5 (2.0) | 0.1 (0.6) | −.045 (4.7) | .001 (0.1) |
| Japan | .73 | .080 | 1.92 | .50 | B | 1.0 | .77 | −1.2 | −1.5 (3.4) | 0.3 (0.6) | .055 (3.2) | −.018 (1.1) |
| **Stone, clay, and glass** | | | | | | | | | | | | |
| U.S. | .74 | .066 | 2.07 | .50 | A | 2.2 | .28 | −1.3 | −0.7 (2.4) | 0.4 (2.6) | −.049 (4.3) | −.047 (3.9) |
| Japan | .91 | .061 | 1.74 | .50 | A | 0.0 | .15 | −1.4 | −1.3 (6.2) | 0.6 (2.6) | −.049 (4.5) | .001 (0.1) |
| **Iron and steel** | | | | | | | | | | | | |
| U.S. | .77 | .144 | 1.37 | 0 | B | 0.5 | .34 | −1.6 | −1.1 (3.0) | 0.4 (0.7) | −.024 (1.6) | −.067 (4.3) |

| | | | | | | | | | | | | |
|---|---|---|---|---|---|---|---|---|---|---|---|---|
| Japan | .97 | .108 | 1.74 | 0 | B | 0.4 | .37 | −1.3 | −1.7 (5.1) | 0.1 (0.7) | .098 (10.1) | .024 (2.3) |
| **Metal products** | | | | | | | | | | | | |
| U.S. | .72 | .046 | 1.43 | .25 | C | 0.2 | .19 | −1.3 | −1.1 (4.8) | 0.6 (3.1) | −.034 (5.2) | −.031 (2.9) |
| Japan | .92 | .067 | 1.70 | .25 | C | 0.2 | .40 | −1.4 | −1.1 (3.1) | 1.0 (3.1) | .070 (7.2) | .045 (2.9) |
| **Machinery, instruments** | | | | | | | | | | | | |
| U.S. | .85 | .034 | 1.97 | .25 | C | 1.0 | .09 | −1.4 | −0.9 (5.2) | 0.3 (2.6) | −.013 (0.2) | −.017 (1.6) |
| Japan | .99 | .052 | 1.61 | .25 | C | 0.9 | .38 | −1.7 | −1.2 (3.0) | 0.7 (2.6) | .103 (8.9) | .073 (4.4) |
| **Electrical machinery** | | | | | | | | | | | | |
| U.S. | .70 | .052 | 2.03 | 0 | B | 0.3 | .14 | −1.4 | −1.2 (5.4) | 0.3 (2.3) | −.032 (4.9) | −.028 (2.6) |
| Japan | .99 | .054 | 2.20 | 0 | B | 0.1 | .23 | −1.6 | −1.3 (4.2) | 0.6 (2.3) | .065 (7.8) | .061 (5.3) |
| **Transportation equipment** | | | | | | | | | | | | |
| U.S. | .07 | .089 | 1.73 | .25 | B | 1.5 | .37 | −1.5 | −0.9 (2.5) | — | −.007 (0.6) | −.047 (2.1) |
| Japan | .94 | .103 | 1.53 | .25 | B | 0.0 | .72 | −1.9 | −1.6 (3.0) | — | .091 (5.7) | −.014 (0.7) |
| **Miscellaneous manufactures** | | | | | | | | | | | | |
| U.S. | .80 | .085 | 1.62 | .25 | C | 0.6 | .33 | −1.3 | −1.0 (3.2) | 0.8 (4.1) | −.082 (8.4) | −.016 (0.9) |
| Japan | .74 | .088 | 1.85 | .25 | C | 0.0 | .55 | −1.5 | −1.7 (3.7) | 1.5 (4.1) | .048 (4.6) | .103 (4.7) |

the following results:
1. $R^2$, the coefficient of determination;
2. SE, the standard error of the estimate;
3. DW, the Durbin-Watson statistic;
4. Rho, the best-fitting value of the autocorrelation coefficient;
5. $L$, the best-fitting shape of the lag distribution on prices;
6. $T1$, the Theil compatibility statistic;
7. $T2$, the Theil measure of the percentage of the posterior estimate attributable to the prior;
8. The prior own-price elasticity;
9. The posterior own-price elasticity;
10. The posterior cross-price elasticity;
11. The trend growth rate until 1971;
12. The trend growth rate after 1971.

Variants of these equations, using alternative specifications, appear in Appendix A. The great detail of these tables, however, does not easily lend itself to overview, and at first the range of the estimates seems bewildering. But closer analysis, aided by aggregated tables (Tables 3.6 through 3.8), provides new insight into the present structure of Japanese-American trade and its evolution over time.

The most obvious general finding is that the share functions fit very well; for example, the median-fitting function — U.S. iron and steel imports from the rest of the world — has an $R^2$ of 0.83, a standard error of 0.14 (since the equation is in double-logarithmic form, this implies a standard percentage error of about 14 percent), and an $F(5,13)$ ratio of 22. In general, the quality of fit is surprising because the dependent variable is not the value of trade (the usual case), but a volatile ratio: the real share of a particular trade flow in domestic demand. Furthermore, the presence of a vast array of priors and restrictions could also have been expected to reduce sample fit.

An overwhelming majority of the estimates have expected signs and magnitudes. With the help of the prior distributions, all own-price elasticities are estimated with the expected negative sign. More will be said about the role of the priors later, but the data themselves, without priors, also yield expected price behavior in all but four of the sixty equations. The price elasticities are

**Table 3.6** Trade-weighted average price elasticities

| | Importer | | | | | | | | | | | |
| --- | --- | --- | --- | --- | --- | --- | --- | --- | --- | --- | --- | --- |
| | U.S. | | | Japan | | | ROW | | | Total exports | | |
| Exporter | $P_{US}$ | $P_J$ | $P_{ROW}$ | $P_{US}$ | $P_J$ | $P_{ROW}$ | $P_{US}$ | $P_J$ | $P_{ROW}$ | $P_{US}$ | $P_J$ | $P_{ROW}$ |
| **U.S.** | | | | | | | | | | | | |
| All goods | | | | −1.19 | 0.92 | 0.28 | −0.84 | 0.19 | 0.65 | −0.87 | 0.26 | 0.62 |
| Mfg. only | | | | −1.19 | 1.15 | 0.03 | −0.90 | 0.24 | 0.66 | −0.92 | 0.30 | 0.62 |
| **Japan** | | | | | | | | | | | | |
| All goods | 1.40 | −2.12 | 0.72 | | | | 0.40 | −1.45 | 1.05 | 0.63 | −1.61 | 0.97 |
| Mfg. only | 1.42 | −2.15 | 0.73 | | | | 0.41 | −1.47 | 1.06 | 0.65 | −1.63 | 0.98 |
| **ROW** | | | | | | | | | | | | |
| All goods | 0.60 | 0.17 | −0.76 | 0.04 | 0.62 | −0.66 | | | | 0.41 | 0.32 | −0.73 |
| Mfg. only | 0.78 | 0.36 | −1.14 | 0.03 | 1.52 | −1.55 | | | | 0.64 | 0.58 | −1.22 |
| **Total imports** | 0.70 | −0.12 | −0.58 | −0.16 | 0.67 | −0.51 | −0.41 | −0.38 | 0.79 | | | |
| | 0.93 | −0.24 | −0.69 | −0.34 | 1.41 | −1.06 | −0.35 | −0.48 | 0.83 | | | |

**Table 3.7** Price-elasticities of all goods: 1960, 1970, and 1980

| | Importer | | | | | | | | | | | |
|---|---|---|---|---|---|---|---|---|---|---|---|---|
| | U.S. | | | Japan | | | ROW | | | Total exports | | |
| Exporter | $P_{US}$ | $P_J$ | $P_{ROW}$ | $P_{US}$ | $P_J$ | $P_{ROW}$ | $P_{US}$ | $P_J$ | $P_{ROW}$ | $P_{US}$ | $P_J$ | $P_{ROW}$ |
| U.S. | | | | | | | | | | | | |
| 1960 | | | | −1.17 | 0.87 | 0.30 | −0.85 | 0.19 | 0.65 | −0.87 | 0.24 | 0.63 |
| 1970 | | | | −1.21 | 0.92 | 0.29 | −0.86 | 0.19 | 0.66 | −0.89 | 0.28 | 0.62 |
| 1980 | | | | −1.19 | 0.92 | 0.28 | −0.84 | 0.19 | 0.65 | −0.87 | 0.26 | 0.62 |
| Japan | | | | | | | | | | | | |
| 1960 | 1.87 | −2.18 | 0.31 | | | | 0.33 | −1.51 | 1.18 | 0.72 | −1.68 | 0.96 |
| 1970 | 1.64 | −2.19 | 0.55 | | | | 0.33 | −1.50 | 1.17 | 0.71 | −1.70 | 0.99 |
| 1980 | 1.40 | −2.12 | 0.72 | | | | 0.40 | −1.45 | 1.05 | 0.63 | −1.61 | 0.97 |
| ROW | | | | | | | | | | | | |
| 1960 | 0.83 | 0.17 | −1.01 | 0.08 | 1.15 | −1.22 | | | | 0.71 | 0.34 | −1.04 |
| 1970 | 0.80 | 0.22 | −1.02 | 0.06 | 0.98 | −1.04 | | | | 0.61 | 0.42 | −1.03 |
| 1980 | 0.60 | 0.17 | −0.76 | 0.04 | 0.62 | −0.66 | | | | 0.41 | 0.32 | −0.73 |
| Total imports | | | | | | | | | | | | |
| | 0.91 | 0.00 | −0.91 | −0.34 | 1.06 | −0.71 | −0.67 | −0.06 | 0.73 | | | |
| | 0.93 | −0.15 | −0.78 | −0.30 | 0.97 | −0.67 | −0.53 | −0.28 | 0.80 | | | |
| | 0.70 | −0.12 | −0.58 | −0.16 | 0.67 | −0.51 | −0.41 | −0.38 | 0.79 | | | |

**Table 3.8** Size variations in sectoral own-price elasticities

| No. | Sector | Average | Largest | | Smallest | |
|---|---|---|---|---|---|---|
| 7 | Iron and steel | −2.20 | −3.17 | R > J[a] | −1.12 | U > R |
| 11 | Transport equipment | −1.78 | −2.37 | J > U | −0.92 | U > R |
| 3 | Textiles, apparel | −1.66 | −2.89 | J > U | −1.37 | U > J |
| 4 | Wood products, paper | −1.62 | −2.21 | R > J | −0.99 | U > R |
| 8 | Metal products | −1.52 | −2.23 | U > J | −1.12 | R > U |
| 12 | Miscellaneous manufactures | −1.34 | −2.48 | J > U | −0.83 | R > U |
| 9 | Machinery, instruments | −1.29 | −1.93 | R > J | −0.85 | U > R |
| 5 | Chemicals | −1.15 | −1.55 | J > U | −0.49 | U > R |
| 10 | Electrical machinery | −0.96 | −1.58 | J > U | −0.33 | R > J |
| 6 | Stone, clay, and glass | −0.88 | −1.28 | J > R | −0.51 | R > J |

a. Indicates type of trade flow; for example, "R > J" means rest-of-the-world exports to Japan.

usually accurately measured; nearly half have standard errors of 0.5 or less, and all but three have $t$-statistics of 1.77 or more, the 5-percent critical level for a one-tailed test.[6] On average, prices respond with a B-type lag; of the three alternative lag forms permitted, 16 percent of the markets analyzed respond to current prices (lag A) and nearly half to prices with a three-period lag (lag C). In sum, own-price elasticities appear to have the expected statistical properties, are accurate, and show about the expected degree of sluggishness.

The cross-price elasticities are not as satisfactory. In some cases even large negative elasticities were obtained. Since imports from different sources are most likely substitutes, these results seem troubling, if not theoretically impossible. In addition, high multicollinearity among the two relative price variables and trend occasionally led to unstable parameter estimates. Accordingly, cross-price elasticity estimates were restricted to a range between zero and the positive absolute value of the share's own-price elasticity. The restriction is binding in nearly half of all equations, although it is often not statistically significant because the variance of the restricted parameter is high.

Nevertheless, the overall pattern of the cross-price elasticities suggests interesting regularities. Estimates with expected magnitudes and signs appeared in 80 percent of rest-of-the-world (ROW) markets (reflecting competition between the United States and Japan) and in 60 percent of U.S. markets, but only in

20 percent of Japanese markets. Since Japan's import structure is highly specialized, it is not surprising that little systematic competition is found between U.S. and rest-of-the-world manufactures in Japanese markets. But in general, cross-price elasticities are less accurately estimated than own-price elasticities; for example, only half of the estimates produce $t$-ratios above the 5-percent level.

Two additive trend terms are used to estimate non-price-related changes: the first measures the rate of change of shares between 1960 and 1971, the second between 1971 and 1980. 1971 was a watershed in Japanese-American trade relations. Near the end of that year, President Nixon's New Economic Policy and the subsequent Smithsonian agreements launched a process that quickly led to a floating dollar and a sharply revalued yen. Alternative specifications with a quadratic trend in place of the two-period variant actually gave very similar but somewhat poorer-fitting results.

Many of the trend terms are important, and some show significant differences between periods. The large, precisely measured growth rates associated with Japanese exports, particularly in the first period, deserve special attention. Japan's entry into foreign markets was not only very rapid but, in terms of the relationships identified by these regressions, occurred in large part independently of market and price changes. Chapter 6 returns to this issue as it tries to untangle different factors behind the growth of trade. But the conclusion is inescapable that something unusual happened to Japan's place in the world economy in the 1960s. Some later results suggest that technical progress was involved; apparently, price statistics significantly underestimate the importance of technology for trade changes during this period.

Other aspects of the elasticity estimates are accessible in aggregate form. Tables 3.6 and 3.7 present aggregations across sectors, highlighting the characteristics of trade by origin and destination. These summary elasticities are individual elasticities weighted by the dollar values of the trade flows involved. The tables also show elasticities of total merchandise trade, obtained by summing the Armington-type elasticities presented in Tables 3.3 – 3.5 with the elasticities (essentially, the excess demand elasticities) of the agriculture and natural resource sectors.[7]

Whether one looks at manufactures or total trade, the esti-

mated elasticities are rather low (see Table 3.6). But beyond this initial impression, there are interesting differences. In manufactures trade, the largest own-price elasticity is observed for Japanese exports to the United States, and the smallest for U.S. exports to the rest of the world. Evidently, Japanese products have good substitutes in U.S. markets (from both U.S. and third producers), whereas U.S. exports consist of goods with especially limited foreign competition. When all goods are counted, most elasticities decline, primarily because natural resource trade is price-inelastic. The difference between the elasticities of manufactures and all trade depends on the natural resource content of the trade flow involved. The Japan/United States elasticity, for example, changes only slightly when all goods are counted, from −2.15 to −2.12, while the ROW/Japan elasticity falls from −1.55 to −0.66. With agricultural and natural resource goods included, the Japan/United States elasticity stands out even more sharply over other elasticities in the table. This point is important in subsequent results.

Elasticities appear to decline over time. Table 3.7 shows how changes in the composition of trade have affected aggregate elasticities between 1960 and 1970. These composition effects support what Richardson (1976) has called the "new elasticity pessimism"; trade increasingly consists of relatively price-inelastic products. Although the bulk of the elasticity decline is due to the increasing share of natural resources in the overall value of trade, similar but smaller effects are also present in the manufactures aggregates.

Elasticity averages by sector have their own story to tell; they also partly explain the decline in the composite price elasticities. The aggregates reported in Table 3.8 are simple averages of each sector's own-price elasticities in the six bilateral share functions (for example, the six nonblank areas of, say, Table 3.7) estimated in the study. Steel, transportation equipment, and textiles lead the list; in each of these products international competition is vigorous and world markets are well established. Perhaps trade in these products has become a routine economic choice rather than a search for novel features not available at home. Trade may have become common because the large national markets represented by these industries were probably the first to justify heavy international marketing investment.

Alternatively, the products involved may have been especially well suited to standardization and large-scale production.

Standardization and stable product characteristics are also associated with slow-growing markets. Thus, as incomes grow, trade tends to shift increasingly to low-price-elasticity products like machinery. At the same time, standardization and price elasticities may rise in these sectors too as production experience accumulates. It would be interesting to know whether standardization is proceeding fast enough in the engineering industries to offset the general shift of demand to these specialized products. Because the decline in price elasticities is extremely important to the future of world trade, the factors that explain differences and changes in price elasticities deserve particular attention. The estimates presented here suggest that at least some determinants of price sensitivity are empirically tractable and might be traced to the interacting properties of suppliers, markets, and products.

At the aggregate level, the estimates fall well within the range of results obtained in many recent studies. To be sure, that range is large. Figures 3.2 through 3.7 show a collection of results culled from the recent literature — "recent" meaning subsequent to Houthakker and Magee's influential multicountry study (1969). The sources of the studies cited in the figures are:

Adams-Junz: as quoted by Branson (1972).

Almon: Almon et al. (1974).

Economic Planning Agency: Economic Planning Agency (1973).

Geraci-Prewo: Geraci and Prewo (1982).

Goldstein-Kahn: Goldstein and Kahn (1976).

Goldstein-Kahn-Officer: Goldstein, Kahn, and Officer (1980).

Haynes-Stone: Haynes and Stone (1983).

Houthakker-Magee: Houthakker and Magee (1969).

Joy-Stolen: Joy and Stolen (1975).

Magee: as quoted by Branson (1972).

Monroe: Monroe (1973).

Murray-Ginman: Murray and Ginman (1976).

Nyhus: Nyhus (1975).

Project LINK: as quoted by Klein (1972).

Warner-Kreinin: Warner and Kreinin (1983).

Wilson-Takacs: Wilson and Takacs (1979).

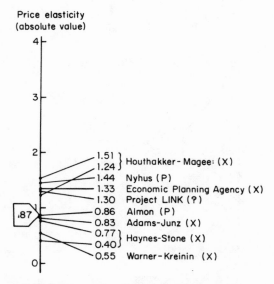

**Figure 3.2**  Recent price elasticity estimates: U.S. exports

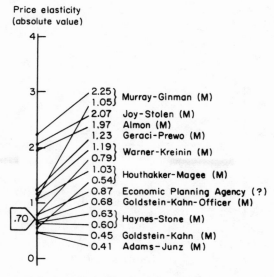

**Figure 3.3**  Recent price elasticity estimates: U.S. imports

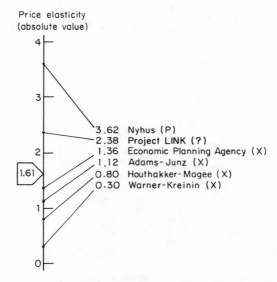

**Figure 3.4** Recent price elasticity estimates: Japanese exports

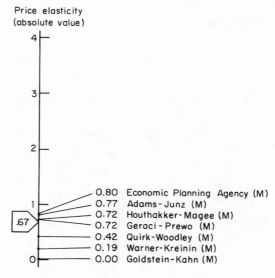

**Figure 3.5** Recent price elasticity estimates: Japanese imports

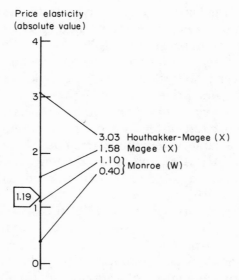

**Figure 3.6**  Recent price elasticity estimates: U.S. exports to Japan

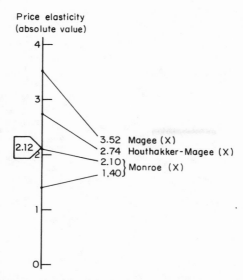

**Figure 3.7**  Recent price elasticity estimates: Japanese exports to the U.S.

The value contained in a large open arrow indicates the results of the present study. The price index used in each of the cited studies is identified in parentheses following the authors' names. "M" and "E" refer to unit value indexes for imports and exports, respectively; "W" stands for a wholesale price index, and "P" for a producers' price index. The present study, of course, relies entirely on producers' price indexes for its estimates.

The estimates cited differ in economic content (choice and definition of variables), technique (functional form, shape of lags, estimation methods), and data (frequency and observation period). In addition, aggregate elasticities, such as those listed in Table 3.8, are sensitive to changes in trade composition over time (see also Joy and Stolen, 1975). But on the whole, the disagreement between the present estimates and the median overall elasticity of past studies is not very large. On average, disaggregated analysis does not appear to yield radically different results from the analysis of aggregate data. There is a substantial amount of underlying variation in disaggregated results, however, and under particular conditions this may lead to great variations in aggregate response.

# 4 Implementing the System

There is abundant information about economic detail at particular moments in time — for example, in disaggregated input-output systems — and about economic aggregates over longer periods of time. However, a Heisenberg-like trade-off appears to apply to empirical modeling: it is very difficult to model both structural detail and sophisticated dynamic response. The problem is that the estimation of dynamic properties usually requires repeated observations of a system in adjustment. Thus, the acquisition of data with adequate structural and time detail represents a serious challenge in empirical general-equilibrium analysis. In the present case, a compromise was struck by joining the time-series variables needed to estimate the trade share functions — a behavioral component which had to be accurately specified — to detailed structural data from a handful of benchmark observations. Estimates of less critical behavioral relationships, to be described below, were based on strong priors and the limited observations of the structural data set.

The sectoral classification of the system is shown in Table 4.1. For the most part, the economic logic of the system argues for detail: for example, both price formation and demand can be more accurately described if sectors are relatively homogeneous. But even aside from the data constraints, too much detail can be counterproductive; the assumption of the separability of intra-

73

**Table 4.1** Composition of sectors

| No. | Sector | United States 1958–1972 Input-output sectors | Japan 1960, 1965 Input-output sectors | Japan 1970 Input-output sectors | Japan 1975 Input-output sectors |
|---|---|---|---|---|---|
| 1 | Agriculture, food | 1–4, 14–15 | 1–6, 12–17 | 1–6, 12–17 | 1–5, 11–16 |
| 2 | Natural resources | 5–10, 31, 38 | 7–11, 31–32, 36 | 7–11, 31–32, 36 | 6–10, 30–31, 35 |
| 3 | Textiles, apparel | 16–19, 33–34 | 18–21, 26 | 18–21, 26 | 17–20, 25 |
| 4 | Wood products, paper | 20–25 | 22–24 | 22–24 | 21–23 |
| 5 | Chemicals | 27–30, 32 | 27–30 | 27–30 | 26–29 |
| 6 | Stone, clay, and glass | 35–36 | 33 | 33 | 32 |
| 7 | Iron and steel | 37 | 34–35 | 34–35 | 33–34 |
| 8 | Metal products | 13, 39–42 | 37 | 37 | 36 |
| 9 | Machinery, instruments | 43–50, 52, 62–63 | 38, 41 | 38, 41 | 37, 40 |
| 10 | Electrical machinery | 51, 53–58 | 39 | 39 | 38 |
| 11 | Transport equipment | 59–61 | 40 | 40 | 39 |
| 12 | Miscellaneous manufactures | 26, 64 | 42, 25 | 42, 25 | 41, 24 |
| 13 | Construction | 11–12 | 43–44 | 43–44 | 42–43 |
| 14 | Utilities | 68, 78–79 | 45–47 | 45–47 | 44–46 |
| 15 | Wholesale, retail trade | 69 | 48 | 48 | 47 |
| 16 | Financial, insurance | 70 | 49 | 49 | 48 |
| 17 | Real estate | 71 | 50 | 50–51 | 49–50 |
| 18 | Transport, communication | 65–67 exc. 65.04 (pt.) | 51–52 | 52–53 | 51–52 |
| 19 | Services | 72–77 | 53–55 | 54–57 | 53–58 |
| 20 | International freight services | 65.04 (pt.) | pt. 51 | pt. 52 | pt. 51 |

sectoral demand (for products distinguished by origin) from intersectoral demand becomes implausible if disaggregation proceeds to far. Unfortunately, this theoretical limit is not reached. Because of the difficulty of matching time-series and structural data, the cost of additional detail begins to rise steeply well before the separability condition becomes suspect.

The principal sources of structural data include U.S. and Japanese national accounts, U.S. input-output systems for 1958, 1963, 1967, and 1972, and Japanese input-output systems for 1960, 1965, 1970, and 1975. Time-series data are added for outputs, prices, and trade flows. Since these data come from a variety of different sources (in some cases, for example Japanese-American bilateral trade, roughly the same data are available in more than one source), numerous inconsistencies must be resolved.[1] The resulting data base, incorporating a range of conceptual and accounting adjustments, is sketched in Figure 4.1. The system provides nationally and internationally consistent "snapshots" of the American and Japanese economies and their interactions in 1960, 1970, and 1980; it also tracks some major variables (output, prices, trade) on an annual basis in the intervening years. The details of data assembly, construction, and adjustment are described in Appendix C.

This chapter completes the technical survey of the model by addressing three outstanding methodological issues: estimation of behavioral functions in production and consumption, principles of general equilibrium solutions, and the actual computerized solution method. The chapter concludes by presenting the three base solutions of the model. These solutions introduce conventions used to present simulation results and provide an initial look at Japanese-American economic structure through the "looking glass" of the model.

## Quantitative Response in Production and Consumption

The theoretical structure of the production and consumption systems was outlined in Chapter 2, in particular in Eqs. (2.6)– (2.8). Estimates of the required parameters are derived by comparing production and consumption data from the input-output systems of different years. Since three points hardly make a

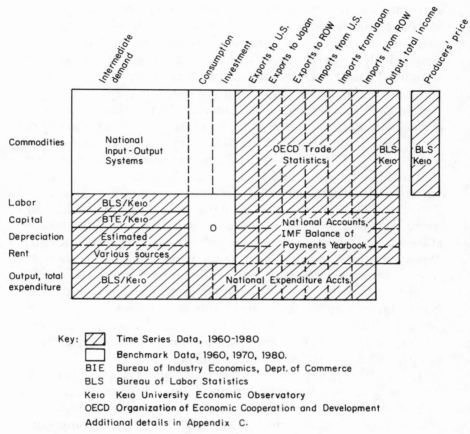

Key:

| ⧄ | Time Series Data, 1960-1980 |
| ☐ | Benchmark Data, 1960, 1970, 1980. |
| BIE | Bureau of Industry Economics, Dept. of Commerce |
| BLS | Bureau of Labor Statistics |
| Keio | Keio University Economic Observatory |
| OECD | Organization of Economic Cooperation and Development |

Additional details in Appendix C.

**Figure 4.1** Schematic view of data and principal sources

significant sample, and since changes between distant input-output systems may include a good deal of measurement noise, the estimated elasticities are carefully controlled to fall within plausible ranges. These ranges are based, in spirit, on studies providing more aggregate input-substitution elasticities (Jorgenson, 1983; Jorgenson and Nishimizu, 1978; Tsujimura, Kuroda, and Shimada, 1981).

The $\beta$ parameters of the production input demand system were estimated for intermediate input-users as a group rather than sector by sector. Although the $\beta$'s are assumed to be the

same throughout each economy, they produce different input price elasticities when applied in different industries. As Eq. (2.8) shows, the price elasticity of a particular input is negatively related to its base consumption level and positively related to the average $\beta$ of the sector's other inputs. In other words, a sector has a large price elasticity for an input if that input is relatively unimportant to the sector and if the sector's other inputs show flexible price response. Using benchmark input-output data for 1960, 1970, and 1980, the equation estimated is

$$\log \Sigma_j a_{ij} x_j = k_i + \beta_i \log \left\{ \frac{q_i}{\Pi_k q_k^{\left(\frac{\beta_k \Sigma_j a_{kj} x_j}{\Sigma_i \Sigma_j \beta_i a_{ij} x_j}\right)}} \right\}, \qquad (4.1)$$

where $q_i$ = price of input $i$ (1970 = 1),
  $a_{ij}$ = input $i$ used per unit of $j$ at time $t$,
  $x_j$ = output weights (1970 base),
  $k_i$ = estimated constant,
  $\beta_i$ = estimated elasticity parameter.

The parameter $\beta$ was restricted to the range $0.1 - 1.5$ for agriculture and natural-resource inputs, and to $0.2 - 2.0$ for other inputs. This procedure implicitly assumes that input changes of the "right" magnitude result from producer responses to relative price changes, while other input shifts reflect technological change. Results are given in Table 4.2.

The linear expenditure system of the consumption sector is estimated with the equation

$$y_i = a_i q_i + b_i (Y - \Sigma_k a_k q_k), \qquad (4.2)$$

where $y_i$ = per capita expenditure on $i$ at time $t$,
  $a_i$ = minimum consumption parameter,
  $b_i$ = marginal expenditure parameter,
  $Y$ = per capita total consumption expenditure.

Since the discretionary income variable (enclosed in parentheses, Eq. 4.2) requires knowledge of the $a_i$, the demand system is iteratively estimated.

Income elasticities provide a convenient point for constraining

**Table 4.2** The model's input substitution parameters

| No. | Sector | United States | Japan |
|---|---|---|---|
| 1 | Agriculture, food | −0.78 | −0.10 |
| 2 | Natural resources | −0.10 | −0.10 |
| 3 | Textiles, apparel | −1.33 | −0.20 |
| 4 | Wood products, paper | −2.00 | −0.36 |
| 5 | Chemicals | −1.46 | −0.66 |
| 6 | Stone, clay, and glass | −0.88 | −2.00 |
| 7 | Iron and steel | −0.20 | −0.20 |
| 8 | Metal products | −1.91 | −1.83 |
| 9 | Machinery, instruments | −2.00 | −0.66 |
| 10 | Electrical machinery | −1.22 | −0.87 |
| 11 | Transport equipment | −1.71 | −0.89 |
| 12 | Miscellaneous manufactures | −0.20 | −0.75 |
| 13 | Construction | −2.00 | −0.24 |
| 14 | Utilities | −2.00 | −0.22 |
| 15 | Wholesale, retail trade | −1.32 | −2.00 |
| 16 | Financial, insurance | −0.21 | −2.00 |
| 17 | Real estate | −1.37 | −2.00 |
| 18 | Transport, communication | −0.84 | −0.20 |
| 19 | Services | −2.00 | −0.20 |
| 20 | International freight services | n.a. | n.a. |
|  | Labor | −0.94 | −0.71 |
|  | Capital | −0.50 | −0.77 |

estimates of the LES demand system. The income elasticities implied by Eq. (4.2) are

$$\xi_i = (\partial y_i / \partial Y)(Y / y_i) = b_i(Y / y_i), \qquad (4.3)$$

where $\xi_i =$ income elasticity of good $i$.

At the 1970 midpoint of the estimating period, the income elasticities were constrained to the range $0-2.0$. This translates into the following lower and upper bounds on $b$ coefficients:

$$0 < b_i < 2(y_i / Y) \qquad (4.4)$$

The implied 1970 income and price elasticities of the estimated linear expenditure system are shown in Table 4.3.

Lastly, econometric functions are also used to describe the determinants of output in the homogeneous sectors, agriculture

**Table 4.3**  The model's income and own-price elasticities in consumption

| No. | Sector | Income elasticities | | Price elasticities | |
|-----|--------|------|-------|------|-------|
| | | U.S. | Japan | U.S. | Japan |
| 1 | Agriculture, food | 0.01 | 0.51 | −0.01 | −0.19 |
| 2 | Natural resources | 0.15 | 1.01 | −0.09 | −0.37 |
| 3 | Textiles, apparel | 0.63 | 1.08 | −0.39 | −0.40 |
| 4 | Wood products, paper | 0.80 | 1.33 | −0.49 | −0.49 |
| 5 | Chemicals | 1.54 | 1.42 | −0.95 | −0.52 |
| 6 | Stone, clay, and glass | 2.77 | 1.77 | −1.71 | −0.65 |
| 7 | Iron and steel | 0.76 | 1.30 | −0.47 | −0.48 |
| 8 | Metal products | 0.43 | 2.20 | −0.27 | −0.81 |
| 9 | Machinery, instruments | 0.98 | 1.20 | −0.60 | −0.44 |
| 10 | Electrical machinery | 1.95 | 2.14 | −1.20 | −0.79 |
| 11 | Transport equipment | 0.72 | 1.88 | −0.44 | −0.69 |
| 12 | Miscellaneous manufactures | 1.08 | 0.99 | −0.67 | −0.36 |
| 13 | Construction | 1.00 | 1.00 | −0.62 | −0.37 |
| 14 | Utilities | 1.25 | 1.18 | −0.77 | −0.44 |
| 15 | Wholesale, retail trade | 1.07 | 1.18 | −0.66 | −0.44 |
| 16 | Financial, insurance | 1.30 | 1.01 | −0.80 | −0.37 |
| 17 | Real estate | 1.77 | 1.61 | −1.09 | −0.60 |
| 18 | Transport, communication | 0.80 | 0.89 | −0.49 | −0.32 |
| 19 | Services | 1.40 | 0.96 | −0.86 | −0.36 |
| 20 | International freight services | n.a. | n.a. | n.a. | n.a. |

and natural resources (see Figure 2.4, Eq. R10). All of these
equations include a price/cost variable to measure incentives to
exploit the resource base and a domestic demand variable to
reflect influences on output in the part of the sector oriented
toward domestic markets (see Chapter 2). One difficulty here is
the lack of annual input-output cost data for estimating the
price/cost ratio. A proxy cost time series is therefore developed
by aggregating input-price time series with a Cobb-Douglas cost
function based on 1970 input use patterns. The equations also
include trend terms to capture technical progress and changes in
the resource base, and yield terms in agriculture to represent the
influence of weather. Because of the domestic demand variable
on the right-hand side, the procedure of two-stage least squares
is used. Results are shown in Table 4.4; all equations yield the
expected signs and fit moderately well.

**Table 4.4**  Regression results for domestic supply

| Coefficient | United States | | Japan | |
|---|---|---|---|---|
| | Agriculture, food | Nonrenewable resources | Agriculture, food | Nonrenewable resources |
| Dependent variable | | | | |
| Value in 1980 ($1970 billions) | 219.42 | 85.70 | 54.82 | 21.57 |
| Independent variables | | | | |
| Constant | −5.05 | 1.74 | −14.14 | −0.47 |
| | (0.0) | (0.1) | (0.9) | (0.4) |
| Price/cost | 21.60 | 1.41 | 11.38 | 0.21 |
| | (1.1) | (0.6) | (1.3) | (0.3) |
| Demand | 0.62 | 0.86 | 0.58 | 0.70 |
| | (0.7) | (3.4) | (1.8) | (10.6) |
| Trend | 1.01 | 1.09 | 0.36 | 0.11 |
| | (0.3) | (1.6) | (0.6) | (0.7) |
| Trend$^2$ | — | −0.06 | — | −0.009 |
| | | (2.2) | | (1.8) |
| Yield | 0.40 | — | 0.03 | — |
| | (1.4) | | (2.0) | |
| $R^2$ | 0.98 | 0.97 | 0.98 | 1.00 |
| Standard error | 4.18 | 2.20 | 1.24 | 0.47 |
| DW | 1.58 | 1.78 | 1.10 | 2.67 |

*Note:* $t$-statistics are in parentheses; demand represents instrumental variable.

## Solving General Equilibrium Models

Although the mathematical literature on the solution of nonlinear equation systems is extensive, it does not address some of the most important issues in designing a solution strategy. The point is that a great deal of simplification is usually possible as the difficult nonlinear core of the system — the part that has to be solved with sophisticated methods — is generally smaller by orders of magnitude than the complete model. Adelman and Robinson (1978) and Dervis, deMelo, and Robinson (1982) are conscious of this problem but limit their discussion to whether the model should be reduced to a system of excess demand equations in factors or in goods. The actual range of options is much greater; the core could equally well contain excess demand equations for some factors, some goods, or some of both. Each

approach requires the elimination (usually numerical solution) of many other variables and equations, and, intuition aside, it is hard to judge the advantages of one over another. A more general theoretical basis is badly needed to guide the simplification strategy. This section does not attempt to fill the gap but does outline the issues involved.

A detailed general equilibrium model contains thousands of equations, most of which deal with the price sensitivity of intermediate and consumption demand. Intuitively, it would be wasteful to solve all of these equations in parallel as a giant simultaneous system. This presumption is based on two common features of nonlinear solution methods: costs per iteration tend to rise sharply with scale, and the speed and likelihood of convergence tend to diminish with scale. Costs rise because the computations involved in generating new trial solutions often require the evaluation or approximation of Jacobian matrices with dimensions equal to the number of equations. There is no general law that relates scale to the speed of convergence, but at the very least, if all variables are iterated in parallel, the convergence of the whole system is slowed down to the speed of its slowest-converging component.

Suppose that the system to be solved consists of the relationships

$$G_i(x_1, \ldots, x_n) = 0, \tag{4.5}$$

where  $G_i$ = equation $i$,
 $x_i$ = unknown $i$,

and that it is partitioned by dividing the variables and equations into two sets: $x_A$, $G_A$ and $x_B$, $G_B$, where $A$ contains difficult (high-feedback) nonlinear relationships and $B$ contains relationships that are easily solved by analytical or numerical methods. If the solution of the $B$ system is given by

$$x_B = S_B(x_A), \tag{4.6}$$

then the core ($A$ system) reduces to

$$G_A[x_A, S_B(x_A)] = G_A'(x_A). \tag{4.7}$$

In the present case, described further below, the $A$ system con-

tains only six equations; thousands of others are solved by numerical methods that take special advantage of the economic content of the relationships involved.

If $n$ equations belong in the core $A$, and $N - n$ are solved in $B$, the overall effort involved in the solution is given by the expression

$$Z = I_A(n)[E_A(n) + I_B(N - n)E_B(N - n)], \qquad (4.8)$$

where   $Z =$ overall solution effort,
$E =$ effort per iteration,
$I =$ number of iterations required,
$A, B =$ subscripts denoting core and noncore computations.

This expression could be used, in principle, to devise an optimal partition for $A$ and $B$. The optimizing rule (readily derived by differentiating Eq. 4.8) would be to move variables (or groups of variables) to $B$ until the transfer of the last imposes the same incremental effort in $B$ as in $A$. In practice, little is known about the functions $I(n)$ and $E(n)$, and quantitative application of Eq. (4.8) is unattainable. But it is likely that an optimal solution involves a fair amount of subdivision if the functions determining effort have the expected shape ($I'(n) > 0$, $E'(n) > 0$), especially if more efficient solution methods can be achieved by fitting techniques to the specific features of smaller problems (and $E_B(n) < E_A(n)$).

Simplification through subdivision can involve further vertical partitions (leading to algorithms with multiple nests) as well as horizontal partitions. In the latter case, subsets of equations are solved separately, and variable values are exchanged among subsets at the beginning of each iteration. These systems are illustrated in Figure 4.2. Horizontal partitions are useful if the variables included in a group depend primarily on others in the group and on a limited number of "global" variables (see Petri, 1979). In most cases, the optimal composite strategy is bound to involve several different mathematical algorithms operating on partitions of the overall equation system.

Using Figure 4.2 as a visual reference, the algorithm assigned to solve the $A$ system represents an "outside" loop, while the

A. Sequential Composite Algorithms

B. Parallel Composite Algorithms

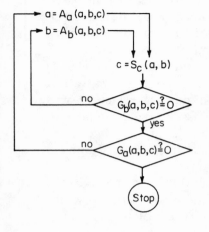

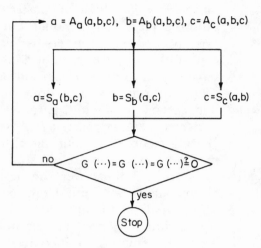

Key: a, b, c,   = vectors of variables grouped for solution purposes
$G_a(a,b,c)$ = subsystem of equations associated with group a
$S_a(b,c)$   = solution of $G_a$ given b,c
$A_a(a,b,c)$ = algorithm for generating a new trial value a

**Figure 4.2**  Solution systems for simultaneous equation models

algorithm operating on the $B$ system represents an "inside" loop. These designations reflect the programming sequence of the computations that need to be performed. First, trial values are introduced for $x_A$, and the $B$ system is solved (also iteratively, if nonlinear). Solutions for $x_B$ are then passed back to the $A$ algorithm, where the functions $G_A(x_A,\ x_B)$ are evaluated and, if necessary, new $x_A$ values are found. The actual method used in this study is presented later in Figure 4.4.

## Nonlinear Algorithms

Once the nonlinear core (or a nonlinear partition) is identified, many solution methods are available (Ortega and Rheinboldt, 1970; Rabinowitz, 1970; Wait, 1979). At one extreme, some elegant algorithms based on Scarf's fixed-point methods (1975) guarantee convergence but have not proved computationally

efficient for models of reasonable size (Taylor, 1975; Ginsburgh and Waelbroeck, 1981). At the other extreme, algorithms based on the economic logic of *tattonement* require very simple computations even for large models but appear to converge only with artfully chosen parameters (Adelman and Robinson, 1978). Recent studies of *tattonement* by Ginsburgh and Waelbroeck (1981) have begun to put the method on a more systematic basis, but much still remains to be done on techniques for selecting, and if necessary modifying, parameters to assure convergence. In between these extremes are several traditional approaches, including steepest descent algorithms and the Newton-Raphson method used in the present study.

Figure 4.3 illustrates the actual solution system used—a nested algorithm built from several methods. The Newton-Raphson algorithm applied to the "outer" problem establishes equilibrium in factor markets and on external account (equivalently, it assures that income equals expenditure). From the viewpoint of this outer loop, the model appears as

$$T = G(C), \tag{4.9}$$

where $T$ = vector of factor and foreign exchange excess demands ("targets"),

$C$ = vector of factor prices and consumption levels ("controls").

The Newton-Raphson algorithm replaces Eq. (4.9) with its linear approximation:

$$T^i = T^{i-1} + \nabla G(C^i - C^{i-1}), \tag{4.10}$$

where $i$ = iteration counter,

$\nabla G$ = matrix of derivatives: $\partial G_i / \partial C_j$.

and solves it for $T^i = 0$:

$$C^i = C^{i-1} - \nabla G^{-1} T^{i-1}. \tag{4.11}$$

If all goes well, successive applications of Eq. (4.11) generate a converging sequence of $C$'s, and the procedure can be terminated arbitrarily close to the solution.

Figure 4.4 illustrates the method in two dimensions. Equation (4.9) is represented by the curve $aa$, Eq. (4.10) by the line $bb$, and

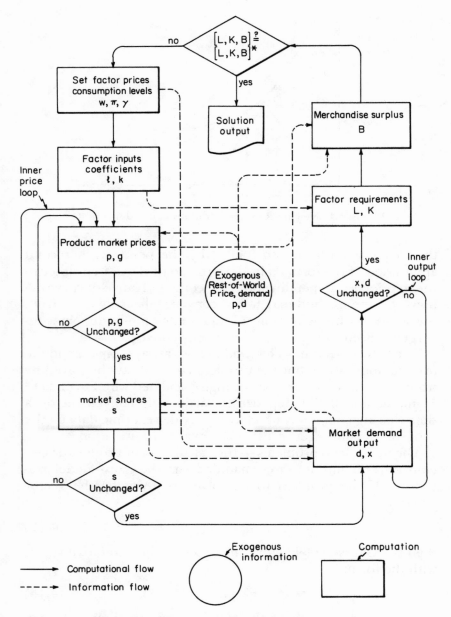

**Figure 4.3**  Composite solution strategy

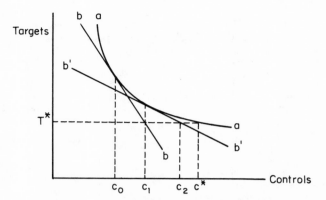

**Figure 4.4** Newton-Raphson iterations in two dimensions

the first evaluation of Eq. (4.11) by the point $c_0$. A second application of the formula leads to the point $c_1$—a step closer to the solution $c^*$. Depending on the second derivative of curve $aa$, however, the method may fail to converge, backing away from the solution with oscillations of increasing amplitude. Nonconvergence is possible even if $aa$ is strictly convex.

The Newton-Raphson method did not always converge in the present application, but the problem could always be solved by scaling down the factor price change calculated with Eq. (4.11).[2] Manipulation of the step size is particularly convenient on a time-sharing computer, which can provide real-time data on the progress of convergence after, say, every fifth iteration.[3]

The inside loop problems — the calculation of product prices, demand, and output — were handled with the Gauss-Seidel procedure. If the problem to be solved is given by the vector equation

$$G(x) = 0, \qquad (4.12)$$

then the Gauss-Seidel algorithm generates new iterative values with the formula

$$x_j^k = x_j^{k-1} + g_j(x_1, \ldots, x_n). \qquad (4.13)$$

Convergence depends on the matching of equations with variables; there are no mathematical reasons to expect the error in a particular equilibrium condition to push any particular variable

toward its equilibrium value. But the economic content of an equation often suggests an obvious equation/variable relationship. For example, product price equations have the form

$$g_j(q_i, p_j) = \Sigma_i a_{ij} q_i - p_j = 0, \qquad (4.14)$$

where $q_i$ = input prices,
$a_{ij}$ = input-output coefficients,
$p_j$ = product prices.

The obvious decision is to match $p_j$ with equation $g_j$, that is, with the equation that "explains" the price. The Gauss-Seidel method then implies

$$p_j^k = \Sigma_i a_{ij} q_i^{k-1}, \qquad (4.15)$$

which is simply the input-output calculation of product prices.

The computational structure represented by Figure 4.3 worked reliably and rapidly; a typical solution of the system required roughly five Newton-Raphson iterations and 20 seconds of central processing time on the DEC-10 computer.

In developing models of this type, computational issues still require substantial investments of time and analysis; there are no "canned"programs for solving general equilibrium models of a reasonable size. Although a unified computational theory for general equilibrium analysis is clearly beginning to emerge, it is hard to see how these models can become sufficiently standardized to make standard computer programs and algorithms worthwhile. Composite algorithms closely matched to the problem at hand are likely to outperform even the most elegant general techniques. What is really needed, therefore, is a clear theoretical basis for the design of composite algorithms.

### Base Solutions

Consistent U.S. and Japanese systems of national account, trade, output, price, and input-output data are available for each of the three benchmark observations of this study (1960, 1970, 1980). When the model is "solved" with these input data (and parameters that capture the disequilibrium nature of each observation through rents and factor unemployment), it replicates all ob-

served values. In this sense, the three benchmark observations are also base-period solutions. Some of the information available in these observations — and routinely generated in simulations — is presented in Table 4.5 and Appendix Tables B-1 through B-3. Table 4.5 shows the national accounts; Tables B-1 through B-3 present sectoral detail relating to prices, outputs, demands, and trade. These tables provide an opportunity to survey variable definitions and the conventions used to report results.

Table 4.5 presents the model's 1980 national accounts in billions of dollars, the unit of measurement used throughout the study. In general, Japanese data are converted with the average annual exchange rate (295.12 yen per dollar in 1980). The external current accounts are somewhat more detailed than is usual. In addition to endogenous merchandise trade and associated international freight (summed directly from the sectoral accounts of a typical solution), the current account also includes several categories of exogenously fixed trade. Exogenous trade consists of the U.S.-Canadian automobile trade,[4] trade in services such as insurance and passenger transportation, and trade in international labor and capital services. In a typical simulation, exogenous transactions are held constant in real terms but are valued at the relevant sectoral prices obtained in the solution.[5] The net balance of all of these items conforms fairly closely to the concept of the current account in the balance of payments, except that the model's current account excludes military transactions. The complement of this modified current account balance is the sum of capital flows, transfers, and net military expenditures.

The model's consumption variable includes both private and government consumption, and, in the case of the United States, also government investment. Because public investment is classified as "consumption" in U.S. statistics and as capital formation in Japan, investment cannot be compared directly in the two economies. This treatment carries through to other variables related to investment; Japanese capital stocks, depreciation, and operating income include public capital, while similar U.S. variables cover only private capital. From the viewpoint of simulations, adequate public capital is thus explicitly assured in the Japanese model, but depends implicitly on having the "right"

**Table 4.5**  The model's national expenditure and income accounts, 1980 (in billions of 1980 dollars)

| National accounts category | United States | | Japan | |
| --- | --- | --- | --- | --- |
| National expenditure | | | | |
| Consumption[a] | 2207.5 | | 712.6 | |
| Investment[b] | 395.4 | | 336.9 | |
| Current account | 23.3 | | −9.8 | |
| (net external saving) | | | | |
| Endogenous exports | | 214.4 | | 133.5 |
| Exogenous exports[c] | | 31.4 | | 10.7 |
| Labor service exports | | 8.1 | | 1.6 |
| Capital service exports | | 86.0 | | 11.6 |
| −Endogenous imports | | 244.4 | | 128.7 |
| −Exogenous imports | | 29.1 | | 26.5 |
| −Labor service imports | | 12.3 | | 0.5 |
| −Capital service imports | | 30.7 | | 11.6 |
| *Total* | 2626.1 | | 1039.6 | |
| National income | | | | |
| Labor | 1704.6 | | 649.1 | |
| Capital | 410.0 | | 187.1 | |
| Depreciation | 304.1 | | 139.3 | |
| Government revenue | 207.7 | | 64.2 | |
| Indirect taxes | | 197.3 | | 55.7 |
| Tariff revenues | | 7.8 | | 5.0 |
| Quota revenues[d] | | 2.5 | | 3.5 |
| *Total* | 2626.1 | | 1039.6 | |

a. Includes government consumption for the U.S. and Japan, government investment for the U.S.
b. Does not include government investment.
c. Includes U.S.-Canadian auto trade and all trade in services excluding international freight services.
d. For accounting purposes, treated as if collected and dispersed by government.

level of consumption (to generate appropriate public investment) in the American model.

The income accounts distinguish between labor, returns on capital, depreciation, and indirect tax revenues. These variables differ somewhat from the corresponding national income concepts, having been modified to better reflect underlying economic principles. Proprietors' income (in Japan called "income of unincorporated enterprises") is allocated to labor and capital income on the basis of separate estimates of the labor and capital

employed in unincorporated businesses. Also, depreciation reflects estimates of physical replacement requirements, at current replacement cost, rather than accounting depreciation. The imputed tariff equivalent of quantitative restrictions has been added to indirect taxes and subtracted from capital income, on the assumption that rents earned from quantitative restrictions are captured as profits in actual statistics. The present accounting system thus treats quota rents first as government tax receipts and then as transfers from government to business.

Appendix Tables B-1 through B-3 describe the three base solutions in additional detail, each in its current dollar prices. (To make real interperiod comparisons, deflators have to be used; see Table 4.6). Note that prices are typically 100, with units implicitly defined as "$1 billion's worth in the home market." In

**Table 4.6**  Price deflators, 1960–1980 (dollar indexes, 1970 = 1)

| No. | Sector | U.S. indexes | | Japan indexes | | ROW indexes[a] | |
|---|---|---|---|---|---|---|---|
| | | 1960 | 1980 | 1960 | 1980 | 1960 | 1980 |
| 1 | Agriculture, food | 0.828 | 2.200 | 0.616 | 3.275 | 0.850 | 2.820 |
| 2 | Natural resources | 0.860 | 4.402 | 0.877 | 6.511 | 0.984 | 7.619 |
| 3 | Textiles, apparel | 0.888 | 1.742 | 0.752 | 2.500 | 0.880 | 2.525 |
| 4 | Wood products, paper | 0.853 | 2.301 | 0.804 | 3.584 | 0.840 | 3.000 |
| 5 | Chemicals | 0.970 | 2.254 | 1.126 | 3.164 | 0.960 | 2.998 |
| 6 | Stone, clay, and glass | 0.849 | 2.336 | 0.797 | 3.820 | 0.775 | 3.054 |
| 7 | Iron and steel | 0.842 | 2.688 | 0.984 | 2.929 | 0.854 | 2.805 |
| 8 | Metal products | 0.793 | 2.294 | 0.848 | 2.992 | 0.687 | 3.083 |
| 9 | Machinery, instruments | 0.807 | 2.023 | 0.919 | 2.312 | 0.688 | 3.091 |
| 10 | Electrical machinery | 0.952 | 1.719 | 1.062 | 1.771 | 0.833 | 2.302 |
| 11 | Transport equipment | 0.856 | 2.018 | 1.023 | 2.326 | 0.833 | 3.068 |
| 12 | Miscellaneous manufactures | 0.778 | 2.150 | 0.769 | 3.436 | 0.775 | 3.334 |
| 13 | Construction | 0.723 | 2.628 | 0.577 | 3.971 | — | — |
| 14 | Utilities | 0.884 | 2.855 | 0.828 | 4.789 | — | — |
| 15 | Wholesale, retail trade | 0.753 | 1.964 | 0.644 | 3.334 | — | — |
| 16 | Financial, insurance | 0.657 | 2.124 | 0.844 | 2.919 | — | — |
| 17 | Real estate | 0.801 | 1.749 | 0.582 | 3.306 | — | — |
| 18 | Transport, communication | 0.808 | 1.920 | 0.742 | 3.965 | — | — |
| 19 | Services | 0.665 | 2.099 | 0.604 | 4.161 | — | — |
| 20 | International freight services | 0.808 | 1.920 | 0.742 | 3.965 | — | — |

a. Rest-of-the-world index not estimated for nontraded sectors.

general, no attempt is made to achieve conformity in the units used to measure a given product in different countries. This rule does not apply to agriculture and natural resources. Since the traded products of these sectors are treated as homogeneous goods, units in all three countries are defined as "$1 billion's worth in the world market." Consequently, the prices of the homogeneous unit are 100 in the rest of the world and 100 in an exporting economy, but higher in an importing economy — by the margin of international transport costs and protection. The solution report used to present base data is calculated for other simulations as well; Appendix B includes such tables for some of the more important solutions analyzed in the book.

# 5 The Structure of Interdependence

Between 1960 and 1980 real Japanese exports to the United States expanded more than fivefold, and interdependence became a fashionable topic for magazine articles, popular books, and legislative debate. In popular discussion, "interdependence" has become a vague and imprecise word, used casually to refer to all bilateral relationships ranging from overall trade to specific business transactions. Thus the question arises: Is the extent of trade between the United States and Japan typical of other major trading relationships? If not, how does the Japanese-American relationship differ qualitatively from a less intensive partnership? And how does trade affect real interdependence, that is, linkages between crucial variables in the two economies? The main tasks of this chapter are to translate interdependence into operational and measurable terms, to analyze how the two economies are presently linked, and to observe how these linkages evolved over the past two decades.

To be sure, interdependence is a broad term with many potential microeconomic and macroeconomic meanings. Cyclical interdependence — the transmission of business cycles among national economies — is perhaps the most frequently mentioned aspect of interdependence, often studied with the aid of linked macroeconomic models (Sawyer, 1979). The present model sheds some light on how business cycles may propagate through

trade, but for the most part it is not designed to analyze adjustment in the short run. Rather, this study examines factors that affect structural interdependence: long-term differences in growth rates, capital accumulation, and technical progress, and changes in world demands, relative prices, and so on. All of these can fundamentally alter the character of a bilateral relationship — by redistributing the gains from trade, shifting the sectoral and factor interests served by trade, and creating new opportunities for intervention.

Interdependence is not simple to define or measure. In any meaningful sense, the concept involves perturbations of a general economic economic equilibrium, requiring both a model of the equilibrium and a choice among many possible perturbations. Cyclical interdependence, for example, brings to mind perturbations of a macroeconomic model and various different results depending on which variables are "shocked." Similarly, structural interdependence could be analyzed by changing a variety of different variables. Some economic mechanisms, however, are particularly interesting because they govern the extent and pattern of international adjustment under many kinds of structural change — namely, mechanisms related to price adjustment and changes in the terms of trade. The bulk of this chapter will be devoted to exploring these mechanisms of interdependence through focused general equilibrium simulations. But it is first helpful to set the context with a brief review of overall magnitudes and trends in the Japanese-American relationship.

## The Bilateral Relationship

Trade between the United States and Japan represents the second largest bilateral exchange of goods in the world, exceeded only by Canadian-American trade. It is also the primary economic link between the two countries; direct investment between the United States and Japan is still quite limited. U.S. investments in Japan, for example, represent just 3 percent of total U.S. investments abroad and rank below those in Australia or Belgium; Japan's investments in the United States amount to just 6 percent of foreign investments in our country and are

smaller than those of the Netherlands, the United Kingdom, and other European countries (Japan Economic Institute, 1982a).

Japanese-American bilateral trade is large for two mutually reinforcing reasons. First, the fit between U.S. and Japanese patterns of comparative advantage, though not optimal, is good; the United States exports agricultural commodities that are very expensive to produce in Japan and is a large market for exports of sophisticated consumer and producer goods. (Both countries specialize, however, in technologically advanced products.) Second, the two economies occupy privileged positions in each other's markets. Thus, U.S. shares of Japanese imports and Japanese shares of U.S. imports in any given product category are typically twice as large as the shares of these countries in the imports of third countries (see Table 5.1).

Trade between the United States and Japan has been important to Japan since the First World War, but it was slow to attract interest in the United States because it was initially small relative to the U.S. economy and because the United States maintained a comfortable bilateral surplus. All this changed between 1960 and 1970. The actual growth of trade is described in Figure 5.1, as ratios of both U.S. and Japanese overall trade. Notwithstanding the rapid growth of the Japanese economy, bilateral trade is still about twice as large compared to Japan's overall trade as relative to U.S. trade. In recent years, however, the relative importance of bilateral trade seems to have stabilized. Accordingly, the popular perception that the bilateral relationship is becoming more intense cannot be explained by the size of bilateral trade, which was no greater, in relative terms, in 1980 than a decade earlier.

An examination of bilateral trade since 1960 (see Figure 5.1) reveals distinct turning points and cyclical patterns. For example, surges appear in U.S. imports relative to U.S. exports in both the late 1960s and the mid-1970s. These surges correspond to periods when the dollar was unusually strong — in the late 1960s because of the continued maintenance of an outdated exchange rate, and in the mid 1970s because of a constellation of factors associated with the deep international recession and the rush of petrodollars into American capital markets. But the important point, from the perspective of structural interdependence, is that

**Table 5.1** Market shares in bilateral and worldwide markets

| No. | Sector | A U.S. share of Japanese market | B U.S. share of ROW market | A/B | C Japanese share of U.S. market | D Japanese share of ROW market | C/D |
|---|---|---|---|---|---|---|---|
| 1 | Agriculture, food | 0.366 | 0.166 | 2.2 | 0.012 | 0.007 | 1.7 |
| 2 | Natural resources | 0.043 | 0.031 | 1.4 | 0.005 | 0.004 | 1.3 |
| 3 | Textiles, apparel | 0.064 | 0.058 | 1.1 | 0.046 | 0.055 | 0.8 |
| 4 | Wood products, paper | 0.315 | 0.097 | 3.2 | 0.015 | 0.017 | 0.9 |
| 5 | Chemicals | 0.337 | 0.166 | 2.0 | 0.092 | 0.063 | 1.5 |
| 6 | Stone, clay, and glass | 0.130 | 0.062 | 2.1 | 0.109 | 0.037 | 2.9 |
| 7 | Iron and steel | 0.069 | 0.056 | 1.2 | 0.390 | 0.180 | 2.2 |
| 8 | Metal products | 0.395 | 0.109 | 3.6 | 0.260 | 0.078 | 3.3 |
| 9 | Machinery, instruments | 0.494 | 0.192 | 2.6 | 0.223 | 0.095 | 2.3 |
| 10 | Electrical machinery | 0.542 | 0.204 | 2.7 | 0.292 | 0.166 | 1.8 |
| 11 | Transport equipment | 0.473 | 0.183 | 2.6 | 0.564 | 0.182 | 3.1 |
| 12 | Miscellaneous manufactures | 0.303 | 0.155 | 2.0 | 0.195 | 0.129 | 1.5 |
| | Median | — | — | 2.2 | — | — | 1.8 |

MODELING JAPANESE-AMERICAN TRADE

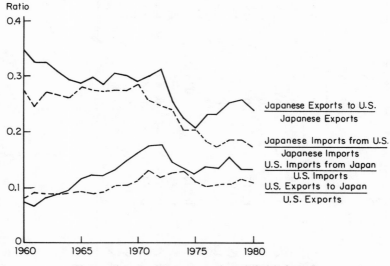

**Figure 5.1** Japanese-American bilateral trade

changes in the bilateral trade balance appear to be closely aligned with changes in the overall U.S. trade balance. Along similar lines, Saxonhouse and Sakakibara (1981) note that annual changes in the U.S. and Japanese overall trade positions are almost always of the opposite sign.

Japanese-American bilateral trade is part of a complex three-way trade; the bulk of Japanese imports are raw or lightly processed materials from the rest of the world. Since the United States is itself an importer of many types of raw materials, it is natural that U.S. exports play a modest role in Japanese imports. Indeed, a quick calculation shows that the bilateral imbalance is about the size one would expect given the commodity structures of the two countries' overall trade. This is illustrated in Table 5.2, where U.S. and Japanese total imports are allocated among exporters with three sets of market shares: actual, "neutral," and "equally privileged." The neutral shares assume that U.S. shares of Japanese markets, for example, are the same, commodity by commodity, as U.S. shares of world markets. As Table 5.2 shows, trade would be smaller under this assumption than it actually was in 1980, but proportionally it would be just as sharply imbalanced. The "equally privileged" shares assume that the bilateral

**Table 5.2** Bilateral trade: Actual and alternative hypothetical market shares (in billions of 1980 dollars)

| No. | Sector | U.S. Exports to Japan | | | Japanese Exports to U.S. | | |
|---|---|---|---|---|---|---|---|
| | | 1980 actual | Worldwide shares | 2 × worldwide shares | 1980 actual | Worldwide shares | 2 × worldwide shares |
| 1 | Agriculture, food | 7.92 | 3.64 | 7.28 | 0.34 | 0.19 | 0.39 |
| 2 | Natural resources | 3.73 | 2.36 | 4.72 | 0.54 | 0.40 | 0.80 |
| 3 | Textiles, apparel | 0.22 | 0.18 | 0.37 | 0.63 | 0.72 | 1.44 |
| 4 | Wood products, paper | 0.92 | 0.27 | 0.54 | 0.15 | 0.17 | 0.34 |
| 5 | Chemicals | 2.74 | 1.34 | 2.68 | 1.07 | 0.73 | 1.46 |
| 6 | Stone, clay, and glass | 0.13 | 0.06 | 0.12 | 0.54 | 0.22 | 0.43 |
| 7 | Iron and steel | 0.06 | 0.04 | 0.08 | 3.14 | 1.59 | 3.18 |
| 8 | Metal products | 0.20 | 0.05 | 0.10 | 1.10 | 0.40 | 0.81 |
| 9 | Machinery, instruments | 2.02 | 0.76 | 1.52 | 4.31 | 2.05 | 4.10 |
| 10 | Electrical machinery | 1.52 | 0.53 | 1.07 | 4.92 | 3.08 | 6.16 |
| 11 | Transport equipment | 0.94 | 0.35 | 0.69 | 12.63 | 5.41 | 10.82 |
| 12 | Miscellaneous manufactures | 6.40 | 0.17 | 0.35 | 1.87 | 1.34 | 2.68 |
| | Total | 20.80 | 9.76 | 19.53 | 31.24 | 16.31 | 32.61 |

trade shares of both the United States and Japan are twice as large as their neutral (world market) shares. These shares generate overall trade imbalances that are almost identical to those observed in 1980.

The statistics of the bilateral trade thus raise several important questions. What are the functional implications—for adjustment, gains from trade, commercial policy—of the special nature of the bilateral relationship? What are the causes and implications of the apparently close association between Japanese and U.S. trade positions? And how do the observed asymmetries in the commodity structure of bilateral trade affect functional interdependence? These and other questions are next explored with extensive simulation studies of the interactions of the two economies.

### The Anatomy of Interdependence

To make the concept of interdependence operational, consider the countries to be components of a general equilibrium system:

$$G(X_1, \ldots, X_n; A_1, \ldots, A_n) = 0, \tag{5.1}$$

where  $X_i$ = variables in country $i$,
$A_i$ = vector of parameters in country $i$.

In this context, interdependence can be formally defined as the derivative (or elasticity) of a particular domestic variable with respect to a particular foreign parameter. If the global system is fully interdependent, changes in any parameter will affect every variable, and a very large number of alternative derivatives could be computed. The implied ambiguity in the definition of interdependence reflects the plain fact that different parts of the economy are unequally affected by external change, and especially by different types of external change.

Economic response to an external event is partly variable-specific and partly change-specific. For example, the effect of an improvement in Japanese steel-making technology on U.S. steel output depends on initial market shares, price elasticities, and the relative sizes of the U.S. and Japanese steel industries. But international linkage also has general dimensions, associated

with the price changes that are required to eliminate potential external imbalance. Most microeconomic changes affect the international accounts; in the example cited, a potential Japanese surplus is likely to emerge as a result of cheaper Japanese steel. If this surplus is not matched by a simultaneous increase in Japan's propensity to save, the yen will appreciate relative to foreign currencies. For most sectors in both economies, the consequences of this price appreciation will ultimately dominate the direct effects of cheaper Japanese steel.

The mechanism of current account adjustment, therefore, warrants special attention in the analysis of interdependence. The next few paragraphs will trace the effects of a one-dollar potential current account imbalance on the welfare of the adjusting country and its partner. The chain linking the original imbalance to ultimate welfare effects includes (1) the exchange-rate effects of the initial imbalance, (2) the terms-of-trade effects of the exchange-rate changes, and (3) the welfare effects of terms-of-trade changes. Each of these components can be analyzed through specially designed simulations.

The first step in the chain is to assess the exchange-rate effects of a current account imbalance. The exchange rate/current account relationship is best analyzed "backward," that is, by seeing how movements in the exchange rate affect the current account. Although exchange rates do not appear explicitly in the model, it is possible to fix each economy's price level (GDP deflator) in terms of a common currency unit. A rise in this price level for one country without a corresponding change for other countries is interpreted in this book as a real exchange rate increase; it could reflect various combinations of domestic inflation and nominal exchange rate changes. GDP deflators are routinely calculated in model simulations and are shown in the "summary" sections of the solution reports included in Appendix B.

Simulations that hold GDP deflators fixed will be referred to as "fixed real exchange rate" simulations. In these simulations the net external savings equations (Table 2.3, Eq. R15) are dropped, and capital flows are assumed to accommodate all changes in the current account. Experiments were run specifying 10-percent increases in the American and Japanese exchange

**Table 5.3** Domestic and bilateral effects of real exchange-rate changes (in billions of 1980 dollars)

| Trade flow affected | 1980 transaction value | Effects of 10-percent U.S. real appreciation | | Effects of 10-percent Japanese real appeciation | |
|---|---|---|---|---|---|
| | | On U.S. current account | On Japanese current account | On U.S. current account | On Japanese current account |
| U.S. exports | | | | | |
| To Japan | 20.8 | −0.3 | 0.3 | 2.4 | −2.4 |
| To ROW | 193.6 | 2.2 | — | 2.8 | — |
| Japanese exports | | | | | |
| To U.S. | 31.2 | −4.3 | 4.3 | 2.4 | −2.4 |
| To ROW | 102.3 | — | 3.2 | — | −2.4 |
| ROW exports | | | | | |
| To U.S. | 213.2 | −16.2 | — | −2.4 | — |
| To Japan | 107.9 | — | −1.3 | — | −6.5 |
| U.S. other[a] | 53.3 | −1.8 | — | 0.5 | — |
| Japan other[a] | −14.7 | — | 0.3 | — | −0.4 |
| Total | | −20.4 | 6.7 | 5.7 | −14.1 |

*Source:* Unpublished simulations 8L1, 8L2.

a. Includes factor and service trade and U.S.-Canadian auto trade; these quantities are exogenously fixed, but their prices are adjusted to solution values.

rates, respectively. Table 5.3 shows results for various types of trade and for the current account as a whole.

The strength of bilateral effects is striking. A 10-percent U.S. appreciation, for example, causes a $20.4 billion deterioration in the U.S. current account and a $6.7 billion improvement in the Japanese account. The ratio of Japan's gain to the U.S. loss (33 percent) is three times as great as Japan's share in U.S. trade. Similarly, about 40 percent of the change in the Japanese current account—nearly twice the share of U.S. trade in Japanese trade —accrues to the United States under yen appreciation. Clearly, the bilateral impact of exchange-rate changes is greater than even the privileged trade relationship suggests.

The effects of American price changes on Japan primarily

involve two trade flows: Japanese exports to the United States and Japanese-American competition in third countries. As shown in Figure 3.6, Japanese exports to the United States are more sensitive to prices than any of the other trade flows analyzed. In addition, Japanese and American products in third markets have relatively large cross-price elasticities. Though smaller, on average, than the elasticities of Japanese exports to the United States, the cross-price elasticities apply to a much larger volume of trade. About half of the effect of American prices on the Japanese current account involves competition in third markets, and half direct bilateral trade.

These exchange-rate findings can be summarized in two matrices. First, using the totals shown in Table 5.3, the relationship between current account changes and exchange rates can be written as

$$dB = \begin{bmatrix} -204 & 57 \\ 67 & -141 \end{bmatrix} dp, \qquad (5.2)$$

where   $dB$ = changes in U.S. and Japanese current
                accounts,
        $dp$ = changes in U.S. and Japanese price levels (in
                the neighborhood of $p = 1$).

Next, Eq. (5.2) can be inverted to show the effects of a current account disturbance on exchange rates:

$$dp = \begin{bmatrix} 0.00565 & 0.00229 \\ 0.00269 & 0.00818 \end{bmatrix} dB. \qquad (5.3)$$

Simulations of the entire model indicate that Eq. (5.3) provides good approximations even for price changes on the order of 20 percent.

The new perspective contributed by Eq. (5.3) is that the dollar and the yen are very closely linked. A potential $10 billion loss in the U.S. current account, for example, would cause a 5.65-percent dollar depreciation (relative to the rest of the world) and a 2.69-percent yen depreciation. Not only are these changes of the same sign, they are also of similar magnitude. It can be said that the dollar extends an exchange-rate "umbrella" over the yen;

the yen will closely follow dollar movements (vis-à-vis third currencies) triggered by the external accounts of the United States.
Even without formal interventions, such as those practiced in the
European Monetary System, the dollar and the yen can be
expected to show smaller bilateral exchange variations than
external variations.

Exchange-rate changes affect welfare through the terms of
trade — that is, the rate of transformation of exports into imports. Because of relative price changes at home and abroad,
changes in exchange rates are not fully translated into terms-of-
trade changes. During appreciation, for example, export prices
fall relative to the domestic price level, and import prices rise
relative to the foreign price level. Since export and import prices
are also routinely calculated in all solutions (see the "summary"
sections in Appendix B), terms-of-trade changes are readily derived from the simulations of real exchange rate movements.
The simulated terms-of-trade effects of exchange-rate changes
are

$$dT = \begin{bmatrix} 0.40 & -0.07 \\ -0.13 & 0.61 \end{bmatrix} dp. \qquad (5.4)$$

The erosion of exchange-rate changes (diagonal values less than
unity in Eq. 5.4) is particularly strong for the United States, since
a large part of U.S. exports consists of agricultural exports with
prices dominated by world markets.

Finally, the impact of terms-of-trade changes on welfare can
be approximated by multiplying base-year imports by the terms-
of-trade change — that is, by the export change required to
maintain imports at base levels at the new prices.[1] In the case of
U.S. price appreciation, for example, the approximation implies
a $12.7 billion increase in consumption possibilities ($316 billion
current account debits times the 4.0 percent terms-of-trade gain
implied by Eq. 5.4), while the actual increase in real consumption
is calculated as $12.9 billion. In the Japanese experiment, the
approximate and actual values are $10.2 billion and $10.5 billion, respectively.

As a whole, the chain of results provides a quantitative sum-

mary of the bilateral effects of current account adjustments:

$$dW = \begin{bmatrix} 0.655 & 0.109 \\ 0.151 & 0.784 \end{bmatrix} dB, \qquad (5.5)$$

where $dW$ = welfare changes in U.S. and Japan.

These are large magnitudes. If the United States diverts one dollar from imports, or captures an additional dollar of export markets, its real income would rise by $0.66. If Japan does the same, its gain is $0.78. In both cases the premium for mercantilist behavior is great; efficiency losses from tariffs, for example, are likely to be small by comparison. Of course, these welfare changes are not global; terms-of-trade effects are implicitly zero-sum.

Because of the close positive association between U.S. and Japanese exchange rates, the off-diagonal elements of the welfare matrix are also positive. If the United States diverts one dollar from imports, Japan gains $0.15. The direct negative effect of a U.S. appreciation is dominated by the umbrella effect: the yen appreciates against third currencies. This means falling import prices and substantial terms-of-trade benefits also for Japan. From a policy viewpoint, the two countries are in the curious position of favoring general protection in the partner's economy while arguing for privileged bilateral access.

## Asymmetric Interdependence

Similar economic events in the United States and Japan can generate highly unequal consequences for their partner's economy. This is not surprising given the unequal sizes of the two countries; in 1980, U.S. GNP was about two and a half times as large as Japan's. But some aspects of asymmetry go beyond the arithmetic of size. The sense of asymmetry is deeply ingrained in Japanese-American economic politics (Destler and Sato, 1982; Monroe, 1982) and is usually traced to Japan's reliance on foreign trade for essential raw materials. The implication is that Japanese welfare is more closely tied to events abroad than U.S. welfare.

The question of asymmetry is examined below in two experi-

ments: (1) increases in each country's rate of external saving, and (2) expansion of each country's factor endowments. In each case we are primarily interested in effects on the partner's economy. The saving experiments provide a general assessment of a country's ability to raise foreign exchange; they are closely related to the current account/welfare linkages studied in the previous section. The factor endowment experiment examines how a specific need for foreign exchange — import requirements for growth — affects the bilateral relationship.

The bottom line of Table 5.4 shows the real income effects of increasing external savings by 2 percent. Changes in real expenditures (real consumption plus real investment) derived in these experiments cannot be identified directly with real income changes since part of the reduction in expenditure is the result of the shifting of income to external savings. Accordingly, the consumption change that is equivalent to the increase in external savings is subtracted from the simulated expenditure change in order to arrive at the net change in real income. This procedure is evident in Table 5.4 and is also used to calculate real income changes elsewhere in this book.

**Table 5.4** Domestic and bilateral effects of changes in external saving (in billions of 1980 dollars)

| Variable affected | Effects of increasing U.S. external saving rate | | Effects of increasing Japanese external saving rate | |
|---|---|---|---|---|
| | On U.S. variables | On Japanese variables | On U.S. variables | On Japanese variables |
| Savings | | | | |
| Change as percentage of GNP | 2.0 | 0.0 | 0.0 | 2.0 |
| In billions of dollars | 49.3 | 0.3 | −0.2 | 20.7 |
| Terms-of-trade (%) | −11.5 | −4.6 | −0.6 | −9.7 |
| Real expenditures | −124.1 | −8.9 | −3.9 | −43.5 |
| Due to change in external savings[a] | −76.9 | 1.1 | −1.0 | −22.5 |
| Due to change in real income | −47.2 | −10.0 | −2.9 | −21.0 |
| Relative to 1980 actual (%) | −1.80 | −0.96 | −0.11 | −2.02 |

*Source:* Appendix Tables B-4 and B-5.
a. Consumption change equivalent to the change in external savings.

When external savings are raised by 2 percent of GDP, the country that increases its external savings loses close to 2 percent of its real income. Thus both experiments generate terms-of-trade changes that create welfare losses that are approximately equal to the expenditures shifted from net imports to external savings. This nearly one-to-one relationship somewhat exceeds the 0.66 and 0.78 ratios obtained in the last section, but the current account adjustment here is two to three times as large as the one examined before.

Although the own-country effects are similar, the cross-country effects — the impacts of an increase in U.S. savings on Japan, and vice versa — are very different. U.S. changes have nearly nine times as large an impact on Japanese welfare as do similar Japanese changes on U.S. welfare. The asymmetry is due to three major factors: (1) the larger size of the initial U.S. "shock," (2) the 50-percent greater "cross" effect of a U.S. current account change on Japanese welfare (compare the off-diagonal terms of Eq. 5.5), and (3) the smaller Japanese consumption base on which the losses are borne. The greater U.S. cross effect on Japan can be traced to the impact of the U.S. current account change on the value of the yen. (Since a dollar depreciation is required to improve the U.S. current account, the yen is also forced to decline.) The downward pressure on the yen is intensified by the high substitutability of U.S. and Japanese goods in both American and third markets and by the price-inelasticity of Japanese raw material imports. The resulting sensitivity of Japanese welfare to the U.S. current account clearly demonstrates the riskiness of relying on price-elastic manufactures to buy price-inelastic raw materials.

Similar but still more skewed results are obtained in experiments that postulate 10-percent increases in each country's factor endowments (Table 5.5). In both experiments welfare improves in the growing country, although by a smaller percentage than the increase in factor supply (because of terms-of-trade losses). Again, the spillover effects are strikingly different: U.S. effects on Japan are thirteen times as large as vice versa. In this case the cross-country effects are negative; the partner does not enjoy the benefit of extra factors but does experience the negative umbrella of exchange depreciation. The main difference

**Table 5.5** Domestic and bilateral effects of changes in factor endowments (in billions of 1980 dollars)

| Variable affected | Effects of increasing U.S. factor endowments | | Effects of increasing Japanese factor endowments | |
|---|---|---|---|---|
| | On U.S. variables | On Japanese variables | On U.S. variables | On Japanese variables |
| Factor endowments | | | | |
| Change as percentage of base | 10.0 | 0.0 | 0.0 | 10.0 |
| Value of change at base prices | 211.5 | 0.0 | 0.0 | 83.6 |
| Current account balance[a] | −33.0 | 2.3 | 2.3 | −16.0 |
| Terms-of-trade (%) | −6.9 | −3.1 | −0.2 | −7.1 |
| Gross real expenditures | 227.4 | −6.3 | −1.6 | 90.4 |
| Due to change in external savings[b] | −7.2 | 0.6 | −0.4 | 2.0 |
| Due to additional capital costs[c] | 32.0 | 0.0 | 0.0 | 14.1 |
| Due to change in real income | 202.6 | −6.9 | −1.2 | 74.3 |
| Relative to 1980 actual (%) | 7.71 | −0.66 | −0.05 | 7.15 |

*Source:* Appendix Tables B-6 and B-7 and unpublished simulations 8L3 and 8L4.
a. Impact before elimination of current account imbalance in final equilibrium.
b. Consumption change equivalent to the change in savings.
c. Depreciation charges associated with increased capital stock.

between the U.S. and Japanese results is the size of the umbrella; dollar depreciation induces a far greater yen depreciation than vice versa (compare off-diagonal terms in Eq. 5.3).

The exercises reported in Tables 5.4 and 5.5 show why the Japanese should be keenly interested in American economic activity and policy. The structural linkages between the United States and Japan place a large part of the burden of a U.S. current account adjustment on U.S.-Japanese competition in American and third markets and, as a result, induce important changes in the Japanese terms of trade. In simulations requiring large U.S. adjustments — as in the growth experiment — these changes imply large Japanese reactions. Japanese welfare changes loom larger still in the context of a smaller economy. Because of both structure and size differences, changes in Japanese variables induced by U.S. actions are typically many times larger than in the reverse case.

## The Evolution of Interdependence

In light of the rapid growth of Japanese-American trade, it is natural to ask how interdependence changed over the past two decades. Did it simply keep pace with the growth of the two economies, and if so, with what implications? What additional biases, if any, emerged from the development patterns of the bilateral relationship? These questions can be directly addressed by repeating the 1980 experiments analyzed earlier in the 1960 and 1970 solution systems. Particular sources of change can be further pinpointed by examining hybrid solutions — systems that combine, say, 1980 economic structure with 1970 commercial policy.

By repeating the savings experiments for earlier years, we find that the capacity of the U.S. economy to adjust on external account increased, while that of Japan's economy diminished. Table 5.6 shows opposing U.S. and Japanese trends in the savings experiments: the terms-of-trade cost of increasing the net external balance (with both cost and saving measured as percentages of national product) declined in the United States but rose in Japan. Equally important, in both the U.S. and Japanese experiments, the external spillover effects grew over time. The combination of growing U.S. flexibility, declining Japanese flexibility, and increasing bilateral interdependence warrants closer analysis.

The difficulty of achieving a particular improvement on current account depends on the size of the transactions to be ad-

**Table 5.6**  Interdependence effects compared for 1960, 1970, 1980 (percentages)

| Experiment and variable affected | 1960 | 1970 | 1980 |
|---|---|---|---|
| U.S. savings increased by 2 percent | | | |
| Real income in U.S. | −1.93 | −2.07 | −1.80 |
| Real income in Japan | −0.47 | −0.71 | −0.96 |
| Japanese savings increased by 2 percent | | | |
| Real income in U.S. | −0.02 | −0.04 | −0.11 |
| Real income in Japan | −0.99 | −1.26 | −2.02 |

*Source:* Appendix Tables B-4 and B-6 and unpublished simulations 7F1, 6F1, 7F2, 6F2.

justed and on their elasticity with respect to price changes. A relatively open economy, for example, should generate larger current account gains with a given exchange-rate change than a closed economy. Similarly, an economy with elastic current account transactions will be better able to avoid adverse terms-of-trade effects. These two issues—openness and price elasticity[2]—are analyzed in some detail in the next few paragraphs.

In the United States, increasing openness has dominated the declining elasticity of external transactions. In 1960 a current account surplus equal to 2 percent of GNP would have represented 29.4 percent of adjustable current account transactions (credits plus debits) and required a very large 58.7 percent depreciation of the dollar. In 1970 the surplus would have come to 23.4 percent of transactions, still requiring a 53.5 percent depreciation. By 1980, however, comparable figures were 10.9 percent of transactions and a 28.6 percent depreciation. The volatile international capital account cycles of the late 1970s would have required far sharper dislocations of economic activity without these sizable increases in the flexibility of the American current account.

The American economy improved its ability to absorb large current account changes despite declines in the price elasticity of its current account. The phenomenon of elasticity decline affected both the United States and Japan and involved virtually all trade flows tracked by the model (see Table 5.7). A large part of the change is explained simply by the expanded share of price-inelastic oil imports in the total import bundle in the 1980 observation. But, as argued in Chapter 3, other compositional changes also played a role.

Japan's current account became significantly less price-elastic during the 1960–1980 period—indeed, much more so than the U.S. current account. The rise in the share of oil and other resources in total import values is largely responsible for this change. And though the Japanese economy became somewhat more open, its increased openness was not sufficient to offset the elasticity decline. Thus, the depreciation required to raise a surplus of 2 percent of GDP increased from only 10.4 percent in 1960 to 15.2 percent in 1970, and to 15.6 percent in 1980. (The surpluses were 10.6, 11.3, and 8.4 percent of current transac-

**Table 5.7** Declining elasticities in external transactions: 1960, 1970, 1980

| Trade flow | Elasticity with respect to increase of U.S. exchange rates | | | Elasticity with respect to increase of Japanese exchange rates | | |
|---|---|---|---|---|---|---|
| | 1960 | 1970 | 1980 | 1960 | 1970 | 1980 |
| U.S. exports | | | | | | |
| To Japan | −1.5 | −1.1 | −0.9 | 1.7 | 1.3 | 1.1 |
| To ROW | −0.9 | −0.8 | −0.7 | 0.1 | 0.1 | 0.1 |
| Japanese exports | | | | | | |
| To U.S. | 1.9 | 1.5 | 1.3 | −1.9 | −1.9 | −1.7 |
| To ROW | 0.5 | 0.4 | 0.3 | −1.3 | −1.2 | −1.0 |
| ROW exports | | | | | | |
| To U.S. | 1.2 | 1.0 | 0.7 | 0.0 | 0.1 | 0.1 |
| To Japan | −0.5 | −0.1 | 0.0 | 1.5 | 1.0 | 0.6 |
| Average of absolute values | 1.0 | 0.9 | 0.7 | 1.4 | 1.2 | 0.9 |

*Source:* Unpublished simulations 6L1, 6L2, 7L1, 7L2, 8L1, 8L2.

tions in the same years.) In 1980 current account adjustments of similar relative size were still easier to accomplish in Japan than in the United States (smaller price and terms-of-trade changes were required), but the difference had narrowed substantially since 1960.

What, then, explains changes in openness? With openness measured as the ratio of current account debits plus credits to gross national product, both the United States and Japan became more open during the twenty-year period of this study. However, for the United States the change was larger and it accelerated in the second decade: external transactions nearly doubled relative to national product. Because of the pervasive influence of openness on the external relations and policies of the United States, it is important to know precisely which factors contributed to this dramatic change.

To answer this question, a series of simulations were run replacing groups of 1980 parameters with their 1970 counterparts. The experiments sought to isolate factors associated with (1) U.S. growth, (2) Japanese growth, (3) the growth of world markets, (4) changes in world relative prices, (5) unexplained

changes in international market shares, and (6) commercial policies. These factors were selected because each could have significantly affected the external exposure of the American and Japanese economies.

Very different factors explain changes in the openness of the American and Japanese economies (see Table 5.8).[3] For the American economy, a major positive contribution is made by autonomous changes in market shares ("share drift"). As described in Chapter 3, the 1970s witnessed important gains in U.S. markets by Japanese and, to a lesser extent, by rest-of-the-world producers — gains that could not be attributed to price changes in the econometric analysis. Tentative results reached in the next chapter suggest that these share changes are associated with technical progress. Whether as a result of improved product quality or marketing skills, foreign producers "caught up" with American producers during this period, and the external interactions of the American economy increased dramatically. In addition to share effects, American openness was enhanced by the fact that foreign economies grew more rapidly than the

**Table 5.8** Factors affecting openness, 1970 – 1980 (Percentages)

| Contributors to openness | U.S. economy | | Japanese economy | |
| --- | --- | --- | --- | --- |
| Exports plus imports as percentage of GNP, 1970 actual | 8.1 | | 18.4 | |
| Effects of introducing: | | | | |
|   1980 commercial policy | 1.0 | | 0.8 | |
|   1970 – 1980 share drift | 4.7 | | 0.6 | |
|   1980 world relative prices | 2.7 | | 8.4 | |
|   1980 growth and structural change[a] | 4.5 | | −7.1 | |
|     In U.S. | | 4.0 | | 1.8 |
|     In Japan | | 0.3 | | −5.6 |
|     In ROW | | −0.7 | | −4.5 |
|     Interaction (residual) | | 0.9 | | 1.2 |
|   Interaction (residual) | −3.5 | | 4.1 | |
| Exports plus imports as percentage of GNP, 1980 actual | 17.5 | | 25.2 | |

Source: Unpublished simulations 8G2, 8G5, 8G6, 8G7, 8G8, 8G9.

a. Factor endowment and technical change for U.S. and Japan, exogenous market demand change for ROW.

American economy; by the increased price of natural resources; and, to a much lesser degree, by changes in commercial policies.

Japan's increased openness is due mainly to world price changes. Higher oil prices raised Japan's import bill and forced it to expand exports more rapidly than it otherwise might have done. One simulation shows, for example, that the yen's exchange rate in 1980 would have been about 150 yen per dollar, rather than 290 yen per dollar, if world relative prices had remained at 1970 levels. Working against the oil price effect, rapid Japanese growth tended to deemphasize external transactions, partly because the yen would have depreciated sharply with balanced expansion. On the whole, the adverse international environment caused Japan to become more open between 1970 and 1980, reversing the slightly negative trend of the previous decade.

## Conclusions

Although the bilateral trade statistics of the United States and Japan suggest a close economic relationship, they understate the true extent of economic interdependence. Functional measures of bilateral interdependence — measures of the spillover effects of economic change in one country on the other — suggest that the two countries are even more intimately linked than their privileged trading relationship indicates. The intensity of this interdependence is in large part due to the close substitutability of U.S. and Japanese products; as a result, the partner bears the brunt of adjustments required in both U.S. and third-country markets. It is not surprising, in this setting, to find that U.S. and Japanese current account positions move in opposite directions. Nor is it surprising that strong bilateral policy pressures arise when economic forces push one or the other country's overall external accounts into politically undesirable territory.

One consequence of close interdependence is that the dollar casts an exchange rate umbrella over the yen. Adjustments in the dollar's rate relative to third currencies result in changes in the yen of the same sign and similar magnitude. Thus dollar appreciations improve not only the American terms of trade but also the Japanese; as long as Japanese goods are not specifically excluded

from U.S. markets, Japan benefits from policies that increase the value of the dollar. The more detailed implications of policy interdependence will be explored in Chapter 7.

The terms-of-trade effects (including especially the real welfare changes induced by the terms of trade) generated by any development that affects the current account are large — not only in the economy that directly experiences the need to adjust but also, through the umbrella effect, in the partner economy. This result is a consequence of relatively price-inelastic trade. The results are all the more significant because elasticities appear to be declining over time.

The real danger posed by declining price elasticities is that international adjustment will be impaired. In the case of the United States, the elasticity declines have been counterbalanced by the increasing openness of the economy. Accordingly, the U.S. economy's capacity to absorb current account perturbations has increased. In Japan, however, declining elasticities have not been offset by increasing openness. Thus, adjustment of the same relative size requires larger price changes and terms-of-trade effects in 1980 than it did in 1960. While this point has important implications for Japanese policy, it is at least partly the result of rapid Japanese growth; Japan is increasingly less able to change its trade without a sizable impact on relative prices and the international terms of trade.

# 6 Sectoral Dimensions of Trade

This chapter explores how and why trade composition changed during the past two decades. In addition, the chapter extends the discussion of interdependence to a sectoral level, that is, it analyzes how the interests of different sectors are affected by various aspects of international adjustment.

Someone familiar with only the recent structure of Japanese-American trade would find it hard to recognize its sectoral composition in the early 1960s (compare Appendix Tables B-1 and B-3). Japanese exports to the United States, in particular, are remarkable not only for their rapid growth but also for their thorough structural transformation. Several different rounds of change can be recognized, with each closely related to changes in Japan's underlying comparative advantage.

An effective visual index of the rate of compositional change is presented in Figure 6.1. The index is calculated from a time series of trade composition vectors (vectors showing the percentage distribution of a particular trade flow across various product categories) by summing the absolute values of year-to-year changes in product categories. Formally:

$$I = \tfrac{1}{2}\Sigma_i |x_i^t/\Sigma_i x_i^t - x_i^{t-1}/\Sigma_i x_i^{t-1}|, \qquad (6.1)$$

where  $I$ = index of compositional change at time $t$,
 $x$ = level of sector $i$ at time $t$.

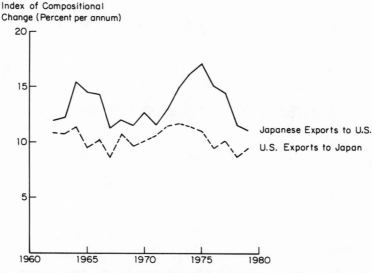

**Figure 6.1** Rate of compositional change of Japanese-American trade

To reduce noise, the calculations are based on three-year moving averages of trade flows. The index would achieve a maximum value of 1.0 if, in a given period, all trade shifted to a sector with previously zero trade. The index is not without flaws (it is sensitive to the level of aggregation), but it provides a simple, broad measure of compositional change.

Of the six types of trade studied (bilateral links among the United States, Japan, and the rest of the world), Japanese exports were by far the most dynamic during the 1960–1980 period: in an average year, 7.3 percent of exports to the United States and 5.5 percent of exports to the rest of the world shifted from one sector to another. Corresponding measures for the United States are 5.2 percent on bilateral trade and 3.3 percent on rest-of-the-world trade. Both U.S. and Japanese imports changed more slowly: 3.0 and 3.8 percent, respectively. Figure 6.1 illustrates the full time-series results for bilateral trade. One interpretation of this figure is that the background rate of change is about the same for U.S. and Japanese exports, but that Japanese exports frequently undergo periods of major restructuring.

The main periods of upheaval in Japanese exports — the

mid-1960s and the mid-1970s — are associated with fundamental changes in the world trading environment and in Japanese economic development. In the first period, the change in trade follows a period of intensive investment activity in Japan — a boom that produced major advances in Japan's heavy industry (Nakamura, 1981, particularly Chap. 3). The second period of upheaval reflects adjustment to the higher price of oil and a more competitive international trade environment. (Since the compositional change index is based on real trade flows, it is not affected by valuation changes caused by the oil price change.) A third period of change, the much-discussed transition to knowledge-based industries, might be under way in the early 1980s; it would be interesting to extend the present analysis to see if the rate of compositional change is as dramatic in this transitional period as in the previous two.

Each period of rapid transformation is associated with specific structural changes in the Japanese trade pattern. Figure 6.2 shows time series of the shares of selected Japanese exports in total exports. The first transition, in the early 1960s, corresponds to the switch from traditional exports, most importantly textiles and metal products, to basic industries such as chemicals and steel. The second transition, in the early 1970s, reflects the rise of Japan's consumer product sector and includes the beginning of the automobile export boom. The hypothesized third transition, which began recently and is not yet confirmed by these graphs, marks the emergence of high-technology exports in the machinery and electrical machinery sectors.

Let us now abstract from the names of the sectors to search for changes in more fundamental characteristics underlying the trade pattern. This kind of analysis, pioneered by Leontief's factor content studies (1954), has been applied to a long list of trade determinants and characteristics (for example, Hufbauer, 1970; Baldwin, 1971). The particular form of the analysis used here involves the evaluation of trade flows (for example, Japanese exports to the United States) with a "common measurement device" (Keesing, 1966). Essentially, measures of a given economic characteristic are constructed for all traded products (assuming that the product characteristic is the same regardless of what country makes it), and average values of the measure are

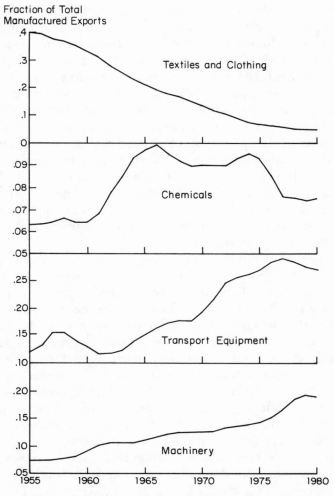

**Figure 6.2** Changes in Japan's export composition

computed for total trade, based on its underlying product composition.

Four product characteristics are analyzed: factor content, income elasticity, dynamism of technology, and growth of markets. The "single measurement device" is constructed, for each sector, by averaging relevant sectoral characteristics observed in 1980 in the United States and Japan. Specifically, factor content

is measured by the direct and indirect capital returns generated per dollar of product's value; income elasticity by the consumption elasticities shown in Table 4.3; technological dynamism by a total factor productivity measure computed from changes in input-output coefficients;[1] and market growth by the real rate of increase of world markets. In the case of factor intensity, these results are extended using other, more sophisticated measurement concepts in the following section.

It is hardly surprising that these several characteristics of trade also underwent rapid change over the 1960–1980 period (see Figures 6.3 through 6.6 and Table 6.1). Factor content moved in unexpected directions. For example, despite the very substantial increase in Japan's relative capital endowment, the role of capital-intensive products in Japanese exports generally declined. Capital intensity did rise a little in the initial transition away from highly labor-intensive traditional products to heavy industry. This is the period observed by Heller (1976) in a study that claimed to find dynamic confirmation of the Heckscher-Ohlin theory in the changing factor content of Japanese trade. In the

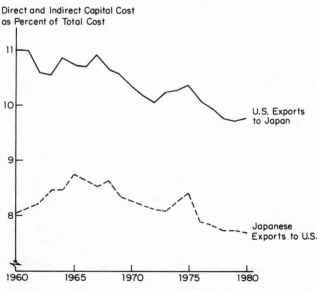

**Figure 6.3** Trade characteristics: capital content

MODELING JAPANESE-AMERICAN TRADE

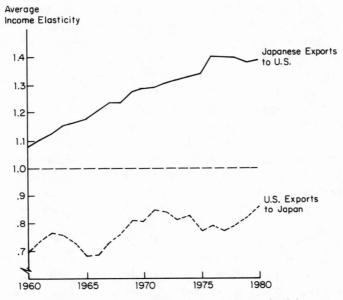

**Figure 6.4** Trade characteristics: income elasticity

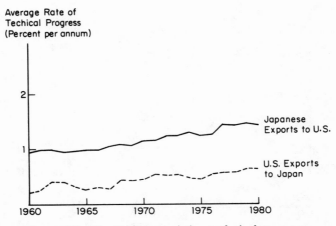

**Figure 6.5** Trade characteristics: technical progress

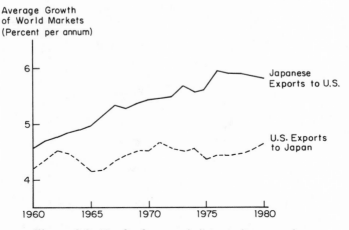

**Figure 6.6** Trade characteristics: market growth

perspective of a longer time horizon, however, the initial in-crease in the capital intensity of Japanese exports is seen to be temporary; the transition to consumer goods and to high-tech-nology exports in the 1970s once again reduced the export role of capital-intensive products. Japanese exports continued to be less capital-intensive than U.S. or ROW exports throughout the period.

Perhaps the decisive transformation in Japanese trade was the shift to products with high income elasticities, fast-growing mar-kets, and rapidly changing technology. By all three of these measures, Japanese exports — bilaterally as well as worldwide — rank substantially above all other trade flows studied (Figures 6.4 – 6.6; Table 6.1). Interestingly, the trade with characteristics most similar to those of Japanese exports is U.S. exports to the rest of the world. Like Japanese exports, but to a more limited extent, this flow also caters to technologically progressive and fast-growing markets.

These findings illustrate some of the major changes in the international positions of the United States and Japan in the 1960s and 1970s. They do not explain, however, why or how such changes took place, or what effect they had on the overall relationship of the two economies. An effort to analyze the

**Table 6.1**  Product characteristics of trade flows: 1960, 1970, 1980

| Trade flow | Year | Capital cost as percentage of total cost | Income elasticity (value) | Technical progress (annual percentage rate) | World market growth (annual percentage rate) |
|---|---|---|---|---|---|
| U.S. exports | | | | | |
| To Japan | 1960 | 0.111 | 0.68 | 0.2 | 4.2 |
| | 1970 | 0.103 | 0.81 | 0.5 | 4.5 |
| | 1980 | 0.098 | 0.86 | 0.6 | 4.7 |
| To ROW | 1960 | 0.093 | 0.94 | 0.7 | 4.8 |
| | 1970 | 0.090 | 1.09 | 0.9 | 5.3 |
| | 1980 | 0.086 | 1.09 | 1.0 | 5.3 |
| Japanese exports | | | | | |
| To U.S. | 1960 | 0.081 | .08 | 1.0 | 4.6 |
| | 1970 | 0.083 | 1.29 | 1.2 | 5.4 |
| | 1980 | 0.076 | 1.39 | 1.4 | 5.8 |
| To ROW | 1960 | 0.080 | 1.07 | 1.1 | 4.7 |
| | 1970 | 0.087 | 1.22 | 1.1 | 5.3 |
| | 1980 | 0.079 | 1.35 | .4 | 5.9 |
| ROW exports | | | | | |
| To U.S. | 1960 | 0.112 | 0.76 | 0.1 | 4.1 |
| | 1970 | 0.105 | 0.88 | 0.4 | 4.5 |
| | 1980 | 0.106 | 0.97 | 0.5 | 4.8 |
| To Japan | 1960 | 0.128 | 0.57 | −0.2 | 3.9 |
| | 1970 | 0.136 | 0.62 | −0.4 | 4.1 |
| | 1980 | 0.130 | 0.70 | −0.2 | 4.3 |

sources of compositional change over the 1960–1980 period is made in the third section of this chapter. This effort is only partially successful; aspects of the dramatic success of Japan's trade strategy are more specifically identified, but the explanations offered are highly tentative. Japan's ability to orient its trade to the most promising world markets is the crux of the Japanese "trade miracle" and may never be fully explained in conventional economic terms.

## The Factor Content of Japanese-American Trade

To better understand the effects of trade in a general equilibrium context, it is useful to look more rigorously at the factor

intensity of Japanese-American trade. This analysis also leads to a new definition of the factor content of trade and provides one more possible explanation for the Leontief paradox.

Factor input results for 1980 are initially computed using the now-standard methodology introduced by Leontief (1953). Thus, total direct and indirect factor requirements for a particular bundle of goods are computed using the equations

$$K = k'(I - A)^{-1}w \quad \text{and} \quad L = l'(I - A)^{-1}w, \qquad (6.2)$$

where  $L$ = direct and indirect labor requirements,
$K$ = direct and indirect capital requirements,
$l$  = labor input coefficients,
$k$  = capital input coefficients,
$A$ = input-output coefficients,
$w$ = demand proportions that sum to unity.

The results from these computations are reported in Table 6.2. Essentially, the demand weights $w$ are successively taken to characterize consumption, investment, and the several different trade flows measured by the model. Each country's own capital and labor coefficients are used. The "relative capital intensities" reported in the table show capital-labor ratios expressed as a percentage of the relevant national capital-labor endowment. The value of 96.4 in the upper left-hand corner of the table means, for example, that the total direct and indirect requirements of U.S. consumption goods involve 96.4 percent as much capital per worker as the amount of capital per worker available to the economy as a whole.

One point illustrated by Table 6.2 is that much of the American capital stock works abroad: all numbers in the first U.S. column are smaller than 100, and the capital/labor intensity applied in all domestic production is only 86 percent of the national endowment. (The data on direct factor trade, in the bottom part of Table 6.2, show that net capital service exports are 13.5 percent of the total capital stock.) In a sense, then, the U.S. economy exports its capital directly, without pausing to build it into capital-intensive goods.

Table 6.2 also shows that consumption is much more capital-intensive than investment and most types of trade in both econo-

MODELING JAPANESE-AMERICAN TRADE

**Table 6.2**  Capital/labor ratios for selected commodity bundles, 1980
(as a percentage of national capital/labor endowment ratio),
and direct factor trade

| | United States | | Japan | |
|---|---|---|---|---|
| Commodity bundle | Average bundles | Marginal bundles | Average bundles | Marginal bundles |
| Consumption | 96.4 | — | 109.9 | — |
| Investment | 44.6 | — | 86.7 | — |
| Commodity trade | | | | |
|   Exports | 56.3 | 52.3 | 98.3 | 96.9 |
|     Excluding raw materials | 49.7 | 48.1 | 97.1 | 96.2 |
|   Imports[a] | 74.2 | 57.3 | 126.1 | 116.2 |
|     Excluding raw materials | 50.0 | 48.8 | 96.7 | 96.4 |
| Bilateral trade | | | | |
|   U.S. imports from Japan | 49.1 | 48.1 | 96.6 | 96.6 |
|     Excluding raw materials | 48.3 | 48.0 | 95.8 | 96.3 |
|   U.S. exports to Japan | 65.3 | 58.8 | 114.3 | 112.5 |
|     Excluding raw materials | 52.9 | 53.2 | 94.3 | 95.4 |
| Direct factor trade (as percentage of factor endowment) | | | | |
|   Labor | | | | |
|     Export | 0.5 | — | 0.2 | — |
|     Import | 0.7 | — | 0.1 | — |
|   Capital | | | | |
|     Export | 21.0 | — | 6.2 | — |
|     Import | 7.5 | — | 6.2 | — |

a. Requirements of import substitutes produced at home.

mies. The main reason for this is the importance of two highly capital-intensive sectors in consumption: services and real estate (the services of rented and owner-occupied housing). Consequently, all model solutions that increase real domestic income and divert resources from traded to nontraded goods also generate an increase in the price of capital relative to labor. The fact that even imports are labor-intensive relative to U.S. consumption has also figured in a possible explanation of the Leontief paradox (Leamer, 1980).

The trade calculations presented by Table 6.2 are generally consistent with earlier results:

1. The original paradox stands: American exports are somewhat less capital-intensive than American import replacements.[2] However, the exclusion of raw materials from the computation (Vanek, 1959) almost completely eliminates the difference.
2. With respect to the paradox, essentially the same results are obtained for Japan as for the United States: trade that includes raw materials involves some net imports of capital-intensive goods, but it is neutral if raw materials are excluded.
3. Japanese-American bilateral trade reflects the factor intensities one might expect, whether or not raw materials are included. The factor content ranking is the same whether computed with Japanese or U.S. input coefficients.

What did come as a surprise, however, is that the standard measures of factor intensity failed to predict the results of various simulations involving changes in trade. A careful analysis of the results indicated that most kinds of trade changes, even broad, economy-wide changes such as those caused by exchange-rate adjustments or economic growth, had very different factor content characteristics from those shown in Table 6.2. It became clear that most simulations affect only limited parts of export and import bundles, and that the factor content of the "marginal" bundles is decisive in predicting overall factor demand effects.

To further explore this hypothesis, factor content computations were performed for "price-marginal" trade bundles, defined as the trade changes caused by a simulated appreciation of the exchange rate. The marginal bundles are compared to average bundles in Table 6.3, and their factor content measures are shown in Table 6.2, columns 2 and 4. The results for average and marginal bundles are generally similar, with one significant exception: U.S. price-marginal imports are substantially less capital-intensive than average imports. Although the paradox is not fully reversed, the difference between the factor intensities of U.S. imports and exports is substantially reduced. Switching from average to marginal imports has an effect similar to that of excluding natural resources from the computations.

The general intent of factor content analysis is to determine

**Table 6.3.A**  Average and price-marginal trade bundles, United States trade

| No. | Sector | Imports from ROW | | Imports from Japan | | Exports to ROW | |
|---|---|---|---|---|---|---|---|
| | | Average | Marginal | Average | Marginal | Average | Marginal |
| 1 | Agriculture, food | 0.1049 | 0.1380 | 0.0103 | 0.0088 | 0.2137 | 0.2505 |
| 2 | Natural resources | 0.4580 | 0.1491 | 0.0174 | 0.0000 | 0.0816 | 0.0027 |
| 3 | Textiles, apparel | 0.0630 | 0.0970 | 0.0203 | 0.0284 | 0.0300 | 0.0516 |
| 4 | Wood products, paper | 0.0486 | 0.0820 | 0.0047 | 0.0066 | 0.0333 | 0.0441 |
| 5 | Chemicals | 0.0509 | 0.0366 | 0.0341 | 0.0241 | 0.1214 | 0.0815 |
| 6 | Stone, clay, and glass | 0.0211 | 0.0227 | 0.0172 | 0.0066 | 0.0117 | 0.0081 |
| 7 | Iron and steel | 0.0237 | 0.0532 | 0.1005 | 0.1094 | 0.0181 | 0.0197 |
| 8 | Metal products | 0.0151 | 0.0150 | 0.0352 | 0.0219 | 0.0234 | 0.0292 |
| 9 | Machinery, instruments | 0.0726 | 0.1447 | 0.1383 | 0.1247 | 0.2179 | 0.2145 |
| 10 | Electrical machinery | 0.0576 | 0.0421 | 0.1575 | 0.1247 | 0.1031 | 0.1344 |
| 11 | Transport equipment | 0.0472 | 0.1535 | 0.4047 | 0.4683 | 0.1125 | 0.1256 |
| 12 | Miscellaneous manufactures | 0.0374 | 0.0660 | 0.0599 | 0.0766 | 0.0333 | 0.0380 |

how changes in the volume of trade (both imports and exports) affect the factor intensity of the economy's product mix. Marginal, rather than average, trade bundles are more appropriate for this purpose because they identify the "changeable" part of product mix. Leontief, for example, excluded "noncompetitive" imports from his original computations because the economy must buy these abroad regardless of how open it is to trade. But this does not go far enough: exports without adequate foreign substitutes should be similarly excluded. More generally, pure complementarity is only an extreme point on the spectrum of substitutability; imports and exports with high price elasticities (presumably reflecting greater substitution opportunities) should receive higher weights in the factor content calculation. Given price-marginal trade bundles, the difference between the factor intensities of exports and imports nearly disappears.

### Determinants of Trade Pattern Changes

It would be pleasing to report that changes in U.S. and Japanese trade patterns are easily traced to the structural properties of the model on which this study is based. Ideally, one would like to show that the change in Japanese-American trade between 1960 and 1980 is due simply to changes in market demands and relative prices. Assuming, in addition, that both price and de-

**Table 6.3.B** Average and price-marginal trade bundles, Japanese trade

| No. | Sector | Imports from ROW | | Imports from U.S. | | Exports to ROW | |
|---|---|---|---|---|---|---|---|
| | | Average | Marginal | Average | Marginal | Average | Marginal |
| 1 | Agriculture, food | 0.1322 | 0.4723 | 0.3804 | 0.4788 | 0.0184 | 0.0176 |
| 2 | Natural resources | 0.6951 | 0.1159 | 0.1799 | 0.0000 | 0.0206 | 0.0000 |
| 3 | Textiles, apparel | 0.0313 | 0.0516 | 0.0107 | 0.0121 | 0.0558 | 0.0529 |
| 4 | Wood products, paper | 0.0194 | 0.0693 | 0.0445 | 0.0667 | 0.0108 | 0.0099 |
| 5 | Chemicals | 0.0521 | 0.1146 | 0.1317 | 0.1515 | 0.0827 | 0.0627 |
| 6 | Stone, clay, and glass | 0.0086 | 0.0126 | 0.0065 | 0.0061 | 0.0134 | 0.0092 |
| 7 | Iron and steel | 0.0073 | 0.0164 | 0.0026 | 0.0061 | 0.1349 | 0.1170 |
| 8 | Metal products | 0.0030 | 0.0126 | 0.0097 | 0.0182 | 0.0323 | 0.0240 |
| 9 | Machinery, instruments | 0.0199 | 0.0668 | 0.0970 | 0.1030 | 0.1933 | 0.1621 |
| 10 | Electrical machinery | 0.0123 | 0.0189 | 0.0730 | 0.0667 | 0.1605 | 0.1424 |
| 11 | Transport equipment | 0.0101 | 0.0302 | 0.0450 | 0.0727 | 0.2234 | 0.3319 |
| 12 | Miscellaneous manufactures | 0.0088 | 0.0189 | 0.0191 | 0.0182 | 0.0539 | 0.0705 |

mand changes can be related to the economic developments of the period, a direct link could be established between the spectacular growth of trade and structural changes in technology and factor endowments.

For some of the six trade flows analyzed, the model indeed provides a fairly complete explanation of the sources of trade growth. It does so, for example, for most U.S. exports and for Japanese imports from the rest of the world. But a large part of the 1960–1980 change in Japanese exports, and in U.S. imports from the rest of the world, cannot be explained by projections based on fixed model structure; exogenous parameter changes have to be introduced. The model can identify what changes are important—primarily market share growth—but it cannot trace these effects to more fundamental causes. In any case, it is useful to see what is explained by model structure and what remains to be explained by other determinants.

Based on the structure of the share equations, it is possible, first of all, to decompose the 1960–1980 growth rates of various trade flows into (1) market growth, (2) price-related changes, and (3) unexplained market share growth ("share drift"). In turn, price-related changes consist of three kinds of effects: the effects of changes in protection on trade volume; the effects of relative price changes on trade volume; and valuation effects—the effects of changes in the import price/domestic price ratio

on the value of trade relative to the value of domestic demand. The last term, market share drift, is derived as residual. It corresponds to the trend terms used in the share equation estimates and is generally close to these estimates in magnitude.

The decomposition of trade growth presented in Tables 6.4 and 6.5 is based on actual changes in the relevant explanatory variables. Market growth, for example, is calculated directly from the time series of demand. The volume effects of price changes are based on actual price changes (converted to a common currency) and the price elasticities estimated in Chapter 3. Similarly, protection effects are calculated with actual changes in tariffs and the tariff equivalents of quotas, translated into volume effects with the estimated trade price elasticities. Calculations are made commodity by commodity, and the results for total trade are summed up from this detail. The analysis is limited to manufactured commodities, since trade in the homogeneous agricultural and natural resource products is determined in a different

**Table 6.4** Factors contributing to the growth of trade in manufactures (annual percentage growth rates)

| Trade flow | Period | Trade growth (value) | Market growth (value) | Valuation effects[a] | Price elasticity effect[b] | Protection effect | Market share drift[c] |
|---|---|---|---|---|---|---|---|
| U.S. exports | | | | | | | |
| To Japan | 1960–70 | 14.8 | 15.3 | 1.1 | −1.3 | 0.1 | −0.2 |
| | 1970–80 | 15.3 | 14.9 | −2.2 | 2.8 | 0.1 | −0.3 |
| To ROW | 1960–70 | 8.5 | 10.5 | −0.5 | 0.3 | 0.0 | −1.8 |
| | 1970–80 | 16.4 | 17.5 | −2.8 | 2.8 | 0.0 | −1.1 |
| Japanese exports | | | | | | | |
| To U.S. | 1960–70 | 17.6 | 5.6 | −0.2 | 0.6 | 0.0 | 11.6 |
| | 1970–80 | 16.9 | 10.2 | 1.6 | −1.7 | 0.4 | 6.4 |
| To ROW | 1960–70 | 15.4 | 9.8 | −0.9 | 1.2 | 0.0 | 5.3 |
| | 1970–80 | 20.0 | 16.9 | −0.7 | 0.6 | 0.0 | 3.2 |
| ROW exports | | | | | | | |
| To U.S. | 1960–70 | 12.2 | 5.6 | 0.4 | −0.8 | 0.0 | 7.0 |
| | 1970–80 | 16.2 | 10.2 | 3.0 | −3.5 | 0.2 | 6.3 |
| To Japan | 1960–70 | 15.9 | 14.3 | 1.5 | −2.6 | 0.6 | 2.1 |
| | 1970–80 | 21.0 | 14.8 | 0.3 | −0.3 | −0.1 | 6.3 |

a. Effects of change in export price relative to market price.

b. Effects of changes in relative producers' prices of competing exporters (includes both own-price and cross-price elasticity changes).

c. Computed as unexplained residual; very close in value to trend effects from estimated market share functions.

**Table 6.5**  Factors contributing to the sectoral growth of Japanese exports to the United States (annual percentage growth rates)

| No. | Sector | Period | Trade growth (value) | Market growth (value) | Valuation effect[a] | Price elasticity effect[b] | Protection effect | Market share drift[c] |
|---|---|---|---|---|---|---|---|---|
| 3 | Textiles, | 1960–70 | 7.7 | 4.8 | 1.7 | −4.8 | 0.2 | 5.8 |
|   | apparel | 1970–80 | −1.3 | 7.7 | 3.3 | −10.4 | 1.5 | −3.4 |
| 4 | Wood products, | 1960–70 | 3.5 | 5.3 | 0.5 | −1.2 | 0.2 | −1.3 |
|   | paper | 1970–80 | 2.0 | 11.5 | 4.3 | −9.4 | 0.3 | −4.1 |
| 5 | Chemicals | 1960–70 | 19.7 | 6.4 | −0.8 | 2.5 | 0.0 | 11.6 |
|   |  | 1970–80 | 15.3 | 11.1 | 3.2 | 0.0 | 0.0 | 1.0 |
| 6 | Stone, clay, | 1960–70 | 7.4 | 4.3 | 0.5 | −0.6 | 0.2 | 3.0 |
|   | and glass | 1970–80 | 12.7 | 10.6 | 4.7 | −4.7 | 0.6 | 1.5 |
| 7 | Iron and steel | 1960–70 | 25.0 | 4.2 | −1.4 | 4.8 | −1.0 | 18.4 |
|   |  | 1970–80 | 11.9 | 10.3 | 0.8 | −2.3 | 0.1 | 3.0 |
| 8 | Metal products | 1960–70 | 14.6 | 6.2 | −0.7 | 2.9 | 0.0 | 6.2 |
|   |  | 1970–80 | 11.6 | 9.6 | 2.6 | 0.4 | 0.0 | −1.0 |
| 9 | Machinery, | 1960–70 | 21.2 | 7.6 | −1.4 | 2.2 | 0.2 | 12.6 |
|   | instruments | 1970–80 | 21.7 | 11.0 | 1.1 | −2.3 | 0.6 | 11.3 |
| 10 | Electrical | 1960–70 | 24.1 | 6.9 | −1.1 | 2.6 | 0.1 | 15.6 |
|   | machinery | 1970–80 | 14.8 | 10.5 | 0.1 | 2.1 | 0.2 | 1.9 |
| 11 | Transport | 1960–70 | 41.2 | 4.7 | −1.8 | 5.0 | 0.0 | 33.3 |
|   | equipment | 1970–80 | 27.1 | 10.0 | 1.2 | 1.2 | 0.0 | 14.7 |
| 12 | Miscellaneous | 1960–70 | 19.4 | 6.2 | 0.1 | −0.3 | 0.4 | 13.0 |
|   | manufactures | 1970–80 | 10.5 | 10.1 | 4.3 | −11.6 | 1.6 | 6.5 |

a. Effects of change in export price relative to market price.

b. Effects of changes in relative producers' prices of competing exporters (includes both own-price and cross-price elasticity changes).

c. Computed as unexplained residual; very close in value to trend effects from estimated market share functions.

way. Table 6.4 provides results for the six total trade flows; Table 6.5 reports on sector-specific results for Japanese exports to the United States.

With only a few exceptions, the bulk of the explanation of long-term trade growth is provided by market growth. This reinforces the need to model trade with general-equilibrium relationships: it is essential to model sectoral demand accurately. At the same time, price changes play a much more limited role than might have been expected. This is due partly to the fact that the estimated price elasticities are generally near unity, and volume effects are canceled by valuation changes. But more important, international relative price changes are not very large. This was especially true in the 1970–1980 period, when differential changes in domestic prices (due to unequal inflation

and productivity change) were mostly offset by exchange-rate movements. This is not to say that prices have no role at all. On a sectoral level (see Table 6.5), the markets for such commodities as steel and transportation equipment were significantly affected by Japan's improving price competitiveness. But even in these industries the market and share terms proved substantially more important.

Unexplained share drift was important for several trade flows, especially during the 1960–1970 period. Share drift was particularly strong for Japanese exports. In the 1970–1980 period, share drift slowed along with economic growth rates but still maintained relative magnitudes consistent with the growth rates of the different parts of the world economy. All in all, there is a close association between economic growth and unexplained share growth in foreign markets. In other words, share growth appears to be partly supply-driven.

According to the expected, conventional scenario, an expanding country would generally devalue to expand exports sufficiently to meet growing import requirements. Although the relative sizes of the American and Japanese economies changed significantly, our price statistics do not indicate devaluations of the expected sign or magnitude. Instead, unexplained share changes account for the required market gains of the faster-growing economy. How does it happen that share drift miraculously rescues rapidly growing economies from deficit and depreciation? It is possible to answer this question only in a tentative way, but the implications for general equilibrium modeling are significant.

Casual observation suggests that share growth is related to "quality" or some other improvement (for example, marketing) in the desirability of imported products. In principle, changes in some of these characteristics should be incorporated in price indexes; in practice, they seldom are. In other words, some part of share drift should really fall in the price elasticity column, but it appears as a residual because the price statistics are not holding quality constant.

Some evidence for this hypothesis can be developed by relating share drift to technological change. Figure 6.7 shows that, at

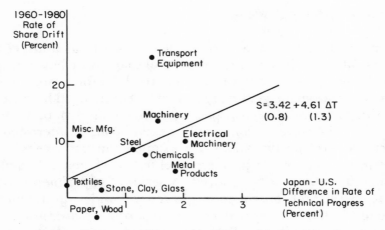

**Figure 6.7**  Relationship between share drift and differential technical progress

least in Japanese exports to the United States, share drift and technological progress were correlated over the 1960–1980 period. Using data from the ten different manufacturing sectors, share drift, defined as the coefficient of the trend term in the market share regression, is plotted against the difference between sectoral total-factor productivity growth rates in Japan and the United States. The correlation is modest ($F$ is just 1.8), partly because two sectors (transport equipment and paper and wood) are well off the apparent regression line. Nevertheless, it suggests that market shares grew particularly fast in sectors where Japanese productivity outpaced U.S. productivity.

The hypothesis of unmeasured quality improvements, suggested by the relationship between share drift and technological progress, is plausible because it explains how a rapidly growing country generates adequate foreign markets. If the technological change that drives growth also generates quality gains relative to foreign products, real devaluation would not be a necessary concomitant to growth.[3] Nevertheless, Chapter 8 argues that this relationship cannot completely explain the importance of share drift and discusses several other factors that are also likely to be involved.

## Sectoral Interdependence

In parallel with the previous chapter's effort to measure economy-wide interdependence, it is useful to quantify how individual sectors are affected by changes abroad. Unfortunately, measures of reasonable generality cannot be constructed because of the importance of sector-specific, rather than economy-wide, issues in the sectoral context. But even if one is interested in sector-specific perturbations (for example, an improvement in the technology of the Japanese steel industry), general equilibrium effects cannot be ignored. A series of experiments show that the sectoral consequences of economy-wide adjustments in the terms of trade and real income, in particular, are varied and surprisingly significant. For many sectors, these effects would dominate the consequences of most specific changes in the behavior of "related" foreign markets or competitors.

To illustrate the relative importance of specific and economy-wide effects, additional analyses are performed on a pair of experiments already utilized in Chapter 5: increases in the factor endowments of the United States and Japan. In reviewing the results of these experiments we are now interested in cross-country effects, that is, in seeing how U.S. growth affects the various sectors of the Japanese economy and how Japanese growth affects the sectors of the U.S. economy.

To trace the relationship between direct (that is, partial equilibrium) and general equilibrium effects, the computations are interrupted at various intermediate points, before all of the equilibrium conditions are satisfied. Specifically, the path from the original equilibrium to the postchange equilibrium is divided into three segments: direct effects (changes before adjustments in the terms of trade and real income), terms-of-trade effects (after exchange-rate adjustments but before real-income changes), and real-income effects. The results of the analysis are presented in Tables 6.6 and 6.7 for the United States and Japan, respectively.

*Direct effects.* Consider, for example, the effects of an expansion in the U.S. economy from the perspective of the Japanese economy. Direct effects consist primarily of the additional Japanese exports generated by the expansion of the American econ-

**Table 6.6** Sectoral interdependence: U.S. effects of 10-percent expansion of Japanese economy (in billions of 1980 dollars)

| No. | Sector | U.S. 1980 output | Total effect | Direct effect | Terms-of-trade effect | Real-income effect |
|-----|--------|--------|--------|--------|--------|--------|
| 1 | Agriculture, food | 482.80 | −0.71 | −0.40 | −0.15 | −0.16 |
| 2 | Natural resources | 377.21 | −3.24 | −0.90 | −2.19 | −0.15 |
| 3 | Textiles, apparel | 111.63 | 0.27 | 0.10 | 0.25 | −0.08 |
| 4 | Wood products, paper | 150.36 | −0.29 | 0.08 | −0.28 | −0.09 |
| 5 | Chemicals | 198.24 | −0.59 | 0.16 | −0.67 | −0.08 |
| 6 | Stone, clay, and glass | 45.66 | −0.12 | 0.00 | −0.10 | −0.02 |
| 7 | Iron and steel | 85.94 | −0.86 | −0.03 | −0.79 | −0.04 |
| 8 | Metal products | 120.85 | −0.84 | −0.13 | −0.67 | −0.04 |
| 9 | Machinery, instruments | 203.73 | −1.41 | 0.08 | −1.41 | −0.08 |
| 10 | Electrical machinery | 133.10 | −0.62 | 0.13 | −0.69 | −0.06 |
| 11 | Transport equipment | 195.35 | −0.60 | 0.10 | −0.60 | −0.10 |
| 12 | Miscellaneous manufactures | 97.59 | −0.64 | 0.08 | −0.77 | −0.05 |
| 13 | Construction | 340.10 | −0.06 | 0.04 | −0.28 | −0.18 |
| 14 | Utilities | 194.87 | −1.82 | −0.47 | −1.32 | −0.03 |
| 15 | Wholesale, retail trade | 570.81 | 0.55 | 0.55 | 0.35 | −0.35 |
| 16 | Financial, insurance | 188.31 | 0.21 | 0.19 | 0.15 | −0.13 |
| 17 | Real estate | 400.49 | 0.83 | 0.38 | 0.70 | −0.25 |
| 18 | Transport, communication | 225.37 | −0.18 | 0.09 | −0.15 | −0.12 |
| 19 | Services | 591.56 | −0.01 | 0.37 | 0.20 | −0.58 |
| 20 | International freight services | 20.45 | −0.07 | 0.00 | −0.06 | −0.01 |

*Source:* Appendix Table B-7 and unpublished simulation 8L4.

omy. To isolate these effects, the size of the American economy is increased, but the eventual general-equilibrium consequences of the change (on exchange rates and the partner's income level) are suppressed. Specifically, computations are interrupted when product markets are cleared, before any adjustments in the prices of domestic factors. This means that product prices are nearly the same as in the base solution.[4] Because of the increased demand for Japanese goods, both factor markets and current account balances are forced out of equilibrium.

Direct effects, as defined here, include both the final and intermediate demand generated by export increases. For example, the $1.21 billion direct impact on Japanese transportation equipment output (Table 6.7, sector 11, column 3) consists of a

**Table 6.7**  Sectoral interdependence: Japanese effects of 10-percent expansion of U.S. economy (in billions of 1980 dollars)

| No. | Sector | Japan 1980 output | Total effect | Direct effect | Terms-of-trade effect | Real-income effect |
|-----|--------|-------------------|--------------|---------------|----------------------|--------------------|
| 1 | Agriculture, food | 179.63 | −0.18 | −0.40 | 0.70 | −0.48 |
| 2 | Natural resources | 140.47 | −1.70 | −0.07 | −1.22 | −0.41 |
| 3 | Textiles, apparel | 56.36 | 0.45 | 0.06 | 0.65 | −0.26 |
| 4 | Wood products, paper | 72.61 | −0.57 | −0.12 | −0.19 | −0.26 |
| 5 | Chemicals | 95.04 | −0.17 | 0.05 | 0.06 | −0.28 |
| 6 | Stone, clay, and glass | 41.24 | −1.44 | −0.27 | −1.00 | −0.17 |
| 7 | Iron and steel | 127.60 | −0.45 | 0.18 | −0.44 | −0.19 |
| 8 | Metal products | 48.20 | −0.96 | −0.03 | −0.75 | −0.18 |
| 9 | Machinery, instruments | 118.44 | −1.80 | 0.57 | −1.93 | −0.44 |
| 10 | Electrical machinery | 96.20 | −0.46 | 0.54 | −0.66 | −0.34 |
| 11 | Transport equipment | 115.72 | 2.36 | 1.21 | 1.40 | −0.25 |
| 12 | Miscellaneous manufactures | 73.14 | −1.21 | 0.31 | −1.26 | −0.26 |
| 13 | Construction | 223.30 | −2.06 | −0.16 | −0.62 | −1.28 |
| 14 | Utilities | 45.96 | −0.46 | −0.01 | −0.25 | −0.20 |
| 15 | Wholesale, retail trade | 200.84 | 1.56 | 1.76 | 0.86 | −1.06 |
| 16 | Financial, insurance | 70.79 | 0.25 | 0.36 | .26 | −0.37 |
| 17 | Real estate | 126.54 | −0.32 | 0.22 | 0.22 | −0.76 |
| 18 | Transport, communication | 80.30 | −0.65 | 0.05 | −0.31 | −0.39 |
| 19 | Services | 376.54 | −1.81 | 0.46 | 0.10 | −2.37 |
| 20 | International freight services | 18.62 | −0.29 | −0.06 | −0.17 | −0.06 |

*Source:* Appendix Table B-5 and unpublished simulation 8L3.

$0.88 increase in final demand (mainly exports to the United States) and a $0.33 increase in intermediate demand (originating in Japanese sectors serving the export market, including the transport equipment sector itself). In some sectors, intermediate demand is very important. Indeed, some of the largest "direct" effects are felt by nontraded sectors such as wholesale and retail trade ($1.76 billion in the Japanese case), which provide inputs to all trading sectors.

Some direct effects are negative. Since world markets are allowed to clear, increased U.S. demand raises the prices of homogeneous products. As the partner begins to economize on these products, demand and output fall in several raw-material-based industries. The most surprising example of this is that

Japanese growth causes a $0.40 billion decline in the U.S. agriculture and food output (Table 6.6); one would have expected this industry to benefit substantially from Japanese expansion. A more detailed look at the solution shows that U.S. exports do increase by $1.18 billion to Japan and by $0.92 billion overall (some exports are diverted from third markets to Japan), but world market price increases cause domestic demand to fall by $1.32 billion. Some of the demand decline frees output for export, but the large part associated with exclusively domestic activities such as processing (Table 2.3, Eq. R12) causes the aggregated output of the agriculture and food industry to decline. This chain of causation is familiar from experience with the oil price shocks of the 1970s: although the effects on domestic oil producers were highly favorable, the industry as a whole —counting downstream refiners and processors—was adversely affected by substitution away from oil-based energy.

*Terms-of-trade effects.* The current account and factor market imbalances implicit in the direct effects induce depreciation by the growing economy. In the second step of the analysis, the computations are allowed to implement these exchange-rate adjustments but are stopped short of imposing the real-income effects implied by the new terms of trade. (In effect, the partner country is allowed to borrow to maintain its real expenditures.) Both currencies depreciate relative to the rest of the world— owing to the umbrella effects described in Chapter 5—but the partner's prices rise relative to the expanding economy's. From the partner's viewpoint this causes a variety of trade effects, including declines in bilateral exports and ROW imports and increases in bilateral imports and ROW exports. The complicated results of these changes depend on the composition and elasticity pattern of the trade structure.

In addition, as the prices of traded goods rise, domestic users substitute nontraded goods for traded goods. An important element in this process is the replacement of intermediate traded inputs with primary factors in production. This mechanism, also familiar from the oil price experience of the 1970s, ultimately leads to a decline in gross output (because of the diminished double-counting of intermediate goods) relative to national product. Thus the sum of output changes is generally negative

for a depreciating economy — the case in both Tables 6.6 and 6.7.

The list of "winners" in the terms-of-trade column includes the partner economy's nontraded industries and its strongest third-country exports. In the case of the United States, even most export industries suffer from the competitive impact of Japanese depreciation, and the nontraded industries emerge as the main beneficiaries. In the case of Japan, transport equipment and, to a lesser extent, textiles and chemicals also gain from the terms-of-trade effect.

*Real-income effect.* The depreciation of both countries' exchange rates implies a reduction in purchasing power. These effects are not large: as it was shown in Table 5.5, the effect of Japanese expansion on U.S. real income is − $1.2 billion, and of U.S. expansion on Japanese income, − $6.9 billion. Multiplied by the input-output structure, these changes nevertheless produce sectoral impacts on the same order of magnitude as the direct and terms-of-trade effects. Since partner real income falls in both experiments and since income elasticities of all products are zero or positive, the results are negative for all sectors. The largest declines appear in the consumption-oriented service industries.

*Total effect.* The varied composition of these effects provides an object lesson in the importance of general equilibrium analysis: one can find at least one industry in which any particular effect dominates all others. Even generalizations about relative changes in traded and nontraded sectors are impossible to make: for some sectors, the positive terms-of-trade effect leads to increased demand; for others, a disproportionately large negative real-income effect leads to decreased demand.

# 7 Alternatives in Commercial Policy

Japanese-American trade is intervention-prone: it is highly visible, and it is imbalanced. Episodes of protectionism have accompanied each of the major periods of change in Japanese-American trade identified in Chapter 6. Japan's initial penetration of American textile markets led to voluntary export restraints (VERs) on cotton textiles as early as 1955, to more formal agreements in the early 1960s, and then to explicit quotas in 1972. Its steel exports led to VERs in 1969 and trigger prices in 1980, and its automobile exports to VERs in 1981. In addition to these prominent industry-wide controls, dozens of cases came before the U.S. Tariff Commission seeking remedies under anti-dumping statutes. At the beginning of the period under study, intervention on the Japanese side was also pervasive, if less discriminatory. Formal measures of protection have been reduced steadily since, although various regulatory practices and high domestic agricultural price supports continue to shelter some important Japanese markets (Japan – United States Economic Relations Group, 1981b).

Each country, then, has seen fit to manipulate its international trade, especially at times when its overall and bilateral trade were in deficit. The reasons for and styles of protection vary enormously between the two economies (Destler and Sato, 1982), but the frequency of trade problems suggests deeper reasons for the

conflict. This chapter explores possible structural reasons for the persistence of interventionist behavior.

The present analysis is focused on a single major rationale for protection, the possibility of national gains from improved terms of trade. The argument has a long and notorious history as the "scientific" or optimum tariff; it results from the fact that large countries face downward-sloping demand curves for their products. Even if policymakers are unfamiliar with the technology of terms-of-trade manipulation, they are generally conscious of the problem of limited foreign demand for exports and of the benefits of a strong currency (for example, lower raw material import prices). As argued in Chapter 1, terms-of-trade considerations are apparently increasing in importance as U.S. economic policy toward Japan is shifting from a sectoral, injury-oriented focus to an export emphasis.

Because terms-of-trade gains are zero-sum gains, it is politically difficult for any country to openly pursue the maximization of its terms of trade. But even if the proximate reasons for protection are more specific and sector-oriented, large positive terms-of-trade effects are likely to erode domestic opposition to protection. These points are emphasized because this study finds potential terms-of-trade effects to be large, both in relation to trade and, as will be shown later, in relation to the efficiency losses likely to result from intervention. Moreover, in the case of Japanese-American trade, distributional questions are especially important because of the unequal threat of unilateral action. Thus, terms-of-trade issues are bound to play a central but quiet role in U.S.-Japanese trade policy.

The terms-of-trade rationale is by no means the only basis for imposing protection. A growing economic literature suggests that adjustment costs are important and may require transitional periods of protection (Baldwin, 1982). Also, "infant industry" protection has been argued to have been especially successful in Japan (General Accounting Office, 1979; Abegglen and Rapp, 1972), and it has even been resurrected to defend the protection of declining American industries (Reich and Magaziner, 1982). But regardless of how protection is justified, it has real-income effects; and if these are as large as they appear to be, they probably play a role in the policy process.

The political significance of these issues notwithstanding, the analysis is limited to examining the economic consequences of protection. In other words, no attempt is made to analyze the intracountry distribution of terms-of-trade gains, as is frequently done in the recent literature on the political economy of protection.[1] Rather, the terms-of-trade issue is viewed from the perspective of the international distribution of the gains from trade. The main question studied is how the structure of trade affects each country's ability to intervene in order to achieve terms-of-trade objectives. The American and Japanese economies appear to differ substantially on this scale, and at least part of their continuing conflict could be explained by these differences.

## Protection in Japanese-American Trade

Not many years ago a study of protection would have focused mainly on tariffs. However, given the steady progress in the multilateral reduction of tariffs and the widening role of government in most industrial economies, protection is increasingly based on nontariff barriers. These range from formal quotas to exclusionary product regulations and "buy national" policies in both the public and private sectors. Thus, although our empirical knowledge of formal protection measures has improved, the estimation of overall protection has become more difficult and uncertain.

In the present analysis, three layers of possible restrictions will be distinguished. The first layer consists of tariffs. Tariffs have predictable effects on prices, and, given the choice mechanisms of the model, their welfare effects are easily analyzed. The second layer includes quotas, both formal and voluntary. These restrictions are relatively well known, but their welfare effects are more uncertain because the quantity and price effects of a quota—the "water" in the quota—are difficult to measure. The third layer of protection includes invisible barriers that are usually not quantified at all. Thus, successively greater subjective judgment is involved in quantifying the effects of each layer of protection.

The evolution of formal U.S. and Japanese protection is traced in Table 7.1. The data present tariffs (and the tariff-

**Table 7.1** Tariff-equivalents of protection in Japanese-American trade (nominal percentage)

| No. | Sector | United States | | | Japan | | |
|---|---|---|---|---|---|---|---|
| | | 1960 | 1970 | 1980 | 1960 | 1970 | 1980 |
| 1 | Agriculture, food | | | | | | |
| | Tariffs | 6.0 | 5.2 | 2.1 | 10.7 | 8.7 | 7.0 |
| | QRs[a] | — | — | — | 1.6 | 4.4 | 5.1 |
| 2 | Natural resources | | | | | | |
| | Tariffs | 2.8 | 2.3 | 0.1 | 6.9 | 5.4 | 1.9 |
| | QRs | — | — | — | 7.2 | 5.3 | 0.7 |
| 3 | Textiles, apparel | | | | | | |
| | Tariffs | 24.9 | 21.8 | 17.7 | 50.7 | 17.9 | 6.9 |
| | QRs | 1.2 | 3.5 | 1.3 | 25.0 | 6.1 | 32.2 |
| 4 | Wood products, paper | | | | | | |
| | Tariffs | 3.3 | 2.8 | 1.3 | 5.4 | 3.6 | 1.6 |
| | QRs | 0.3 | — | — | 2.2 | — | — |
| 5 | Chemicals | | | | | | |
| | Tariffs | 7.1 | 6.1 | 5.9 | 7.0 | 8.1 | 4.9 |
| | QRs | — | — | — | 1.8 | — | 5.5 |
| 6 | Stone, clay, and glass | | | | | | |
| | Tariffs | 13.0 | 11.2 | 5.0 | 11.3 | 3.0 | 1.2 |
| | QRs | — | — | — | — | — | — |
| 7 | Iron and steel | | | | | | |
| | Tariffs | 7.8 | 6.8 | 5.1 | 6.4 | 1.8 | 1.8 |
| | QRs | — | 6.0 | 7.0 | — | — | — |
| 8 | Metal products | | | | | | |
| | Tariffs | 10.3 | 8.9 | 5.9 | 11.5 | 11.4 | 5.7 |
| | QRs | — | — | — | 0.5 | — | — |
| 9 | Machinery, instruments | | | | | | |
| | Tariffs | 9.6 | 8.3 | 4.5 | 10.7 | 11.6 | 6.3 |
| | QRs | — | — | — | — | — | — |
| 10 | Electrical machinery | | | | | | |
| | Tariffs | 10.0 | 8.7 | 5.5 | 4.1 | 8.9 | 6.8 |
| | QRs | — | — | 0.8 | — | — | — |
| 11 | Transport equipment | | | | | | |
| | Tariffs | 3.0 | 2.6 | 2.5 | 4.9 | 3.8 | 10.3 |
| | QRs | — | — | — | — | — | — |
| 12 | Miscellaneous manufactures | | | | | | |
| | Tariffs | 11.6 | 9.9 | 3.0 | 27.6 | 17.1 | 16.1 |
| | QRs | — | — | — | — | — | — |
| | Total trade | | | | | | |
| | Tariffs | 13.7 | 8.9 | 4.1 | 8.9 | 8.2 | 5.7 |
| | QRs | 0.4 | 1.4 | 0.9 | 2.8 | 2.7 | 3.1 |

a. Quantitative restrictions on bilateral trade; tariff-equivalents estimated by Turner (1981). U.S. restrictions include voluntary export restraints actually imposed by the government of Japan.

equivalents of quotas) as a fraction of total imports by commodity category. Changes in rates defined this way tend to understate the extent of across-the-board reductions in protection;[2] thus the decline of formal protection during the 1960–1980 period was probably sharper than Table 7.1 indicates.

The quota equivalents shown in Table 7.1 are based on an impressive detailed study of U.S. and Japanese quotas by Turner (1981). Turner's study starts with the end of Japan's import-licensing system in 1962; the Japanese quantitative restrictions shown for 1960 for Japan are really 1962 restrictions. (Japanese import statistics do not suggest a dramatic impact between 1960 and 1962.) Turner used a variety of methods to estimate quota equivalents. In a number of cases he compared protected and unprotected prices by studying time-series price changes following the introduction or removal of quotas. In other cases, when quotas were applied only in specific markets, he compared changes in the price of the product in the protected market with changes in other, unprotected markets. The analysis was conducted on a four-digit Standard International Trade Classification level and has been significantly aggregated for the purposes of this book. Turner's estimates represent a major empirical breakthrough in the analysis of U.S. and Japanese protection; without these estimates, the present study could have made only very rough guesses about the importance of nontariff restrictions.

Between 1960 and 1980 Japanese protection underwent a series of major transitions (see Ozaki, 1972; Ichikawa, 1981; Japan Economic Institute, 1982b). The first broad revision of the trade control system in 1962 abolished import licensing, which had effectively placed all import decisions under government control, and introduced a "negative list" of explicitly restricted commodities. This list initially included 493 commodities and was gradually narrowed to 27 commodities, most of which were agricultural, by 1980. The list is now short enough to compare favorably with the equivalent protected lists of other major developed economies (Japan Economic Institute, 1982b). Nevertheless, according to Turner's data, the growing potential for trade in restricted categories has kept the overall price effect

of Japanese quantitative restrictions approximately stable over the 1960–1980 period (Table 7.1).

With the dismantling of formal quantitative controls in the 1960s, the burden of protecting Japanese markets fell increasingly on tariffs. Products where Japan expected to enter world markets were protected especially heavily: in 1967, for example, the Japanese tariff on automobiles was 40 percent, and on color television receivers, 30 percent (General Accounting Office, 1979). Tariffs were sharply reduced following the Kennedy Round agreements of 1967. The cuts were accelerated relative to the original five-year implementation schedule and were followed by a unilateral 20-percent reduction in tariffs in 1972. By the late 1970s Japanese tariffs stood at levels only slightly higher than those prevailing in the United States and Europe. Further cuts negotiated in the Tokyo Round are expected to bring Japanese tariffs below those of other industrialized countries by 1987 (Deardorff and Stern, 1979).

The principal remaining elements of Japanese protection include key agricultural price controls—the Japanese domestic price of rice, for example, is still pegged at about three times world levels (Japan–United States Economic Relations Group, 1981b)—and various informal barriers. Some of these barriers are explicitly exclusionary.[3] But other barriers are probably more important and less tangible: "buy Japanese" attitudes by Japanese producers and close relationships among Japanese companies, including the trading companies that handle the distribution of most imported products (Committee on Ways and Means, 1979).

The history of U.S. protection is not nearly as dynamic. Like Japan, the United States also gradually reduced tariffs during the 1960–1980 period. Unlike Japan, the United States had no general system of exchange controls to dismantle, and U.S. protection relied primarily on tariffs at the start of the period. U.S. tariffs were therefore initially higher than Japan's. U.S. tariffs declined sharply (Table 7.1), however, and were somewhat lower than Japanese tariffs by 1980. But there is another side to American protectionism. Not shown in these tables is the effect of the threat of intervention: the number of complaints brought under U.S. trade law has risen considerably in recent

years. Although each judgment affects products of limited general importance, the threat of costly legal proceedings, severe retroactive penalties, and the loss of market investments constitutes a powerful informal trade barrier. These unmeasurable factors are not investigated in this study.

## The Analytics of Protection

Before turning to the analysis of existing protection and alternative strategies, it is best to establish how intervention operates in the context of the model. We start with a brief look at the theoretical effects of protection and move to quantitative simulations of various types of protection.

The effects of a tariff are illustrated in Figure 7.1, which introduces protection into the earlier Figure 2.6. To simplify the discussion, only consumption effects are considered (that is, a one-sector model is used) and production is assumed to remain at the full employment level $X$. Because of intervention, consumers no longer face the true terms of trade line $TT$ but the flatter line $TT_P$, which adds the tariff to the price of imports. If the true terms of trade are fixed, a new consumption equilibrium is reached at $C'$, with an obvious welfare loss relative to $C$. The point $C'$ is on the home country's new offer curve: this is now its

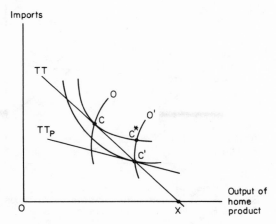

**Figure 7.1** Protection in a one-sector Armington-type model

offer at terms of trade *TT*. Thus, the home offer curve has shifted from *O* to *O'*. Equilibrium can be found by adding a foreign offer curve to the diagram. If the foreign offer curve intersects *O'* above the point $C^*$, home welfare improves with protection; if not, home welfare declines. Note, in particular, that *TT* itself represents a perfectly elastic "offer curve." Welfare necessarily falls if protection is applied with this curve; a small country cannot gain by protecting its markets.

Are the United States and Japan small countries in the sense of Figure 7.1? To flesh out this abstract view of protection, simulation results are collected from several experiments to sketch the "actual" curves facing the American and Japanese economies (Figures 7.2 and 7.3). Each of the three simulations used in these figures changes some aspect of the U.S. (or Japanese) economy while leaving the other structures of the other two economies unchanged. In effect, the home offer curve is perturbed to "feel out" the position of the foreign offer curve. Although a multi-sector model has multisectoral offer curves, the figures show only aggregate import-export relationships. Consequently, the for-

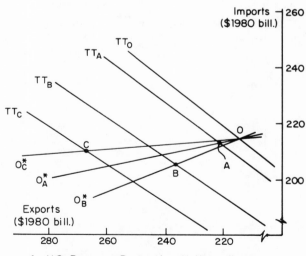

A = U.S. Removes Protection Unilaterally
B = U.S. Factor Endowments Increase by 10 Percent
C = U.S. External Savings Increase by 2 Percent

**Figure 7.2**  Trade offer facing the United States in 1980

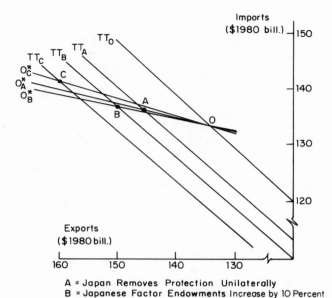

A = Japan Removes Protection Unilaterally
B = Japanese Factor Endowments Increase by 10 Percent
C = Japanese External Savings Increase by 2 Percent

**Figure 7.3** Trade offer facing Japan in 1980

eign offer curves ($O_a^*$, $O_b^*$, $O_c^*$) found in the several experiments differ, since each experiment involves a slightly different combination of sectoral trade changes. Nevertheless, the simulated offer curves are similar and clearly show that neither the United States nor Japan faces elastic world markets.[4]

These results are further reinforced by simulated increases in U.S. and Japanese protection. Table 7.2 reports on the implications of adding 10 percentage points to tariffs across the board, on all trade and on bilateral trade alone, by the United States and Japan. If the United States increases all of its tariffs, its real income grows by $15.7 billion, or 0.6 percent. If Japan raises all tariffs, its income grows by $8.7 billion, or 0.8 percent of national income. The cost of consumption distortions is roughly estimated by the "efficiency effect"—the difference between the real income gain and the change in the real trade balance (real exports minus real imports). In the U.S. experiment the real trade balance improves by $17.5 billion, and all but $1.8 billion of this becomes a real income gain. The difference is similarly

**Table 7.2** Effects of increased protection (billions of 1980 dollars)

| Variable | Base solution | Effects of 10% tariff increases | | | |
|---|---|---|---|---|---|
| | | By United States | | By Japan | |
| | | MFN[a] | Bilateral[b] | MFN | Bilateral |
| U.S. variables | | | | | |
| Exchange rate (index) | 100.0 | 11.5 | 1.0 | 1.4 | −0.2 |
| Real income | 2626.1 | 15.7 | 2.5 | 0.5 | −1.1 |
| Exports | 214.2 | −14.8 | −3.1 | −0.2 | −0.5 |
| Imports | 244.5 | 2.7 | −0.6 | 0.1 | −1.2 |
| Efficiency effect | — | −1.8 | 0.0 | — | — |
| Japanese variables | | | | | |
| Exchange rate (index) | 100.0 | 2.4 | −3.2 | 8.5 | 1.9 |
| Real income | 1039.6 | 0.7 | −4.5 | 8.7 | 1.0 |
| Exports | 157.4 | 0.1 | 0.4 | −12.2 | −2.7 |
| Imports | 167.3 | 0.2 | −3.1 | −2.9 | −0.8 |
| Efficiency effect | — | — | — | −0.6 | −0.9 |
| Bilateral trade variables | | | | | |
| U.S. exports to Japan | 20.8 | −1.6 | −1.3 | −0.7 | −1.8 |
| Japanese exports to U.S. | 31.2 | −0.9 | −3.6 | −3.8 | −0.9 |
| Rest-of-world net imports | — | −17.6 | 1.0 | −9.6 | −1.2 |

*Source:* Unpublished simulations 8H8, 8H9, 8HA, 8HB.
a. MFN (most favored nation) tariff increase is applied to all imports.
b. Applied to bilateral imports only.

small for Japan. Thus, efficiency losses due to consumption distortions are on the order of 10 percent of the terms-of-trade gains generated by protection.

The effects of discriminatory bilateral protection are highly asymmetric. A 10-percentage-point increase in U.S. tariffs on imports from Japan would increase U.S. income by $2.5 billion and reduce Japanese income by $4.5 billion; a similar Japanese tariff would raise Japanese income by $1.0 billion and reduce U.S. income by $1.1 billion. Economic negotiations between the United States and Japan are undoubtedly conditioned by the fact that the consequences of unilateral action are so different for the two countries.

Finally, the tariff experiments suggest that the bilateral effects of general protection may have opposite signs. The magnitudes involved are relatively small (only about one-twentieth of the

gains experienced by the protectionist country itself), but they demonstrate still another aspect of the close dollar/yen relationship. The effects of Japanese tariffs on U.S. welfare are of the conventional sign; the dollar and U.S. real income fall. But U.S. protection raises Japanese real income. Evidently, the dollar appreciation induces a sufficient increase in the third-currency purchasing power of the yen to outweigh the negative direct effects of increased U.S. protection.

## The Effects of Existing Protection

The first seven of the experiments address the removal of the easily quantified barriers, namely, tariffs and quantitative restrictions (see Table 7.3 and also Table 7.4, which repeats the first two experiments of Table 7.3 for different base years). Experiments A, B, and C hypothesize the complete elimination of tariffs and quantitative restrictions by the United States, Japan, and both countries simultaneously. Experiments D and E then sepa-

**Table 7.3**  Effects of eliminating protection (percentage changes)

|  | United States | | Japan | |
|---|---|---|---|---|
| Experiment | Exchange rate | Real income | Exchange rate | Real income |
| A. U.S. removes tariffs, quotas unilaterally | −5.1 | −0.32 | −0.7 | 0.06 |
| B. Japan removes tariffs, quotas unilaterally | −1.3 | 0.02 | −8.1 | −0.81 |
| C. U.S., Japan both remove tariffs, quotas | −6.3 | −0.24 | −8.8 | −0.77 |
| D. U.S., Japan both remove tariffs only | −4.4 | −0.23 | −4.9 | −0.45 |
| E. U.S., Japan both remove quotas only | −1.7 | −0.09 | −3.6 | −0.35 |
| F. U.S., Japan remove bilateral tariffs, quotas | −0.7 | −0.03 | −0.3 | 0.04 |
| G. U.S., Japan both remove tariffs, quotas, with share elasticities tripled | −5.0 | −0.18 | −5.0 | −0.21 |

*Source:* Appendix Tables B-8 and B-9 and unpublished simulations 8H3–8H7.

**Table 7.4**  Effects of eliminating protection, 1960–1980
(percentage changes)

| | | Simulated changes | | | |
|---|---|---|---|---|---|
| | | United States | | Japan | |
| Experiment | Year | Exchange rate | Real income | Exchange rate | Real income |
| A. U.S. removes tariffs, quotas unilaterally | 1960 | −5.6 | −0.08 | 1.2 | 0.62 |
| | 1970 | −9.1 | −0.28 | −0.7 | 0.24 |
| | 1980 | −5.1 | −0.32 | −0.7 | 0.06 |
| B. Japan removes tariffs, quotas unilaterally | 1960 | −0.8 | 0.00 | −10.4 | −0.73 |
| | 1970 | −0.9 | 0.02 | −8.6 | −0.63 |
| | 1980 | −1.3 | 0.02 | −8.1 | −0.81 |

*Source:* Appendix Tables B-8 and B-9 and unpublished simulations 6H1, 6H2, 7H1, 7H2.

rate the effects of tariffs and quantitative restrictions in the case where both countries remove barriers. Experiment F examines the special case where only bilateral barriers are removed; essentially, it represents the formation of a Japanese-American customs union. Finally, the case of joint elimination of all barriers is repeated under a substantially more price-elastic trade structure than the one estimated and used elsewhere in the book (Experiment G).

An important feature of the results is their near-perfect additivity. For example, results when both countries eliminate protection simultaneously are about equal to the sum of the results when the two countries remove barriers separately. Similarly, the results when both tariffs and quantitative restrictions are eliminated are about equal to the sum of the results when these two types of barriers are removed individually. Evidently, protection effects are small enough to be near-linear.

Other results of the experiments include the following.

1. Both the United States and Japan have substantial terms-of-trade gains built into their present protective structure.

Japan's structure provides larger gains relative to national product, partly because of the greater openness of the Japanese economy and the higher level of protection.

2. Each country's protective structure imposes costs on its partner's economy. The positive spillover effects of U.S. protection on Japan, noted in the previous section for across-the-board changes in protection, are not present in the actual structure of U.S. protection. If the United States unilaterally eliminates its tariffs, the United States loses but Japan gains. Evidently, the existing structure of U.S. protection is biased against bilateral imports.

3. Quantitative restrictions play a more important role in Japan than in the United States, but in 1980 the consequences of eliminating tariffs were still twice as large as those of eliminating quantitative restrictions. Tariffs played a somewhat larger role in U.S. protection.

4. The bilateral elimination of formal protection would have a negative effect on U.S. welfare and a positive effect on Japanese welfare, but in both cases the impact would be small.

5. Despite a decline in the nominal rate of protection, the value of protection has grown relative to the American GNP over time (see Table 7.4). This finding is largely due to the greater openness of the U.S. economy and to the declining elasticity of its exports and imports.

6. The effect of U.S. multilateral protection on the Japanese economy has sharply diminished over time, mainly because the direct effect of reduced access to U.S. markets is increasingly offset by the appreciation of the yen induced by dollar appreciation.

The sectoral effects of these experiments provide a direct view of how protection alters economic structure. As in the sectoral analysis of Chapter 6, several major factors are involved in determining sectoral response. One direct effect of removing protection is stiffer price competition (from imports) for formerly protected industries. Another direct effect operates on the input side: cost declines in sectors that use imports or can easily substitute imports for domestic inputs. (This is the problem solved in effective rate of protection [ERP] analysis.) In addition to these direct effects, each sector experiences terms-of-trade

and real-income effects similar to those outlined in Chapter 6. Since the elimination of protection usually leads to terms-of-trade and real-income losses, the output of traded sectors as a whole increases at the expense of nontraded services (although in any particular sector the net impact depends on the relative magnitudes of the tariffs and various domestic demand effects).

The sectoral impacts of complete elimination of formal protection in the United States and Japan, respectively, are shown in Table 7.5. The table also compares these results to two measures of the protection, the nominal rate of protection (including tariffs and the tariff equivalent of quantitative restrictions) and a standard ERP measure.[5] It is clear from this comparison that

**Table 7.5** Sectoral effects of eliminating protection (percentage change)

| No. | Sector | United States | | | Japan | | |
| | | Output change | Nominal rate | ERP | Output change | Nominal rate | ERP |
|---|---|---|---|---|---|---|---|
| 1 | Agriculture, food | −0.3 | 6.6 | 9.3 | −0.9 | 12.1 | 18.3 |
| 2 | Natural resources | −1.1 | 0.1 | −1.0 | 0.1 | 2.6 | 2.9 |
| 3 | Textiles and apparel | −1.7 | 24.2 | 37.9 | −1.6 | 39.1 | 78.5 |
| 4 | Wood products, paper | 0.0 | 1.3 | −0.5 | 1.2 | 1.6 | −5.6 |
| 5 | Chemicals | −0.2 | 5.9 | 9.1 | 0.7 | 10.4 | 19.2 |
| 6 | Stone, clay, and glass | −0.3 | 5.0 | 7.8 | −2.0 | 1.2 | −0.5 |
| 7 | Iron and steel | −0.9 | 10.1 | 17.9 | 3.3 | 1.8 | 1.3 |
| 8 | Metal products | −0.4 | 5.9 | 7.0 | −0.7 | 5.7 | 9.7 |
| 9 | Machinery, instruments | 0.6 | 4.5 | 4.6 | 2.1 | 6.3 | 9.6 |
| 10 | Electrical machinery | 0.6 | 5.5 | 7.4 | 2.2 | 6.8 | 10.5 |
| 11 | Transport equipment | 0.5 | 2.5 | −0.2 | 4.4 | 10.3 | 18.5 |
| 12 | Miscellaneous manufactures | 0.2 | 3.0 | 3.8 | 1.3 | 16.1 | 28.8 |
| 13 | Construction | −0.5 | — | −2.8 | −1.0 | — | −4.6 |
| 14 | Utilities | −1.5 | — | −0.3 | −0.3 | — | −2.2 |
| 15 | Wholesale, retail trade | −0.1 | — | −0.1 | −0.1 | — | −0.5 |
| 16 | Financial, insurance | −0.1 | — | −0.1 | 0.2 | — | −0.5 |
| 17 | Real estate | 0.2 | — | −0.1 | −0.7 | — | −0.1 |
| 18 | Transport, communication | −0.3 | — | −0.3 | −0.5 | — | −5.9 |
| 19 | Services | −0.3 | — | −0.3 | −0.7 | — | −3.0 |
| 20 | International freight services | −0.3 | — | −0.3 | −0.5 | — | −5.9 |

*Source:* Appendix Tables B-8 and B-9.

neither index provides a good prediction of the final results. Superior ERP formulas could be devised to better approximate the results of the model, but they would require a great deal of additional information of the type actually incorporated in the model's structural relationships. The fact is that any reasonable general equilibrium structure produces much more complicated interactions than simple indicators of protection are likely to track.

We turn finally to the popular issue of intangible barriers in the Japanese market. The list of barriers that are frequently cited is long, ranging from specific government regulations, say, on acceptable food additives to nationalistic attitudes of Japanese decision makers in business and government. Because it is impossible to assess these barriers directly, the implicit effects of the barriers have to be judged by comparing Japanese trade to the trade of "open" economies of similar size and level of advancement. The country most frequently mentioned in this respect is West Germany. A host of factors make such a comparison questionable, not the least of which is Germany's close physical and economic proximity to its neighbors. But it is still intriguing to ask what Japanese trade patterns might look like if Japan's openness approached that of Germany.

Previous attempts to make such comparisons have raised the question, What would Japan's manufactured imports be if the same proportion of Japan's imports as Germany's consisted of manufactured goods?[6] This is a curious question, since it implies that Japan might somehow go without the raw material imports that now dominate its import structure. A more appropriate formulation of the comparison would permit technological and endowment considerations to determine the composition of exports, while "forcing" overall openness to match that of a comparable economy.

To get the Japanese economy to be as open as the German (that is, to raise exports plus imports from 25 to 45 percent of GNP), we introduce an across-the-board subsidy of Japanese imports. (This subsidy can be interpreted also as the removal of present positive barriers.) The driving force behind most of the experiment's results is a 22-percent depreciation in the value of the yen (Table 7.6). In the final equilibrium solution, the desired

**Table 7.6** Effects of massive increase in openness of Japanese economy (in billions of 1980 dollars)

| Variable affected | United States | | Japan | |
|---|---|---|---|---|
| | Base year | Simulated change | Base year | Simulated change |
| Exchange rate (percent) | 100.0 | −4.5 | 100.0 | −21.9 |
| Real income | 2626.1 | −0.8 | 1039.6 | −33.8 |
| Exports | 214.4 | 2.1 | 133.5 | 43.6 |
| Bilateral | 20.8 | 2.2 | 31.1 | 13.8 |
| Imports | 244.4 | 3.1 | 128.7 | 9.4 |
| Bilateral | 31.1 | 13.8 | 20.8 | 2.2 |
| Value of exports + imports relative to GNP (percent) | 0.17 | 0.01 | 0.25 | 0.09 |

*Source:* Appendix Table B-10.

level of openness is mainly achieved by depreciating to the point where imports, slightly expanded in physical quantity and in world market value, represent the high required percentage of devalued national product. In the process, Japanese markets become more open to U.S. and rest-of-the-world products, and U.S. manufactured exports to Japan increase from 12 to 30 percent, depending on the sector. But in order to pay for these exports, given a depreciated currency, Japan must increase manufactured exports even more drastically: exports to the United States rise 45 percent in quantity terms and 16 percent in value terms.

By becoming substantially more open, Japan would be forced to do a great deal more of what it now does: exporting manufactures to pay for raw materials. Many of these exports would find U.S. markets. Although Japan's own manufactured imports would also increase, Japan's manufactured exports would expand still more rapidly, yielding an increased real trade surplus in manufactured goods. Though apparently designed to serve the interest of U.S. manufacturing industries, the policy would create sharp price competition in manufactures in both U.S. and rest-of-the-world markets. The overall equilibrium effects of the change would move U.S. resources from traded to nontraded industries, primarily from sectors that had faced the strongest

Japanese competition in the recent past. Although U.S. exports to Japan would increase by 11 percent, the bilateral trade balance would become still more negative, both in value and especially in real terms. Given the structure of Japanese-American trade, the U.S. market would naturally absorb an important share of the Japanese export increases generated in the experiment.

If Japanese exports are inherently limited by the relatively slow growth of foreign markets, it is difficult to see how the general reductions of Japanese barriers would contribute to the solution of trade conflicts. Bilateral problems with the United States would almost certainly be more severe. What increased openness does is to improve the terms of trade of Japan's trade partners. However, these terms-of-trade effects benefit only the rest of the world; the tight relationship between the dollar and the yen causes slight depreciation and terms-of-trade losses by the United States as well.

## Strategies in Bilateral Trade

The reasons for imbalance in bilateral trade have already been analyzed in Chapter 5; imbalance results naturally from the general export and import patterns of the United States and Japan. Moreover, the previous experiment shows that the imbalance does not diminish if the general protection in Japanese markets is reduced, even if extreme assumptions are made about the effects of intangible barriers.

Despite the fact that bilateral imbalance is the product of fundamental economic forces, it is a critical political issue. For example, the Subcommittee on Trade of the House Ways and Means Committee regards it as the primary reason for "concentrating on trade problems in the Far East" (Committee on Ways and Means, 1979, p. 1). Political interest in the bilateral imbalance may be explained by the apparently large terms-of-trade effects of intervention. Even if bilateral imbalance can be justified from the viewpoint of global efficiency, imbalanced bilateral trade crucially affects negotiating positions in the allocation of the gains from trade between the United States and Japan.

It might seem possible to eliminate bilateral imbalance by

purely "cosmetic" means, for example by diverting Japanese raw-materials purchases to the United States from the rest of the world, even for products that the United States itself imports. Cosmetic devices are ineffective, however, because they do not change the fundamental asymmetry of threats involved in the bilateral relationship. U.S. protection, for example, would have the same effect on Japan regardless of the world trade pattern in homogeneous goods. To increase its leverage over U.S. policy, Japan would have to import goods which the United States cannot easily sell in third markets (products with low price elasticities in U.S.–rest of the world trade), and which, therefore, constitute a net increase in U.S. export markets.

During recent years a number of plans have been advanced to reduce the bilateral imbalance, ranging from formal restrictions in U.S. markets to informal measures to improve American access to Japanese markets. The congressional report already cited listed the options in simple, direct terms: "(1) Japan can buy more from the United States; (2) Japan can invest in U.S. production facilities, thus returning capital and jobs to America; or (3) the United States can buy less from Japan" (Committee on Ways and Means, 1979, p. 3). The report went on to urge options 1 and 2, but it clearly held out the threat of option 3 if satisfactory progress were not made.

The strategies outlined in the congressional report can be implemented by various means: incentives to expand a particular trade flow could be applied by either the exporting or the importing economy. To assess these alternatives, five final simulations will be examined:

1. U.S. protection of imports from Japan.
2. Japanese restraint of exports to the United States.
3. Increased Japanese direct investment in the United States.
4. U.S. subsidies of exports to Japan.
5. Japanese subsidies of imports from the United States.

In practice, the alternatives need not be implemented by explicit trade taxes or subsidies; preferential taxation, loan guarantees and subsidies, changes in regulatory policies, and various other interventions are common elements of modern commercial policy. We do assume, however, that the effects of all of these policies except alternative 3 (increased Japanese direct invest-

ment) can be translated into an equivalent tax or subsidy on exports or imports.

Increased Japanese direct investment in the United States is modeled as a transfer of technology, including marketing and management know-how; the capital flows that might be associated with direct investment are ignored. This is done for both conceptual and practical reasons. Conceptually, it is not clear whether Japanese direct investment in the United States would alter capital flows; this depends on the crowding-out effects of Japanese investment on other U.S. investment and on changes in the American and Japanese external saving rates. If capital flows are triggered, they have a complicated intertemporal effect on the current account: at first, a capital inflow into the United States would induce a current account deficit; later, the profits of the investment would generate a negative U.S. "capital service" flow, forcing other current account items such as trade to become more positive. It would not be possible to model all phases of this cycle in the present steady-state approach.

From a practical viewpoint, the critical aspect of direct investment is the international transfer of technology and, most important, the markets that have been captured by this technology. An apt model of such capital-free "investment" is Toyota's agreement to produce a Japanese-designed car in a Japanese-managed plant in California, with the plant to be provided by General Motors. Technology transfer is actually simulated by shifting a part of Japan's share of U.S. markets to the relevant U.S. industry. In effect, the United States becomes a producer, in Armington's terms, of goods usually distinguished by a Japanese place of production. In addition, Japanese input-output coefficients are applied in the part of the American industry that serves this extra market share.

In the simulations performed, each of the five policies is applied uniformly to all sectors: equal percentage point taxes and subsidies are applied to all sectors, and the technology transfer alternative shifts a fixed percentage of all Japanese market shares (that is, exports) to U.S. producers. The actual level of intervention is chosen so as to halve the bilateral imbalance (a reduction of $5.2 billion) in all five experiments. Results are collected in Table 7.7.

**Table 7.7**  Effects of policies to reduce bilateral imbalance (in billions of 1980 dollars)

| Variable affected | Base year | Simulated changes | | | | |
|---|---|---|---|---|---|---|
| | | U.S. protection | Japanese restraint | Technology transfer | U.S. export subsidy | Japanese import aid |
| Scale of intervention required to halve imbalance (%) | — | 15.3 | 11.6 | 27.0[a] | 27.5 | 26.8 |
| U.S. exports to Japan | 20.8 | −1.3 | −0.5 | −1.6 | 5.2 | 6.7 |
| Japanese exports to U.S. | 31.2 | −5.4 | −5.2 | −5.5 | 0.7 | 3.5 |
| U.S. variables | | | | | | |
| Exchange rate | 100.0 | 1.3 | 0.0 | 3.2 | −1.5 | 0.7 |
| Real income | 2626.1 | 2.5 | −2.4 | 6.2 | −8.6 | 3.2 |
| Japanese variables | | | | | | |
| Exchange rate | 100.0 | −4.6 | −2.1 | −4.3 | −3.1 | −6.1 |
| Real income | 1039.6 | −7.2 | 0.0 | −8.1 | 4.6 | −7.2 |
| Rest-of-the-world net imports | — | 1.9 | 1.4 | −0.2 | 4.0 | 4.0 |

*Source:* Appendix Tables B-11 through B-15.
a. Percentage of Japanese export markets transferred to U.S. producers.

Reducing the bilateral imbalance is, at least from the viewpoint of the United States and Japan, a negative-sum enterprise. Although the results for U.S. and Japanese welfare differ widely depending on policy, the gains of the winner never approach the losses of the loser. This is illustrated also in Figure 7.4, which plots the several outcomes for direct comparison. The line roughly connecting the alternative results passes about $3.5 billion below the origin, the point representing welfare in the initial, imbalanced trading position.

Not all of the $3.5 billion that the United States and Japan lose in trying to balance their bilateral trade is due to allocational inefficiency. Depending on the experiment, a large part of the loss becomes a terms-of-trade gain by third countries. An estimate of this gain, obtained by calculating the change in the rest of the world's real trade balance with the United States and Japan, is reported in the last line of Table 7.7.

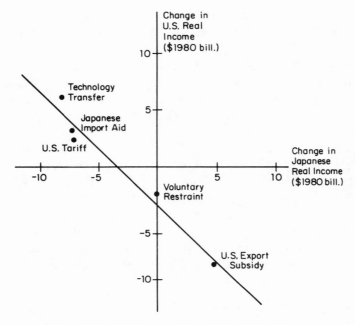

**Figure 7.4**  Policies to reduce bilateral imbalance

The most favorable policy from the U.S. viewpoint is the technology transfer alternative. A transfer of about 22 percent of Japanese markets in the United States is required, in this case, to halve the bilateral deficit. The United States gains markets at no tangible cost; the distortions usually associated with protection are absent. Indeed, Japanese techniques provide a slightly more efficient use of some U.S. resources. But this policy is also the least attractive from the Japanese viewpoint: large export revenue losses in the U.S. market must be replaced by depreciation in U.S. and other markets. The result is a deterioration in the Japanese terms of trade and large gains by the United States and the rest of the world.

At the opposite end of the scale, Japanese benefits are largest when the imbalance is narrowed by U.S. export subsidies. The required subsidy is estimated at 28 percent. This approach directly improves the Japanese terms of trade by subsidizing Japanese consumers at the expense of U.S. consumers. This policy is

in fact practiced to a limited extent through the subsidization of export credit and the preferential tax treatment of export earnings.

The strategy providing the smallest departures from the original equilibrium involves the Japanese restriction of exports to the United States. The export tax equivalent of voluntary export restraints is 17 percent; these "revenues" are captured by Japan. Consequently, the Japanese terms of trade improve and real income rises slightly. The effects on the United States are negative; U.S. terms-of-trade benefits are nill, and the economy faces an efficiency loss of $2.4 billion. But the U.S. losses are not large, and they may be offset, in an appropriate sectoral context, by savings in adjustment costs or by special political advantages to those who impose protection. Thus the propensity to agree on VERs is probably relatively high, at least when compared to other measures with more drastic distributional consequences.

## Summary and Conclusions

The initial sections of this chapter used the estimated positions of offer curves facing the United States and Japan to suggest that each country could gain by protecting its markets. In actual simulations with moderate additional tariffs, the terms-of-trade effects of protection proved to be about ten times as large as efficiency losses. The "value" of the existing formal protection structure, estimated in another set of experiments, proved modest relative to national product but large when compared to trade or to efficiency losses. In addition, the benefits implicit in the existing structure of protection have grown relative to GNP over the 1960–1980 period, despite significant reductions in the rate of protection. In short, although tariffs have been steadily reduced by multilateral negotiations, the incentives for protection appear to have generally increased over the past decade.

The effects of protection are complicated and often surprising in a general equilibrium setting. This is true not only for sectoral effects, which depend on a sequence of interindustry, exchange-rate, and real-income mechanisms, but also for the country-to-country allocation of benefits. For example, experiments hypothesizing a broad general opening of the Japanese market

produce losses not only in Japan but also in the United States. Given the substantial competitive interdependence of the two economies, the ultimate effects of policy are very sensitive to general equilibrium reactions, including especially changes in Japanese-American competition in third markets.

Policies designed to reduce the bilateral trade imbalance involve a sharp trade-off between U.S. and Japanese gains. Moreover, all such policies showed joint losses by the two economies. Not surprisingly, the most frequent form of bilateral intervention in the past has been based on the device with the most limited distributional implications, Japanese voluntary export restraints. At the same time, there is growing political interest in the United States in shifting bilateral intervention away from VERs to policies that would help to open Japanese markets to U.S. products. The shift to export-oriented strategies may be explained by the fact that VERs, in general, fail to deliver the gains that U.S. politicians feel should be attainable, given the asymmetric bargaining positions of the two countries. In any case, the results of the previous section indicate that the barriers to be eliminated would have to be very large (on the order of 28 percent in tariff equivalent) to halve the existing bilateral deficit.

Despite distributional conflict over bilateral trade, there are important areas of agreement between U.S. and Japanese economic interests. For example, the experiments that deal with the bilateral allocation of gains typically generate large windfalls to third countries. The reasons for these losses can again be traced to the competitive position of U.S. and Japanese exports; if Japan has to depreciate to recapture revenue lost in U.S. markets, the dollar will follow to some extent. Thus, the most persuasive case against an escalation of bilateral conflict may be the prospect of large joint losses to the rest of the world, and not the cost of allocational inefficiency. What these and other results imply is that the interests of the United States and Japan, as two major exporters of manufactured goods and importers of resource goods, are generally aligned regarding trade with third countries. This alliance may be the main force that holds bilateral trade disputes in check.

# 8 Implications

In less than two decades, Japanese-American trade has become a symbol of the opportunities and frustrations of international commerce. Perhaps because of the very visibility and commercial value of this trade, considerable confusion surrounds its economic structure and benefit. The demand for answers that are simple, definitive, and constructive (from the viewpoint of policy) has given rise to a literature that is predominantly sectoral and institutional in focus, and often anecdotal and speculative in style. Surprisingly little work has been done on the issues examined in this book: the structural determinants of Japanese-American trade, changes in these determinants over time, and the distribution of the gains from the trade.

This analysis has been undertaken for pragmatic as well as academic reasons. It is likely that an overabundance of specific, descriptive information — now generated by many popular and academic writers about Japan — has hindered policymaking by giving the appearance of analytical structure without its benefits. It is easy to argue, for example, that U.S. exporters would benefit from lowered Japanese import restrictions. It is far more difficult to judge the complete implications of such a policy change, however, given complex reactions by rest-of-the-world exporters and changes in Japan's exchange rate. In the past the absence of a consistent conceptual basis for policy, especially in

the United States, has led to conflict over minor issues and complacency on major ones. Thus, a great deal more political effort was recently spent on discussing irritating Japanese regulations against American baseball bats than on opening Japanese markets in financial and business services—areas of decided American comparative advantage.

## Lessons on Modeling Trade

The model as a whole has proved to be a versatile and sometimes surprising analytical tool. Its results clearly underscore the need for general equilibrium approaches in trade analysis: a variety of indirect effects turn out to be large and often counterintuitive. Even the sign of a policy effect may be unclear before simulation —as some experiments reported in Chapter 6 suggest—because strong indirect mechanisms work with opposing signs. To provide intuition on the working of the model, the study has identified the sectoral implications of different aspects of general equilibrium adjustment in a number of simulations. Further development of this typology may be useful for approximating policy effects in some "typical" economic settings. But accurate general prediction evidently requires fairly sophisticated models and cannot depend on simple formulas such as those commonly used to calculate effective rates of protection.

Several problems that might have been expected to arise in building the model proved easily surmountable. The data needs of the system were indeed large, but by focusing data collection on areas in which precision was most important—by combining annual time-series data on key relationships with benchmark data for other purposes—it was possible to meet broad requirements with manageable effort. The job of solving a large, nonlinear simultaneous equation system (the potential difficulties of which are anticipated by an extensive mathematical literature) was handled with conventional methods; the overall algorithm, based on nested Newton-Raphson and Gauss-Seidel components, was easily programmed and produced satisfactory convergence. Even in the occasionally difficult to reach solution, minor modifications of the conventional approach were sufficient. Improved solution strategies, particularly in the area of multiple-

loop iterations, would doubtless help to sharpen the performance of the present algorithm and streamline its formulation.
But simple solution strategies seem quite adequate for dealing
with models on a scale justified by present theoretical knowledge
and data availability. Finally, the estimation of the trade share
functions, the empirical core of the study, produced robust
statistical results, with properties consistent with theoretical ex-
pectations and prior estimates.

But the results of the study also point to empirical difficulties
in using conventional substitution relationships to model long-
term structural change. The problem has not received much
attention so far, primarily because general equilibrium trade
models have rarely been used to simulate actual changes in trade
flows over time. In the present case, unexplained changes in
market shares proved surprisingly important in fitting and repli-
cating some of the trade flows covered by the model. In other
words, changes in the size of markets and prices (multiplied by
estimated price elasticities), the two main endogenous determinants of market shares, sometimes leave a large part of trade
changes unexplained. The explanatory power of the model
varies greatly from trade flow to trade flow, with the greatest
difficulties encountered in tracking rapidly changing trade flows
such as Japanese exports to the United States. An analysis of
these unexplained market share changes (called share drift in
Chapter 6) suggests that supply-related determinants may be
involved; positive market share drift — a steady increase in market share — is typically correlated with growth and technical
progress in the exporting economy.

The problem of share drift may have multiple origins. In
general, share drift is probably a hidden price effect, that is, a
result of inaccurately estimated price changes or price elasticities. One reason why price changes may be measured inaccurately is that quality changes are sometimes inadequately translated into price changes. Statistical estimates of Japanese prices,
for example, may fail to hold quality constant (relative to American quality) and thus result in a price index that rises faster (or
falls less rapidly) than the "true" index. If the deviation is
serious, the same price elasticity structure is consistent with
substantially larger Japanese market gains.

In practice, the true Japanese export price index would have had to decline by about 5.3 percent per annum relative to the observed index in the 1960s and by 2.9 percent in the 1970s. This implies that a 123-percent relative quality improvement (over the 1960–1980 period) is now missing from the price data. The figure seems implausibly large: if all Japanese products improved at this pace, Japanese GNP would have to be revalued similarly, making Japanese GNP per capita considerably higher than that of other industrial countries. Hidden quality increases may account for some, but probably not all, of market share drift.

Another possibility is that trade price elasticities are systematically underestimated. (There is no special reason to believe that this is true, since the elasticities are generally within the range of previous estimates.) But even if trade elasticities were underestimated, replacing them with higher values would offer only a partial explanation of share drift because in some of the subperiods of the study, share drift and the effect of relative price changes moved in opposite directions. For example, Japanese market shares continued to grow during the 1970s even as some Japanese relative prices increased over this period, principally as a result of exchange revaluations. Coupled with some hidden quality change, however, higher price elasticities do suggest a possible explanation. If quality adjustments are large enough to make Japanese relative prices fall even during periods when current price data suggest the opposite, then larger price elasticities coupled with moderate price corrections (to eliminate the distortion of improving quality) provide a reasonable compound explanation.

Finally, the trade price elasticities may be measured with an inappropriately short time horizon. A two- to three-year lag structure is now standard in international trade analysis, supported by several explicit studies of the lag distributions involved in international trade. This period is certainly long enough to permit adjustments in the market shares of established, competing products. Over the long term, however, certain marketing investments are undertaken by both sellers (in sales facilities, product design, and brand image) and buyers (in information about and adaptations to new sources of supply). These invest-

ments, in turn, can be expected to yield steady market share changes in subsequent periods. The relevant lags in this process may be even on the order of decades. Thus, although accurate estimates can be obtained of short-term price elasticities (adjustment without market investment), long-term response remains obscure because the lag is long relative to the estimation period.

From a statistical viewpoint, incorrectly specified lags do not bias parameter estimates (on average, the estimated elasticities will not be too low) but can lead to significant unexplained autocorrelation. This may explain the significance of trend terms in the problematic market share equations. In fact, strong share drift generally occurred in unusually rapidly changing trade flows. It is intuitively plausible, for example, that at least some of Japan's rapid export growth in the 1960s (which now registers as share drift) is a result of large productivity gains experienced in the 1950s followed by systematic, prolonged investments in product design, market image, and distribution.

In principle, product design and image are aspects of quality, and the problem of long lags would disappear if prices correctly accounted for such intangible aspects of quality as brand image. In practice, the observed price index is even less likely to allow for changes in these aspects of quality than in the more measurable aspects considered above. The implications of market investment differ from the consequences of general quality distortions (discussed earlier). The market investment hypothesis implies a specific timing relationship between domestic productivity change and export performance: export quality change will be a delayed consequence of domestic productivity advance. This hypothesis is consistent with the empirical relationship between share drift and productivity progress reported in Chapter 5. But the lag explanation is not plausible as a single cause either; Japanese market shares continued to grow rapidly into the early 1980s despite a measured deterioration in Japanese price competitiveness starting in the early 1970s.

If none of these hypotheses offers a satisfactory explanation by itself, each contributes insights about the model's limited ability to predict certain trade changes. Some experiments were therefore performed to assess the implications of possible specification

errors of the type outlined. For example, several simulations were rerun with elasticities three times as large as those estimated. The signs and relative magnitudes of the results on which the main conclusions depend were unchanged. Thus, for example, the ratio of distributional transfers to allocational efficiency losses in protectionist intervention remained high, changing from 10 : 1 under the estimated elasticities to about 6 : 1 under elasticities three times as high. But other results (for example, the relative magnitudes of direct and indirect effects calculated in Chapter 6) are sensitive to the price specification used, and therefore the mystery of share drift deserves high priority in future empirical research. The problem will doubtless become more prominent as general equilibrium models are increasingly turned to empirically demanding applications.

### The Structure of Bilateral Trade

Although much has been written about the institutional complexity and special character of Japanese-American trade, its most significant economic features rest on simple, basic national characteristics. Most importantly, key structural properties of bilateral trade, including its extreme imbalance, appear to be indirect consequences of relative resource endowments. Japan's intense dependence on foreign raw materials and food supplies is well known. But Japan is not just another resource-poor economy: its economy is huge, and Japan is unusually distant, in both geographic and cultural terms, from its logical trading partners.

From early on in its modern history, these factors have caused Japan to adopt, on both private and public levels, a cautious, quasi-mercantilist strategy toward international commerce. The value of foreign raw materials and technology was clearly recognized, but to achieve the most favorable terms possible (that is, to keep the required export effort within reasonable bounds), trade had to be held to essentials. As recently as 1962, the Japanese government exercised detailed control over all foreign transactions. Informal codes of business conduct also developed—at times under the encouragement of MITI's administrative guidance—giving domestic producers an advantage over foreign

competitors. Examples of this strategy and its implementation are provided by Johnson (1982).

For a while, growing foreign exchange reserves were viewed as financial insurance against future risks to Japan's raw material supply. (In fact, Japan did run large current account deficits following both the 1973 and 1979 oil shocks.) But eventually, wide-ranging adjustments had to be made in strategies and institutions designed to ration foreign exchange and to protect what was perceived as a limited market for Japanese products abroad. Viewed in historical perspective, the subsequent liberalization of Japan's international transactions has been rapid and thorough; in less than two decades Japan passed from complete exchange controls to an economy largely free of formal trade restrictions. Thus, defenders of Japanese trade policy can point to an impressive history of liberalization at the same time that critics can argue that Japanese markets are still more restricted — particularly through informal barriers — than markets in most other industrial economies.

The structure of Japan's trade and the controls that it engendered during the better part of the postwar period have left Japanese trade extremely specialized. More than 75 percent of Japanese imports consist of raw materials; more than 95 percent of exports are manufactured goods. In this context, Chapter 5 has shown that Japanese-American trade follows the expected bilateral pattern, with the exception that bilateral trade is about twice as intense as are the two countries' relationships with other trade partners. The large bilateral imbalance is also consistent with existing trade specializations. (Europe, in the absence of important raw material exports, runs a proportionally much larger bilateral imbalance with Japan.) In other words, if Japan's overall level of openness is accepted as given, the observed bilateral trade and imbalance follow as a natural consequence. Furthermore, if the Japanese economy did become more open, as postulated in the experiments reported in Chapter 7, the imbalance would become still larger.

The adjustment characteristics of bilateral trade also follow from the commodity structure. Since Japan's specialized imports are largely necessities, Japanese imports, on the whole, are price-

inelastic. By contrast, Japanese exports, built on Japan's comparative advantage in manpower, consist virtually entirely of manufactured products that compete with products made in many other countries. Specifically, as the composition of the Japanese export bundle has adjusted to rising Japanese wages and productivity, Japanese exports have become increasingly competitive with American products. The United States now produces nearly all goods it imports from Japan. Thus, Japanese products are generally better substitutes for American products than products from other countries, and Japanese exports to the United States are therefore quite elastic with respect to American prices. These observations are amply confirmed by the empirical analysis of elasticities governing the trade patterns of the two economies (Chapter 3).

In a general equilibrium context, the high price elasticity of Japanese exports to the United States makes them a buffer in overall U.S. trade. Major U.S. current account adjustments resulting, say, from a substantial increase in capital inflows affect imports from Japan to a much greater extent than other trade flows. Although Japanese trade accounts for about 12 percent of U.S. trade overall, about a third of price-induced current account adjustment falls on this trade. Consequently, bilateral trade is more volatile than either country's overall trade. The dollar/yen exchange rate is also affected by these characteristics; a general dollar appreciation is likely to "pull along" the yen vis-à-vis third currencies.

Finally, the same structural characteristics also make the trade linkage considerably more important from the Japanese viewpoint; experiments using the model suggest that Japanese economic variables are many times as sensitive to U.S. policy variables than in the reverse case. This sensitivity is partly due to the substitutable nature of Japanese exports to the United States and partly to the fact that Japan could not easily find new markets if its present exports to the United States diminished. Taken together, the experiments clearly illustrate the closeness of U.S.-Japanese linkages and explain why the economic underpinnings of the linkage make it asymmetrically more important to Japan than to the United States.

## Policy Consequences of Economic Structure

The persistent imbalance and volatility that are evidently structural features of Japanese-American trade make this trade highly
visible and intervention-prone. Since the bilateral trade imbalance usually accompanies large general U.S. current account
deficits, efforts to "cure" a perceived U.S. balance-of-payments
problem inevitably converge on the control of bilateral trade.
This makes some economic sense: by limiting inflows of goods
for which reasonable substitutes exist at home, the United States
can pursue domestic goals that conflict with trade at only moderate allocational cost. Not surprisingly, the protectionist option
became increasingly popular in the early 1980s as a powerful
dollar and a recession combined to depress several major im-
port-competing industries in the United States.

In general, the goal of a free global trading system has been
aggressively pursued by both the United States and Japan in
international negotiation. But a close analysis of the bilateral
relationship illustrates the temptations of protectionism: the
efficiency gains generated by free trade are often small relative
to the welfare gains that can be achieved by intervention. According to the experiments described in Chapter 7, the terms-
of-trade benefits of protection — the negative-sum transfers
achieved by imposing protection — may be an order of magnitude larger than the efficiency losses involved. Thus Japan and
especially the United States face strong incentives to protect
their markets — provided they can avoid international retaliation. The gains available from protection probably have not
been openly pursued by the two countries because of their stake
in global multilateral trade.

The structure of bilateral trade makes it especially vulnerable
to conflict. Due to the overall trade imbalance as well as the
elasticity structure of bilateral trade, U.S. intervention could
inflict economic injuries on Japan that are several times as large
as those that Japan could inflict on the United States. Thus,
Japanese retaliation poses no significant economic dangers for
the United States. To put it another way, the threat positions are
not balanced enough to produce the economic equivalent of

"mutual deterrence," and constant friction over the gains from trade ensues.

For reasons already discussed, the friction intensifies with deficits in overall U.S. trade; this helps to explain the timing of several major periods of conflict since the late 1960s. Given the growing volatility of U.S. trade and the increasingly competitive structures of the American and Japanese economies, it is unlikely that the conflict will diminish. At the same time, following modern patterns of intraindustry specialization, the trade should continue to expand. This implies a permanent state of conflict that is enormously frustrating to the direct participants. Put in perspective, however, the bickering is as much a part of the trading relationship as the gains that issue from it.

It is a measure of the success of the postwar multilateral trading system that Japanese-American trade has remained relatively open through the difficult economic conditions of the late 1970s and early 1980s. Especially in the United States, protective steps have become difficult to implement in the 1980s. Due to detailed international agreements, unilateral changes in tariffs or quantitative barriers have become infrequent and therefore more visible and politically charged. Formal protection thus carries an increased risk of retaliation. Moreover, the greater visibility of formal protection makes it a better target for domestic opposition; it is more difficult to build special-interest coalitions in public. Against this background, the United States now relies mainly on slow, case-by-case approaches to intervention, ranging from antidumping legislation to negotiated voluntary export restraints.

No similar trends apply in the murkier world of nonquantitative barriers. In fact, countries comfortable with such instruments have sometimes substituted them for formal barriers. Although both the United States and Japan made substantial progress in removing formal protection, Japan's insular economic culture apparently left a greater residue of informal restrictive tools. Thus, despite the relatively greater clout of a U.S. trade threat, bilateral trade appears to be somewhat more restricted by Japan than by the United States. But removing these restrictions would do little for the trade imbalance or the Ameri-

can terms of trade. It has been shown earlier that, contrary to common perception, the multilateral elimination of Japanese protection (even on the largest conceivable scale) would not significantly benefit the United States. Nevertheless, the discrepancy between the potential U.S. threat and the actual balance of intervention is a constant irritant to American negotiators.

What light, then, does this study shed on solutions to the problems of bilateral trade? Its central finding, of course, is that conflict is a natural, if regrettable, consequence of trade structure. This suggests that mechanisms must be found to divert the distributional struggle from trade intervention, or at least to focus it on negotiations that tend to enhance rather than limit trade. For example, as long as barriers exist, negotiations can focus on removing them rather than on adding new ones. It is encouraging, therefore, that the bilateral debate has recently shifted to an emphasis on increasing U.S. exports rather than decreasing Japanese exports. Unfortunately, this avenue is limited by the existing protective structure; with the exception of some recent voluntary export restrictions, the United States has little general protection to bargain away.

The safest approach to defusing the distribution problem is to shift zero-sum issues from trade policy to other types of transfer mechanisms. (The problems faced by individual U.S. import competitors would then still have to be solved by intra-U.S. transfers.) The intercountry transfer mechanisms might include technology transfers from Japan to severely affected U.S. industries (the conceptual rationale for plans to increase Japanese direct investment in the United States), greater Japanese participation in common investment (such as fusion and medical research), and greater Japanese contributions to common "consumption" such as foreign aid and defense.

Some of these suggestions, of course, are recognized by present American negotiating positions. However difficult it may be to justify such transfers, flowing as they would from a poorer to a richer nation, they offer a low-cost alternative to the forcible balancing of bilateral trade. The need for transfers is generated by the fundamental dilemma of Japanese-American trade: its structure leads to a market distribution of gains that is inconsistent with the market powers of the two countries. Hence

the difficult but essential mission of U.S.-Japanese politics: to subordinate the frustrations of conflict to the greater advantage of vigorous economic and political partnership. No economic analysis can determine whether this is possible, but it is hopeful that the relationship has already survived grave crises. One of the contributions of this book is to show that the conflict does not turn on personalities or differences in national character. Perhaps this notion will help to advance the dispassionate analysis and reasoned compromise needed to keep the partnership vital.

# Alternative Market Share Equations

$R^2$ = Standard $R$

CS = Compatibility statistic

* = $t$ significant at 1% level

· = $t$ significant at 10% level

DW = Durbin-Watson statistic

PP = Percent from prior

+ = $t$ significant at 5% level

APPENDIX A

Table A-1.  Alternative share equations for U.S. markets

| Equation | Statistics | | | | Const | Price Elast | | Trend | |
|---|---|---|---|---|---|---|---|---|---|
|  | R2 | DW | T1 | T2 |  | Own | Cross | 1971- | 1971+ |
| **TEXTILES** | | | | | | | | | |
| Imports from Japan | | | | | | | | | |
| Standard | 0.96 | 2.28 | 0.50 | 0.16 | -4.4* | -2.9* | 0.0* | 0.05* | -0.00 |
| 2SLS | 0.95 | 1.95 | 0.20 | 0.17 | -4.4* | -2.9* | 0.0* | 0.05* | 0.01 |
| No Prior | 0.96 | 2.30 | | | -4.4* | -3.0* | 0.0* | 0.05* | 0.00 |
| Imports from ROW | | | | | | | | | |
| Standard | 0.98 | 1.62 | 1.40 | 0.13 | -3.7* | -1.2* | 0.0* | 0.08* | 0.10* |
| 2SLS | 0.98 | 1.54 | 1.40 | 0.12 | -3.7* | -1.1* | -0.0* | 0.08* | 0.10* |
| No Prior | 0.98 | 1.63 | | | -3.8* | -1.0* | 0.0* | 0.08* | 0.10* |
| **PAPER AND WOOD PRODUCTS** | | | | | | | | | |
| Imports from Japan | | | | | | | | | |
| Standard | 0.91 | 1.37 | 4.90 | 0.55 | -5.8* | -2.1* | -0.0* | -0.01. | -0.06* |
| 2SLS | 0.90 | 1.25 | 4.70 | 0.63 | -5.8* | -2.0* | 0.0* | -0.02. | -0.05+ |
| No Prior | 0.93 | 1.58 | | | -5.8* | -3.1* | 0.0* | -0.01 | -0.02 |
| Imports from ROW | | | | | | | | | |
| Standard | 0.58 | 1.94 | 0.00 | 0.27 | -2.9* | -1.4* | 0.0* | 0.01. | 0.03* |
| 2SLS | 0.56 | 1.92 | 0.00 | 0.24 | -2.9* | -1.2* | 0.0* | 0.01. | 0.03* |
| No Prior | 0.59 | 1.93 | | | -2.9* | -1.4* | 0.0* | 0.01. | 0.03* |
| **CHEMICALS** | | | | | | | | | |
| Imports from Japan | | | | | | | | | |
| Standard | 0.93 | 2.48 | 0.00 | 0.70 | -7.2* | -1.5* | 1.6+ | 0.14* | 0.02. |
| 2SLS | 0.93 | 2.29 | 0.40 | 0.63 | -7.3* | -1.2* | 0.9. | 0.15* | 0.02. |
| No Prior | 0.93 | 2.48 | | | -7.2* | -1.6+ | 1.6+ | 0.13* | 0.02. |
| Imports from ROW | | | | | | | | | |
| Standard | 0.93 | 2.53 | 1.50 | 0.19 | -4.0* | -0.8* | 0.3+ | 0.05* | 0.05* |
| 2SLS | 0.91 | 2.64 | 3.20 | 0.24 | -3.9* | -0.5+ | 0.1. | 0.04* | 0.05* |
| No Prior | 0.93 | 2.65 | | | -4.0* | -0.7+ | 0.3+ | 0.04* | 0.05* |
| **STONE, CLAY, AND GLASS** | | | | | | | | | |
| Imports from Japan | | | | | | | | | |
| Standard | 0.23 | 1.83 | 3.40 | 0.05 | -4.8* | -1.0* | -0.0* | 0.01 | 0.02. |
| 2SLS | 0.15 | 1.81 | 3.00 | 0.11 | -4.8* | -1.2* | 0.0* | 0.02. | 0.03. |
| No Prior | 0.27 | 1.73 | | | -4.8* | -0.8* | -0.0* | 0.01 | 0.02. |
| Imports from ROW | | | | | | | | | |
| Standard | 0.75 | 1.69 | 2.40 | 0.10 | -3.4* | -0.8+ | -0.0* | 0.05* | 0.05* |
| 2SLS | 0.75 | 1.93 | 1.80 | 0.16 | -3.5* | -0.8+ | 0.0* | 0.06* | 0.04* |
| No Prior | 0.75 | 1.65 | | | -3.5* | -0.6+ | 0.0* | 0.05* | 0.04* |
| **IRON AND STEEL** | | | | | | | | | |
| Imports from Japan | | | | | | | | | |
| Standard | 0.88 | 1.30 | 2.00 | 0.45 | -5.0* | -3.1* | 0.8+ | 0.16* | 0.02. |
| 2SLS | 0.90 | 1.43 | 2.10 | 0.38 | -5.1* | -3.0* | 1.0+ | 0.16* | 0.02 |
| No Prior | 0.89 | 1.35 | | | -4.9* | -3.9* | 0.9+ | 0.15* | 0.03. |
| Imports from ROW | | | | | | | | | |
| Standard | 0.83 | 2.86 | 0.20 | 0.24 | -4.4* | -1.6* | 0.8+ | 0.12* | 0.01 |
| 2SLS | 0.79 | 2.82 | 0.00 | 0.38 | -4.3* | -2.0* | 1.1+ | 0.12* | 0.01 |
| No Prior | 0.83 | 2.87 | | | -4.4* | -1.6* | 0.9+ | 0.12* | 0.01 |

Table A-1 (continued)

| Equation | Statistics | | | | Const | Price Elast | | Trend | |
|---|---|---|---|---|---|---|---|---|---|
| | R2 | DW | T1 | T2 | | Own | Cross | 1971- | 1971+ |
| METAL PRODUCTS | | | | | | | | | |
| Imports from Japan | | | | | | | | | |
| Standard | 0.77 | 2.51 | 0.90 | 0.24 | -6.0* | -1.4* | 1.3* | 0.09* | -0.00 |
| 2SLS | 0.79 | 2.07 | 0.60 | 0.28 | -5.9* | -1.4* | 1.5* | 0.09* | -0.01 |
| No Prior | 0.77 | 2.55 | | | -6.0* | -1.1+ | 1.4* | 0.09* | -0.01 |
| Imports from ROW | | | | | | | | | |
| Standard | 0.91 | 2.49 | 1.30 | 0.09 | -5.2* | -1.1* | 1.0* | 0.07* | 0.06* |
| 2SLS | 0.87 | 2.79 | 1.20 | 0.18 | -5.3* | -1.2* | 1.1* | 0.07* | 0.06* |
| No Prior | 0.91 | 2.61 | | | -5.2* | -1.0* | 1.0* | 0.07* | 0.05* |
| MACHINERY | | | | | | | | | |
| Imports from Japan | | | | | | | | | |
| Standard | 1.00 | 2.15 | 1.60 | 0.20 | -6.0* | -1.7* | 0.0* | 0.13* | 0.13* |
| 2SLS | 0.99 | 1.63 | 4.30 | 0.39 | -6.0* | -1.9* | 0.0* | 0.12* | 0.14* |
| No Prior | 1.00 | 2.25 | | | -6.0* | -1.9* | 0.0* | 0.12* | 0.14* |
| Imports from ROW | | | | | | | | | |
| Standard | 0.96 | 1.27 | 0.00 | 0.26 | -4.1* | -0.9* | 0.0* | 0.10* | 0.06* |
| 2SLS | 0.96 | 1.23 | 0.00 | 0.36 | -4.1* | -0.9* | -0.0* | 0.10* | 0.05* |
| No Prior | 0.96 | 1.28 | | | -4.1* | -1.0* | -0.0* | 0.10* | 0.06* |
| ELECTRICAL MACHINERY | | | | | | | | | |
| Imports from Japan | | | | | | | | | |
| Standard | 0.93 | 1.94 | 2.90 | 0.63 | -5.5* | -1.6* | 0.6. | 0.17* | 0.03. |
| 2SLS | 0.93 | 1.93 | 7.30 | 0.71 | -5.4* | -1.7* | 1.4+ | 0.15* | 0.00 |
| No Prior | 0.94 | 2.10 | | | -5.3* | -2.5* | 0.5. | 0.16* | 0.04+ |
| Imports from ROW | | | | | | | | | |
| Standard | 0.94 | 1.41 | 0.60 | 0.55 | -5.1* | -0.5. | 0.7. | 0.16* | 0.07* |
| 2SLS | 0.94 | 1.53 | 0.00 | 0.67 | -5.4* | -0.8+ | 1.6+ | 0.17* | 0.07* |
| No Prior | 0.94 | 1.45 | | | -5.1* | -0.2 | 0.6. | 0.15* | 0.07* |
| TRANSPORT EQUIPMENT | | | | | | | | | |
| Imports from Japan | | | | | | | | | |
| Standard | 0.98 | 1.82 | 0.30 | 0.59 | -8.4* | -2.4* | 1.1+ | 0.37* | 0.13* |
| 2SLS | 0.98 | 1.76 | 0.00 | 0.72 | -8.3* | -2.7* | 1.7+ | 0.36* | 0.10+ |
| No Prior | 0.98 | 1.82 | | | -8.5* | -1.9. | 0.9. | 0.38* | 0.12* |
| Imports from ROW | | | | | | | | | |
| Standard | 0.81 | 1.49 | 0.20 | 0.52 | -5.1* | -2.5* | 1.4+ | 0.13* | 0.08+ |
| 2SLS | 0.84 | 1.76 | 0.10 | 0.38 | -5.3* | -2.5* | 2.3+ | 0.14* | 0.06+ |
| No Prior | 0.81 | 1.49 | | | -5.0* | -2.3+ | 1.2. | 0.13* | 0.08+ |
| MISCELLANEOUS MANUFACTURES | | | | | | | | | |
| Imports from Japan | | | | | | | | | |
| Standard | 0.98 | 1.47 | 1.40 | 0.02 | -5.2* | -2.5* | 0.0* | 0.13* | 0.09* |
| 2SLS | 0.99 | 2.05 | 0.10 | 0.03 | -5.0* | -4.0* | 0.0* | 0.13* | 0.17* |
| No Prior | 0.98 | 1.49 | | | -5.2* | -2.4* | 0.0* | 0.12* | 0.08* |
| Imports from ROW | | | | | | | | | |
| Standard | 0.98 | 2.44 | 4.20 | 0.03 | -4.2* | -0.8* | 0.0* | 0.08* | 0.08* |
| 2SLS | 0.97 | 2.34 | 4.30 | 0.03 | -4.3* | -0.7+ | 0.0* | 0.08* | 0.07* |
| No Prior | 0.98 | 2.45 | | | -4.2* | -0.7+ | 0.0* | 0.08* | 0.07* |

APPENDIX A

Table A-2. Alternative share equations for Japanese markets

| Equation | Statistics | | | | Const | Price Elast | | Trend | |
|---|---|---|---|---|---|---|---|---|---|
| | R2 | DW | T1 | T2 | Const | Own | Cross | 1971- | 1971+ |
| **TEXTILES** | | | | | | | | | |
| Imports from U.S. | | | | | | | | | |
|   Standard | 0.73 | 1.70 | 0.00 | 0.60 | -6.9* | -1.3* | 0.3 | 0.07. | 0.11+ |
|   2SLS | 0.73 | 1.76 | 0.00 | 0.64 | -6.8* | -1.4* | 0.1 | 0.06. | 0.11+ |
|   No Prior | 0.72 | 1.56 | | | -6.9* | -0.8. | -0.3 | 0.07+ | 0.13+ |
| Imports from ROW | | | | | | | | | |
|   Standard | 0.92 | 1.48 | 0.00 | 0.19 | -5.9* | -1.4* | 0.1 | 0.21* | 0.15* |
|   2SLS | 0.92 | 1.63 | 0.00 | 0.25 | -5.7* | -1.6* | 0.0 | 0.19* | 0.16* |
|   No Prior | 0.92 | 1.53 | | | -5.9* | -1.2* | -0.1 | 0.21* | 0.14* |
| **PAPER AND WOOD PRODUCTS** | | | | | | | | | |
| Imports from U.S. | | | | | | | | | |
|   Standard | 0.66 | 2.02 | 0.80 | 0.56 | -4.7* | -1.6* | 0.0 | 0.03. | -0.02 |
|   2SLS | 0.61 | 1.77 | 0.00 | 0.59 | -4.8* | -1.2* | 1.1 | 0.03. | 0.01 |
|   No Prior | 0.69 | 2.22 | | | -4.7* | -2.2* | 0.3 | 0.02. | -0.04. |
| Imports from ROW | | | | | | | | | |
|   Standard | 0.86 | 1.79 | 3.30 | 0.70 | -5.4* | -2.2* | 0.0 | 0.12* | 0.02 |
|   2SLS | 0.77 | 1.60 | 0.50 | 0.79 | -5.4* | -1.9* | 1.0. | 0.13* | 0.07+ |
|   No Prior | 0.87 | 1.61 | | | -5.4* | -4.1* | 0.2 | 0.12* | 0.01 |
| **CHEMICALS** | | | | | | | | | |
| Imports from U.S. | | | | | | | | | |
|   Standard | 0.79 | 1.90 | 0.00 | 0.31 | -3.4* | -1.2* | 0.0* | -0.04* | 0.03+ |
|   2SLS | 0.78 | 1.87 | 0.20 | 0.49 | -3.4* | -1.5* | 0.0* | -0.04* | 0.02. |
|   No Prior | 0.78 | 1.88 | | | -3.3* | -1.0* | 0.0* | -0.04* | 0.04+ |
| Imports from ROW | | | | | | | | | |
|   Standard | 0.66 | 1.68 | 0.90 | 0.57 | -3.1* | -1.5* | -0.0* | -0.01. | 0.04* |
|   2SLS | 0.67 | 1.78 | 0.10 | 0.35 | -3.1* | -1.1* | 0.0* | -0.02+ | 0.04* |
|   No Prior | 0.66 | 1.67 | | | -3.1* | -1.5+ | -0.0* | -0.01 | 0.04* |
| **STONE, CLAY, AND GLASS** | | | | | | | | | |
| Imports from U.S. | | | | | | | | | |
|   Standard | 0.59 | 1.99 | 0.10 | 0.62 | -5.6* | -1.0* | 0.0* | 0.04* | -0.05+ |
|   2SLS | 0.59 | 1.92 | 0.00 | 0.76 | -5.6* | -1.2* | 0.0* | 0.04* | -0.06+ |
|   No Prior | 0.57 | 1.96 | | | -5.7* | -0.3 | 0.0* | 0.04* | -0.01 |
| Imports from ROW | | | | | | | | | |
|   Standard | 0.72 | 1.50 | 6.90 | 0.80 | -4.5* | -0.5. | -0.0* | 0.06* | 0.03. |
|   2SLS | 0.73 | 1.48 | 0.80 | 0.87 | -4.5* | -0.8+ | 0.0* | 0.07* | 0.01 |
|   No Prior | 0.79 | 1.71 | | | -4.7* | 2.2+ | -0.0* | 0.06* | 0.12* |
| **IRON AND STEEL** | | | | | | | | | |
| Imports from U.S. | | | | | | | | | |
|   Standard | 0.36 | 1.77 | 0.30 | 0.77 | -6.3* | -2.5* | 0.0* | -0.13+ | 0.01 |
|   2SLS | 0.32 | 1.81 | 0.00 | 0.78 | -6.3* | -2.4* | 0.0* | -0.13+ | 0.01 |
|   No Prior | 0.37 | 1.69 | | | -6.4* | -3.2+ | 0.0* | -0.12+ | -0.00 |
| Imports from ROW | | | | | | | | | |
|   Standard | 0.54 | 2.13 | 3.60 | 0.78 | -3.6* | -3.2* | 0.0* | -0.14+ | 0.00 |
|   2SLS | 0.44 | 1.93 | 0.70 | 0.83 | -3.4* | -2.6* | 0.0* | -0.15+ | 0.01 |
|   No Prior | 0.61 | 2.27 | | | -4.0* | -6.0* | 0.0* | -0.09. | -0.03 |

Table A-2 (continued)

| Equation | R2 | DW | T1 | T2 | Const | Own | Cross | 1971- | 1971+ |
|---|---|---|---|---|---|---|---|---|---|
| | | Statistics | | | | Price Elast | | Trend | |
| **METAL PRODUCTS** | | | | | | | | | |
| Imports from U.S. | | | | | | | | | |
| Standard | 0.46 | 1.81 | 0.70 | 0.48 | -5.2* | -2.2* | 0.0* | -0.04* | -0.03. |
| 2SLS | 0.45 | 1.81 | 0.60 | 0.52 | -5.1* | -2.5* | 0.0* | -0.04* | -0.04. |
| No Prior | 0.47 | 1.82 | | | -5.2* | -2.1+ | 0.0* | -0.04* | -0.03 |
| Imports from ROW | | | | | | | | | |
| Standard | 0.63 | 2.10 | 0.10 | 0.60 | -6.0* | -2.1* | 0.0* | 0.05+ | 0.10* |
| 2SLS | 0.65 | 2.18 | 0.20 | 0.70 | -6.0* | -2.7* | 0.0* | 0.05+ | 0.09* |
| No Prior | 0.63 | 2.13 | | | -5.9* | -1.8+ | 0.0* | 0.04. | 0.10* |
| **MACHINERY** | | | | | | | | | |
| Imports from U.S. | | | | | | | | | |
| Standard | 0.72 | 1.06 | 1.40 | 0.16 | -3.2* | -1.0* | 0.0* | -0.06* | 0.00 |
| 2SLS | 0.75 | 1.25 | 0.50 | 0.20 | -3.2* | -1.3* | 0.0* | -0.06* | -0.00 |
| No Prior | 0.72 | 1.09 | | | -3.2* | -0.9* | 0.0* | -0.06* | 0.01 |
| Imports from ROW | | | | | | | | | |
| Standard | 0.88 | 2.26 | 0.10 | 0.36 | -3.6* | -1.9* | 0.0* | -0.02. | 0.04* |
| 2SLS | 0.83 | 2.08 | 0.40 | 0.38 | -3.5* | -1.3* | -0.0* | -0.03+ | 0.02. |
| No Prior | 0.88 | 2.25 | | | -3.6* | -1.9* | 0.0* | -0.02. | 0.04+ |
| **ELECTRICAL MACHINERY** | | | | | | | | | |
| Imports from U.S. | | | | | | | | | |
| Standard | -0.03 | 2.03 | 2.60 | 0.32 | -3.7* | -0.9+ | 0.0* | -0.00 | -0.01 |
| 2SLS | 0.01 | 2.10 | 1.50 | 0.46 | -3.7* | -1.1+ | 0.0* | 0.00 | -0.01 |
| No Prior | 0.03 | 2.03 | | | -3.7* | -0.2 | 0.0* | -0.00 | -0.00 |
| Imports from ROW | | | | | | | | | |
| Standard | -0.07 | 1.64 | 9.80 | 0.53 | -4.3* | -0.3 | -0.0* | 0.01 | 0.02. |
| 2SLS | -0.01 | 1.69 | 15.40 | 0.59 | -4.3* | -0.1 | 0.0* | 0.00 | 0.01 |
| No Prior | 0.21 | 1.98 | | | -3.9* | 1.5+ | 0.0* | -0.04. | -0.03. |
| **TRANSPORT EQUIPMENT** | | | | | | | | | |
| Imports from U.S. | | | | | | | | | |
| Standard | -0.01 | 1.69 | 0.80 | 0.75 | -4.6* | -1.5+ | 0.3 | 0.02 | -0.06. |
| 2SLS | 0.08 | 1.80 | 0.00 | 0.83 | -4.7* | -1.9* | -0.1 | 0.03 | -0.05. |
| No Prior | 0.02 | 1.73 | | | -4.4* | -0.5 | 0.1 | 0.01 | -0.03 |
| Imports from ROW | | | | | | | | | |
| Standard | 0.54 | 2.51 | 0.60 | 0.89 | -4.2* | -1.7+ | 0.2 | -0.08* | 0.13* |
| 2SLS | 0.52 | 2.46 | 1.60 | 0.85 | -4.2* | -1.5+ | -0.1 | -0.09* | 0.11* |
| No Prior | 0.56 | 2.67 | | | -3.9* | -0.2 | 0.1 | -0.11+ | 0.08. |
| **MISCELLANEOUS MANUFACTURES** | | | | | | | | | |
| Imports from U.S. | | | | | | | | | |
| Standard | 0.74 | 2.04 | 1.40 | 0.47 | -5.5* | -0.7+ | 0.0* | 0.10* | -0.06+ |
| 2SLS | 0.76 | 2.16 | 0.20 | 0.66 | -5.4* | -1.1+ | 0.0* | 0.09* | -0.08+ |
| No Prior | 0.74 | 2.02 | | | -5.6* | -0.0 | 0.0* | 0.11* | -0.02 |
| Imports from ROW | | | | | | | | | |
| Standard | 0.88 | 1.32 | 0.50 | 0.73 | -5.6* | -1.4* | 0.0* | 0.13* | -0.01 |
| 2SLS | 0.90 | 1.38 | 0.00 | 0.73 | -5.6* | -1.4* | 0.0* | 0.13* | -0.01 |
| No Prior | 0.88 | 1.41 | | | -5.7* | -0.9. | 0.0* | 0.13* | 0.00 |

APPENDIX A

Table A-3.  Alternative share equations for ROW markets

| Equation | R2 | DW | T1 | T2 | Const | Own | Cross | 1971− | 1971+ |
|---|---|---|---|---|---|---|---|---|---|
| | Statistics | | | | | Price Elast | | Trend | |
| **TEXTILES** | | | | | | | | | |
| Imports from U.S. | | | | | | | | | |
| Standard | 0.95 | 1.45 | 0.10 | 0.15 | −2.6* | −1.6* | 0.2. | −0.06* | 0.00 |
| 2SLS | 0.97 | 1.95 | 0.30 | 0.11 | −2.6* | −1.6* | −0.2. | −0.05* | 0.00 |
| No Prior | 0.95 | 1.48 | | | −2.6* | −1.6* | 0.1 | −0.06* | 0.00 |
| Imports from Japan | | | | | | | | | |
| Standard | 0.94 | 2.02 | 0.50 | 0.22 | −2.5* | −1.6* | 0.2. | −0.00. | −0.04* |
| 2SLS | 0.92 | 1.75 | 0.30 | 0.31 | −2.5* | −1.6* | −0.2. | −0.01. | −0.05* |
| No Prior | 0.94 | 1.99 | | | −2.5* | −1.7* | 0.1 | −0.00 | −0.04* |
| **PAPER AND WOOD PRODUCTS** | | | | | | | | | |
| Imports from U.S. | | | | | | | | | |
| Standard | 0.59 | 1.16 | 0.60 | 0.13 | −2.0* | −1.0* | 0.0* | −0.02* | −0.03* |
| 2SLS | 0.46 | 1.24 | 1.00 | 0.15 | −2.0* | −0.9* | −0.0* | −0.02+ | −0.03* |
| No Prior | 0.59 | 1.18 | | | −2.0* | −0.9* | 0.0* | −0.02* | −0.03* |
| Imports from Japan | | | | | | | | | |
| Standard | 0.70 | 2.43 | 0.10 | 0.24 | −3.9* | −1.4* | −0.0* | 0.01. | −0.03+ |
| 2SLS | 0.69 | 2.33 | 0.00 | 0.27 | −4.0* | −1.6* | −0.0* | 0.02. | −0.03+ |
| No Prior | 0.70 | 2.44 | | | −3.9* | −1.4* | −0.0* | 0.01. | −0.03+ |
| **CHEMICALS** | | | | | | | | | |
| Imports from U.S. | | | | | | | | | |
| Standard | 0.70 | 2.32 | 1.90 | 0.23 | −1.3* | −0.5+ | 0.1 | −0.05* | 0.00 |
| 2SLS | 0.67 | 2.36 | 2.80 | 0.27 | −1.3* | −0.4+ | 0.1 | −0.05* | 0.00 |
| No Prior | 0.71 | 2.49 | | | −1.3* | −0.3. | 0.2 | −0.04* | 0.01 |
| Imports from Japan | | | | | | | | | |
| Standard | 0.73 | 1.92 | 1.00 | 0.77 | −3.3* | −1.5* | 0.3 | 0.05* | −0.02. |
| 2SLS | 0.78 | 2.14 | 0.70 | 0.58 | −3.3* | −1.6* | 0.2 | 0.05* | −0.02. |
| No Prior | 0.74 | 1.92 | | | −3.1* | −2.3* | 0.3 | 0.04. | −0.01 |
| **STONE, CLAY, AND GLASS** | | | | | | | | | |
| Imports from U.S. | | | | | | | | | |
| Standard | 0.73 | 2.07 | 2.20 | 0.28 | −1.9* | −0.7+ | 0.4* | −0.05* | −0.05* |
| 2SLS | 0.70 | 2.04 | 0.70 | 0.41 | −1.8* | −1.0* | 0.6* | −0.06* | −0.06* |
| No Prior | 0.74 | 2.03 | | | −1.8* | −0.4. | 0.5* | −0.05* | −0.04* |
| Imports from Japan | | | | | | | | | |
| Standard | 0.91 | 1.74 | 0.00 | 0.15 | −2.5* | −1.3* | 0.6* | −0.05* | 0.00 |
| 2SLS | 0.90 | 2.09 | 0.30 | 0.27 | −2.5* | −1.5* | 0.8* | −0.04* | 0.02. |
| No Prior | 0.91 | 1.76 | | | −2.5* | −1.2* | 0.7* | −0.05* | 0.00 |
| **IRON AND STEEL** | | | | | | | | | |
| Imports from U.S. | | | | | | | | | |
| Standard | 0.77 | 1.37 | 0.50 | 0.34 | −2.5* | −1.1* | 0.4 | −0.02+ | −0.07* |
| 2SLS | 0.77 | 1.40 | 0.40 | 0.41 | −2.4* | −1.1* | −0.0 | −0.03+ | −0.07* |
| No Prior | 0.77 | 1.39 | | | −2.4* | −0.9+ | 0.3 | −0.03+ | −0.06* |
| Imports from Japan | | | | | | | | | |
| Standard | 0.97 | 1.74 | 0.40 | 0.37 | −3.0* | −1.7* | 0.1 | 0.10* | 0.02+ |
| 2SLS | 0.96 | 1.46 | 0.20 | 0.49 | −3.0* | −1.6* | −0.0 | 0.10* | 0.02+ |
| No Prior | 0.97 | 1.76 | | | −3.0* | −1.8* | 0.1 | 0.10* | 0.02+ |

Table A-3 (continued)

| Equation | Statistics | | | | | Price Elast | | Trend | |
|---|---|---|---|---|---|---|---|---|---|
| | R2 | DW | T1 | T2 | Const | Own | Cross | 1971- | 1971+ |
| **METAL PRODUCTS** | | | | | | | | | |
| Imports from U.S. | | | | | | | | | |
| Standard | 0.72 | 1.43 | 0.20 | 0.19 | -1.7* | -1.1* | 0.6* | -0.03* | -0.03* |
| 2SLS | 0.76 | 1.50 | 0.00 | 0.19 | -1.7* | -1.2* | 0.7* | -0.03* | -0.03* |
| No Prior | 0.73 | 1.44 | | | -1.7* | -1.0* | 0.6* | -0.03* | -0.03+ |
| Imports from Japan | | | | | | | | | |
| Standard | 0.92 | 1.70 | 0.20 | 0.40 | -3.5* | -1.1* | 1.0* | 0.07* | 0.04* |
| 2SLS | 0.94 | 1.83 | 0.70 | 0.44 | -3.4* | -1.7* | 1.2* | 0.06* | 0.05* |
| No Prior | 0.92 | 1.70 | | | -3.5* | -0.9+ | 0.9* | 0.07* | 0.04* |
| **MACHINERY** | | | | | | | | | |
| Imports from U.S. | | | | | | | | | |
| Standard | 0.85 | 1.97 | 1.00 | 0.09 | -1.6* | -0.9* | 0.3* | -0.00 | -0.02+ |
| 2SLS | 0.84 | 1.78 | 0.40 | 0.14 | -1.6* | -1.0* | 0.3+ | -0.00. | -0.02+ |
| No Prior | 0.85 | 1.97 | | | -1.6* | -0.8* | 0.3+ | -0.00 | -0.01. |
| Imports from Japan | | | | | | | | | |
| Standard | 0.99 | 1.61 | 0.90 | 0.38 | -4.1* | -1.2* | 0.7* | 0.10* | 0.07* |
| 2SLS | 0.99 | 1.70 | 0.40 | 0.40 | -4.1* | -1.4* | 0.8+ | 0.10* | 0.07* |
| No Prior | 0.99 | 1.62 | | | -4.2* | -0.9+ | 0.6+ | 0.11* | 0.08* |
| **ELECTRICAL MACHINERY** | | | | | | | | | |
| Imports from U.S. | | | | | | | | | |
| Standard | 0.70 | 2.03 | 0.30 | 0.14 | -1.3* | -1.2* | 0.3+ | -0.03* | -0.03* |
| 2SLS | 0.71 | 2.03 | 0.10 | 0.20 | -1.2* | -1.3* | 0.4+ | -0.03* | -0.03+ |
| No Prior | 0.71 | 2.03 | | | -1.3* | -1.1* | 0.3+ | -0.03* | -0.03+ |
| Imports from Japan | | | | | | | | | |
| Standard | 0.99 | 2.20 | 0.10 | 0.23 | -3.2* | -1.3* | 0.6+ | 0.06* | 0.06* |
| 2SLS | 0.99 | 1.59 | 0.10 | 0.46 | -3.2* | -1.5* | 0.7+ | 0.06* | 0.06* |
| No Prior | 0.99 | 2.18 | | | -3.2* | -1.2* | 0.6+ | 0.07* | 0.06* |
| **TRANSPORT EQUIPMENT** | | | | | | | | | |
| Imports from U.S. | | | | | | | | | |
| Standard | 0.07 | 1.73 | 1.50 | 0.37 | -1.6* | -0.9+ | -0.0* | -0.01 | -0.05+ |
| 2SLS | 0.03 | 1.75 | 2.00 | 0.37 | -1.6* | -0.8+ | -0.0* | -0.01 | -0.04+ |
| No Prior | 0.10 | 1.88 | | | -1.6* | -0.6. | 0.0* | -0.00 | -0.03. |
| Imports from Japan | | | | | | | | | |
| Standard | 0.94 | 1.53 | 0.00 | 0.72 | -2.9* | -1.6* | 0.0* | 0.09* | -0.01 |
| 2SLS | 0.96 | 2.18 | 1.30 | 0.53 | -2.8* | -2.3* | 0.0* | 0.08* | -0.03+ |
| No Prior | 0.94 | 1.53 | | | -2.9* | -1.7+ | 0.0* | 0.09* | -0.02 |
| **MISCELLANEOUS MANUFACTURES** | | | | | | | | | |
| Imports from U.S. | | | | | | | | | |
| Standard | 0.80 | 1.62 | 0.60 | 0.32 | -1.1* | -1.0* | 0.8* | -0.08* | -0.02. |
| 2SLS | 0.81 | 1.83 | 0.00 | 0.41 | -1.1* | -1.3* | 1.1* | -0.09* | -0.04+ |
| No Prior | 0.80 | 1.63 | | | -1.1* | -0.8+ | 0.8* | -0.08* | -0.01 |
| Imports from Japan | | | | | | | | | |
| Standard | 0.74 | 1.85 | 0.00 | 0.55 | -3.0* | -1.7* | 1.5* | 0.05* | 0.10* |
| 2SLS | 0.68 | 1.79 | 0.40 | 0.64 | -3.0* | -1.3* | 2.0* | 0.05* | 0.12* |
| No Prior | 0.74 | 1.82 | | | -3.0* | -1.9* | 1.5* | 0.05* | 0.10* |

# Selected Simulation Results

The "summary" section of each simulation report shows the values of aggregates (summed from underlying product detail) that correspond to the national accounts concepts shown in Table 4.5. The aggregates are measured in constant base solution prices. (For example, all simulations derived from the 1980 base solution are reported in 1980 billions of dollars.) Directly below the aggregates are price deflators showing changes in an appropriate price index from base (for example, 1980) levels. The consumption deflator is calculated from the underlying preference function (see Eq. 2.10); other deflators are Paasche indexes. The current account balance (which is defined to equal net external saving) is calculated only in nominal terms. The items "credits" and "debits" include merchandise trade, factor trade, and trade in factor services.

The "detailed" section of each report shows real quantities in base-year units. For most commodities this means that prices equal 100 in the 1980 base solution. The units of homogeneous products (agriculture and natural resources) are chosen so that base-year ROW prices are equal to 100; consequently, base-year U.S. and Japanese prices are not necessarily equal to 100. This convention also accounts for the slight difference between the "quantity" and "value" column totals for exports and imports in the base solution; the quantity sum values homogeneous goods at base-year world prices, while the value sum uses domestic prices.

The "real exchange rate" is calculated as the ratio of a given country's GDP deflator to the ROW export deflator. "Terms of trade" are measured as the ratio of the credit deflator to the debit deflator. "Real expenditures" are defined as real consumption plus real investment.

178

Table B-1. 1980 base solution

## SUMMARY FEATURES OF SOLUTION

| | GDP | CONSUME | INVEST | CURRENT ACCOUNT | CREDIT | EXPORT | DEBIT | IMPORT | LABOR | CAPITAL | TARIFF EQUIV |
|---|---|---|---|---|---|---|---|---|---|---|---|
| United States | 2626.1 100.0 | 2207.5 100.0 | 395.4 100.0 | 23.30 | 339.80 100.0 | 214.40 100.0 | 316.51 100.0 | 244.44 100.0 | 1704.6 100.0 | 410.0 100.0 | 10.34 |
| Japan | 1039.6 100.0 | 712.6 100.0 | 336.9 100.0 | -9.87 | 157.39 100.0 | 133.45 100.0 | 167.27 100.0 | 128.70 100.0 | 649.1 100.0 | 187.1 100.0 | 8.52 |

## DETAILED FEATURES OF SOLUTION

| | United States | | | | | Japan | | | | | Bilateral | |
|---|---|---|---|---|---|---|---|---|---|---|---|---|
| | PRICES | OUTPUT | DEMAND | EXPORT | IMPORT | PRICES | OUTPUT | DEMAND | EXPORT | IMPORT | US>JPN | JPN>US |
| Agriculture | 100.0 | 482.80 | 456.30 | 48.49 | 21.99 | 124.2 | 144.63 | 164.59 | 1.68 | 21.63 | 7.92 | 0.27 |
| Resources | 114.2 | 330.31 | 408.80 | 16.86 | 95.29 | 118.2 | 118.84 | 192.06 | 2.10 | 75.35 | 3.28 | 0.45 |
| Textiles | 100.0 | 111.63 | 119.40 | 5.90 | 13.68 | 100.0 | 56.36 | 53.90 | 5.92 | 3.47 | 0.22 | 0.63 |
| Paper, wood | 100.0 | 150.36 | 153.32 | 7.25 | 10.23 | 100.0 | 72.61 | 74.38 | 1.18 | 2.93 | 0.92 | 0.15 |
| Chemicals | 100.0 | 198.24 | 184.04 | 25.80 | 11.59 | 100.0 | 95.04 | 94.27 | 8.90 | 8.15 | 2.74 | 1.07 |
| Stone, clay | 100.0 | 45.66 | 48.22 | 2.35 | 4.91 | 100.0 | 41.24 | 40.45 | 1.81 | 1.02 | 0.13 | 0.54 |
| Steel | 100.0 | 85.94 | 90.48 | 3.50 | 8.04 | 100.0 | 127.60 | 112.47 | 15.93 | 0.81 | 0.06 | 3.14 |
| Metal products | 100.0 | 120.85 | 120.42 | 4.64 | 4.21 | 100.0 | 48.20 | 44.54 | 4.16 | 0.51 | 0.20 | 1.10 |
| Machinery | 100.0 | 203.73 | 179.68 | 43.41 | 19.35 | 100.0 | 118.44 | 99.88 | 22.64 | 4.09 | 2.02 | 4.31 |
| Electrical | 100.0 | 133.10 | 128.83 | 21.11 | 16.84 | 100.0 | 96.20 | 78.86 | 20.14 | 2.80 | 1.52 | 4.92 |
| Vehicles | 100.0 | 195.35 | 195.46 | 22.31 | 22.40 | 100.0 | 115.72 | 83.88 | 33.82 | 1.99 | 0.94 | 12.63 |
| Miscel mfg | 100.0 | 97.59 | 100.50 | 6.71 | 9.62 | 100.0 | 73.14 | 67.47 | 6.98 | 1.32 | 0.40 | 1.87 |
| Construction | 100.0 | 340.10 | 340.10 | | | 100.0 | 223.30 | 223.30 | | | | |
| Utilities | 100.0 | 194.87 | 194.87 | | | 100.0 | 45.96 | 45.96 | | | | |
| Trade serv | 100.0 | 570.81 | 570.81 | | | 100.0 | 200.84 | 200.84 | | | | |
| Finance | 100.0 | 188.31 | 188.31 | | | 100.0 | 70.79 | 70.79 | | | | |
| Real estate | 100.0 | 400.49 | 400.49 | | | 100.0 | 126.54 | 126.54 | | | | |
| Transport | 100.0 | 225.37 | 225.37 | | | 100.0 | 80.30 | 80.30 | | | | |
| Services | 100.0 | 591.56 | 591.56 | | | 100.0 | 376.57 | 376.57 | | | | |
| Freight | 100.0 | 20.45 | 22.84 | 3.71 | 6.09 | 100.0 | 18.62 | 15.46 | 7.37 | 4.22 | 0.00 | 0.00 |
| QUANTITY SUM | | | | 212.04 | 244.25 | | | | 132.64 | 128.26 | 20.35 | 31.08 |
| VALUE SUM | | | | 214.45 | 244.41 | | | | 133.44 | 128.73 | 20.82 | 31.23 |

Table B-2. 1970 base solution

## SUMMARY FEATURES OF SOLUTION

| | GDP | CONSUME | INVEST | CURRENT ACCOUNT | CREDIT | EXPORT | DEBIT | IMPORT | LABOR | CAPITAL | TARIFF EQUIV |
|---|---|---|---|---|---|---|---|---|---|---|---|
| United States | 992.7 | 841.9 | 144.2 | 6.66 | 65.67 | 41.08 | 59.01 | 38.93 | 663.6 | 141.0 | 4.57 |
| | 100.0 | 100.0 | 100.0 | | 100.0 | 100.0 | 100.0 | 100.0 | 100.0 | 100.0 | |
| Japan | 197.2 | 117.1 | 77.9 | 2.17 | 22.97 | 19.91 | 20.80 | 16.42 | 100.3 | 66.8 | 1.85 |
| | 100.0 | 100.0 | 100.0 | | 100.0 | 100.0 | 100.0 | 100.0 | 100.0 | 100.0 | |

## DETAILED FEATURES OF SOLUTION

| | United States | | | | | Japan | | | | | Bilateral | |
|---|---|---|---|---|---|---|---|---|---|---|---|---|
| | PRICES | OUTPUT | DEMAND | EXPORT | IMPORT | PRICES | OUTPUT | DEMAND | EXPORT | IMPORT | US>JPN | JPN>US |
| Agriculture | 100.0 | 178.55 | 177.57 | 8.30 | 7.32 | 125.3 | 35.33 | 39.47 | 0.54 | 4.68 | 1.82 | 0.14 |
| Resources | 133.7 | 58.51 | 62.14 | 2.84 | 6.46 | 127.5 | 12.83 | 18.55 | 0.21 | 5.93 | 0.64 | 0.06 |
| Textiles | 100.0 | 53.49 | 55.99 | 0.97 | 3.47 | 100.0 | 17.72 | 15.72 | 2.28 | 0.28 | 0.02 | 0.72 |
| Paper, wood | 100.0 | 47.13 | 48.45 | 1.52 | 2.85 | 100.0 | 16.87 | 16.95 | 0.33 | 0.41 | 0.17 | 0.13 |
| Chemicals | 100.0 | 63.15 | 60.81 | 4.46 | 2.12 | 100.0 | 19.30 | 18.68 | 1.55 | 0.93 | 0.36 | 0.23 |
| Stone, clay | 100.0 | 16.28 | 16.80 | 0.49 | 1.01 | 100.0 | 7.52 | 7.30 | 0.35 | 0.13 | 0.04 | 0.15 |
| Steel | 100.0 | 31.66 | 32.49 | 1.39 | 2.22 | 100.0 | 32.31 | 28.78 | 3.76 | 0.22 | 0.03 | 0.95 |
| Metal products | 100.0 | 46.16 | 46.23 | 0.86 | 0.93 | 100.0 | 10.60 | 9.95 | 0.72 | 0.06 | 0.03 | 0.34 |
| Machinery | 100.0 | 65.15 | 60.09 | 8.17 | 3.12 | 100.0 | 26.43 | 25.19 | 2.16 | 0.92 | 0.51 | 0.49 |
| Electrical | 100.0 | 47.09 | 45.34 | 4.58 | 2.84 | 100.0 | 21.43 | 19.55 | 2.52 | 0.64 | 0.45 | 1.12 |
| Vehicles | 100.0 | 73.53 | 72.19 | 4.35 | 3.01 | 100.0 | 21.53 | 18.67 | 3.19 | 0.33 | 0.25 | 0.84 |
| Miscel mfg | 100.0 | 35.91 | 36.80 | 1.08 | 1.98 | 100.0 | 13.66 | 12.76 | 1.15 | 0.25 | 0.13 | 0.65 |
| Construction | 100.0 | 129.97 | 129.97 | | | 100.0 | 44.94 | 44.94 | | | | |
| Utilities | 100.0 | 54.39 | 54.39 | | | 100.0 | 6.82 | 6.82 | | | | |
| Trade serv | 100.0 | 221.88 | 221.88 | | | 100.0 | 40.30 | 40.30 | | | | |
| Finance | 100.0 | 61.81 | 61.81 | | | 100.0 | 12.93 | 12.93 | | | | |
| Real estate | 100.0 | 139.48 | 139.48 | | | 100.0 | 18.90 | 18.90 | | | | |
| Transport | 100.0 | 89.51 | 89.51 | | | 100.0 | 19.23 | 19.23 | | | | |
| Services | 100.0 | 194.92 | 194.92 | | | 100.0 | 55.88 | 55.88 | | | | |
| Freight | 100.0 | 2.57 | 3.04 | 1.11 | 1.58 | 100.0 | 1.20 | 1.66 | 0.95 | 1.41 | 0.00 | 0.00 |
| QUANTITY SUM | | | | 40.12 | 38.89 | | | | 19.72 | 16.20 | 4.43 | 5.83 |
| VALUE SUM | | | | 41.07 | 38.94 | | | | 19.91 | 16.42 | 4.65 | 5.89 |

Table B-3. 1960 base solution

## SUMMARY FEATURES OF SOLUTION

| | GDP | CONSUME | INVEST | CURRENT ACCOUNT | CREDIT | DEBIT | EXPORT | IMPORT | LABOR | CAPITAL | TARIFF EQUIV |
|---|---|---|---|---|---|---|---|---|---|---|---|
| United States | 506.5 100.0 | 425.2 100.0 | 75.9 100.0 | 5.46 | 28.87 100.0 | 23.41 100.0 | 19.13 100.0 | 14.52 100.0 | 328.2 100.0 | 81.6 100.0 | 1.42 |
| Japan | 43.0 100.0 | 28.3 100.0 | 14.6 100.0 | 0.17 | 4.92 100.0 | 4.75 100.0 | 4.19 100.0 | 3.99 100.0 | 21.1 100.0 | 14.5 100.0 | 0.51 |

## DETAILED FEATURES OF SOLUTION

| | United States | | | | | Japan | | | | | Bilateral | |
|---|---|---|---|---|---|---|---|---|---|---|---|---|
| | PRICES | OUTPUT | DEMAND | EXPORT | IMPORT | PRICES | OUTPUT | DEMAND | EXPORT | IMPORT | US>JPN | JPN>US |
| Agriculture | 100.0 | 120.06 | 119.05 | 5.04 | 4.02 | 124.4 | 14.39 | 15.65 | 0.25 | 1.51 | 0.55 | 0.08 |
| Resources | 124.2 | 37.29 | 39.08 | 1.51 | 3.30 | 131.4 | 3.06 | 4.26 | 0.03 | 1.24 | 0.27 | 0.01 |
| Textiles | 100.0 | 34.58 | 34.93 | 0.66 | 1.01 | 100.0 | 6.39 | 5.17 | 1.24 | 0.02 | 0.00 | 0.34 |
| Paper, wood | 100.0 | 27.75 | 28.60 | 0.58 | 1.42 | 100.0 | 4.17 | 4.04 | 0.16 | 0.03 | 0.03 | 0.09 |
| Chemicals | 100.0 | 33.59 | 32.27 | 2.11 | 0.79 | 100.0 | 5.07 | 5.22 | 0.21 | 0.36 | 0.15 | 0.03 |
| Stone, clay | 100.0 | 10.76 | 10.93 | 0.19 | 0.36 | 100.0 | 1.45 | 1.28 | 0.17 | 0.01 | 0.00 | 0.07 |
| Steel | 100.0 | 21.85 | 21.72 | 0.68 | 0.55 | 100.0 | 7.72 | 7.39 | 0.41 | 0.07 | 0.02 | 0.08 |
| Metal products | 100.0 | 25.04 | 24.85 | 0.43 | 0.25 | 100.0 | 1.65 | 1.49 | 0.17 | 0.01 | 0.00 | 0.08 |
| Machinery | 100.0 | 30.98 | 28.26 | 3.19 | 0.47 | 100.0 | 4.95 | 4.86 | 0.31 | 0.22 | 0.13 | 0.06 |
| Electrical | 100.0 | 23.71 | 22.81 | 1.22 | 0.32 | 100.0 | 3.89 | 3.68 | 0.28 | 0.07 | 0.05 | 0.10 |
| Vehicles | 100.0 | 46.48 | 45.45 | 1.70 | 0.68 | 100.0 | 3.82 | 3.46 | 0.44 | 0.07 | 0.05 | 0.01 |
| Miscel mfg | 100.0 | 20.33 | 19.96 | 0.77 | 0.35 | 100.0 | 3.04 | 2.02 | 0.24 | 0.02 | 0.01 | 0.09 |
| Construction | 100.0 | 78.20 | 78.20 | | | 100.0 | 8.84 | 8.84 | | | | |
| Utilities | 100.0 | 27.13 | 27.13 | | | 100.0 | 1.80 | 1.80 | | | | |
| Trade serv | 100.0 | 111.70 | 111.70 | | | 100.0 | 7.25 | 7.25 | | | | |
| Finance | 100.0 | 28.47 | 28.47 | | | 100.0 | 2.32 | 2.32 | | | | |
| Real estate | 100.0 | 64.06 | 64.06 | | | 100.0 | 2.27 | 2.27 | | | | |
| Transport | 100.0 | 49.81 | 49.81 | | | 100.0 | 4.70 | 4.70 | | | | |
| Services | 100.0 | 82.33 | 82.33 | 0.68 | 0.96 | 100.0 | 12.45 | 12.45 | 0.22 | 0.29 | 0.00 | 0.00 |
| Freight | 100.0 | 0.94 | 1.22 | | | 100.0 | 0.33 | 0.40 | | | | |
| QUANTITY SUM | | | | 18.76 | 14.50 | | | | 4.12 | 3.93 | 1.27 | 1.05 |
| VALUE SUM | | | | 19.13 | 14.52 | | | | 4.19 | 3.99 | 1.34 | 1.07 |

Table B-4. U.S. external savings rate increased 2 percent

SUMMARY FEATURES OF SOLUTION

| | GDP | CONSUME | INVEST | CURRENT ACCOUNT | CREDIT | EXPORT | DEBIT | IMPORT | LABOR | CAPITAL | TARIFF EQUIV |
|---|---|---|---|---|---|---|---|---|---|---|---|
| United States | 2603.9 71.8 | 2102.3 72.4 | 376.5 73.2 | 72.58 | 391.74 80.4 | 266.34 75.6 | 266.66 90.8 | 194.59 95.4 | 1705.8 68.2 | 410.0 62.6 | 7.41 |
| Japan | 1037.6 86.3 | 706.6 86.8 | 334.0 87.3 | -9.53 | 159.36 88.5 | 135.42 87.8 | 162.32 92.8 | 123.75 92.0 | 649.2 85.7 | 187.1 84.9 | 7.98 |

DETAILED FEATURES OF SOLUTION

| | United States | | | | | Japan | | | | | Bilateral | |
|---|---|---|---|---|---|---|---|---|---|---|---|---|
| | PRICES | OUTPUT | DEMAND | EXPORT | IMPORT | PRICES | OUTPUT | DEMAND | EXPORT | IMPORT | US>JPN | JPN>US |
| Agriculture | 80.1 | 469.12 | 421.93 | 61.65 | 14.89 | 109.4 | 145.25 | 163.42 | 1.86 | 19.79 | 8.81 | 0.21 |
| Resources | 103.6 | 304.50 | 372.95 | 17.07 | 85.85 | 110.9 | 116.98 | 188.67 | 2.06 | 73.69 | 3.26 | 0.41 |
| Textiles | 71.8 | 117.74 | 115.25 | 9.36 | 9.07 | 87.0 | 57.72 | 53.89 | 6.52 | 2.99 | 0.31 | 0.36 |
| Paper, wood | 71.7 | 149.38 | 145.00 | 9.76 | 6.28 | 87.0 | 72.18 | 73.44 | 1.31 | 2.68 | 1.20 | 0.09 |
| Chemicals | 72.9 | 195.08 | 174.29 | 29.56 | 9.31 | 87.9 | 95.43 | 93.33 | 9.69 | 7.77 | 3.31 | 1.22 |
| Stone, clay | 73.0 | 45.27 | 45.95 | 2.72 | 3.72 | 89.0 | 39.01 | 38.31 | 1.64 | 0.95 | 0.16 | 0.43 |
| Steel | 74.2 | 87.53 | 88.09 | 4.53 | 5.80 | 89.6 | 128.37 | 111.93 | 17.02 | 0.62 | 0.08 | 2.35 |
| Metal products | 73.7 | 113.01 | 110.35 | 5.95 | 3.43 | 88.0 | 46.63 | 43.30 | 3.83 | 0.51 | 0.28 | 1.19 |
| Machinery | 72.5 | 205.67 | 163.47 | 54.13 | 13.06 | 87.2 | 115.54 | 98.93 | 20.52 | 3.98 | 2.40 | 2.89 |
| Electrical | 72.6 | 133.09 | 119.36 | 28.12 | 14.67 | 87.5 | 95.11 | 78.08 | 19.99 | 2.96 | 1.75 | 4.51 |
| Vehicles | 72.6 | 199.78 | 185.78 | 29.39 | 16.55 | 87.2 | 119.43 | 84.19 | 37.27 | 2.08 | 1.27 | 11.04 |
| Miscel mfg | 71.0 | 98.61 | 96.73 | 8.02 | 6.79 | 86.7 | 70.94 | 66.64 | 5.46 | 1.20 | 0.45 | 1.11 |
| Construction | 71.7 | 326.47 | 326.47 | | | 87.5 | 220.26 | 220.26 | | | | |
| Utilities | 74.9 | 175.07 | 175.07 | | | 39.1 | 45.34 | 45.34 | | | | |
| Trade serv | 69.1 | 562.77 | 562.77 | | | 86.0 | 201.56 | 201.56 | | | | |
| Finance | 68.8 | 184.77 | 184.77 | | | 86.0 | 71.18 | 71.18 | | | | |
| Real estate | 67.2 | 404.70 | 404.70 | | | 85.9 | 126.00 | 126.00 | | | | |
| Transport | 70.0 | 219.96 | 219.96 | | | 88.1 | 79.34 | 79.34 | | | | |
| Services | 70.0 | 573.16 | 573.16 | | | 86.4 | 373.85 | 373.85 | | | | |
| Freight | 70.1 | 17.57 | 18.91 | 3.71 | 5.04 | 88.1 | 18.22 | 14.92 | 7.37 | 4.07 | 0.00 | 0.00 |
| QUANTITY SUM | | | | 263.97 | 194.47 | | | | 134.53 | 123.28 | 23.28 | 25.81 |
| VALUE SUM | | | | 201.35 | 185.56 | | | | 118.84 | 113.87 | 18.57 | 22.74 |

Table B-5. Japanese external savings rate increased 2 percent

## SUMMARY FEATURES OF SOLUTION

| | GDP | CONSUME | INVEST | CURRENT ACCOUNT | CREDIT | EXPORT | DEBIT | IMPORT | LABOR | CAPITAL | TARIFF EQUIV |
|---|---|---|---|---|---|---|---|---|---|---|---|
| United States | 2624.6<br>94.9 | 2204.2<br>95.0 | 394.8<br>95.0 | 23.06 | 339.89<br>96.3 | 214.49<br>95.4 | 314.29<br>96.9 | 242.22<br>97.0 | 1704.5<br>94.4 | 410.0<br>93.9 | 10.16 |
| Japan | 1035.0<br>84.5 | 683.1<br>85.7 | 322.9<br>86.2 | 10.79 | 183.74<br>87.7 | 159.80<br>86.9 | 154.82<br>97.1 | 116.25<br>98.1 | 649.2<br>83.2 | 187.1<br>80.9 | 7.09 |

## DETAILED FEATURES OF SOLUTION

| | United States | | | | | Japan | | | | | Bilateral | |
|---|---|---|---|---|---|---|---|---|---|---|---|---|
| | PRICES | OUTPUT | DEMAND | EXPORT | IMPORT | PRICES | OUTPUT | DEMAND | EXPORT | IMPORT | US>JPN | JPN>US |
| Agriculture | 95.5 | 482.13 | 454.48 | 48.58 | 20.72 | 112.7 | 145.20 | 158.12 | 2.36 | 15.51 | 5.91 | 0.36 |
| Resources | 111.8 | 326.63 | 403.69 | 16.81 | 93.98 | 113.8 | 117.03 | 188.75 | 2.21 | 73.93 | 3.23 | 0.44 |
| Textiles | 95.0 | 112.36 | 119.07 | 6.21 | 13.13 | 85.8 | 57.88 | 52.95 | 7.42 | 2.83 | 0.21 | 0.83 |
| Paper, wood | 95.0 | 150.01 | 152.05 | 7.42 | 9.52 | 86.4 | 71.14 | 71.81 | 1.41 | 2.20 | 0.78 | 0.17 |
| Chemicals | 95.2 | 197.24 | 182.74 | 25.68 | 11.24 | 87.3 | 97.04 | 92.98 | 10.60 | 6.85 | 2.45 | 1.28 |
| Stone, clay | 95.2 | 45.54 | 47.97 | 2.31 | 4.76 | 88.6 | 37.89 | 36.77 | 1.99 | 0.88 | 0.12 | 0.57 |
| Steel | 95.3 | 84.90 | 89.69 | 3.50 | 8.25 | 89.4 | 134.22 | 115.76 | 19.02 | 0.60 | 0.05 | 3.90 |
| Metal products | 95.2 | 119.66 | 119.31 | 4.44 | 4.13 | 86.9 | 46.52 | 42.18 | 4.70 | 0.38 | 0.16 | 1.31 |
| Machinery | 95.0 | 202.14 | 178.20 | 43.18 | 19.28 | 85.9 | 122.67 | 99.61 | 26.29 | 3.36 | 1.81 | 5.04 |
| Electrical | 95.0 | 132.12 | 128.16 | 21.01 | 17.07 | 86.5 | 99.26 | 78.12 | 23.69 | 2.59 | 1.38 | 5.87 |
| Vehicles | 94.9 | 194.62 | 195.45 | 23.20 | 24.14 | 86.1 | 125.69 | 83.96 | 43.34 | 1.68 | 0.84 | 16.56 |
| Miscel mfg | 94.9 | 96.56 | 100.24 | 6.09 | 9.79 | 85.3 | 73.65 | 66.11 | 6.56 | 1.09 | 0.36 | 2.39 |
| Construction | 94.9 | 339.38 | 339.38 | | | 86.3 | 212.74 | 212.74 | | | | |
| Utilities | 95.5 | 192.57 | 192.57 | | | 88.6 | 44.88 | 44.88 | | | | |
| Trade serv | 94.6 | 571.27 | 571.27 | | | 83.6 | 200.74 | 200.74 | | | | |
| Finance | 94.5 | 188.44 | 188.44 | | | 83.7 | 71.56 | 71.56 | | | | |
| Real estate | 94.4 | 401.46 | 401.46 | | | 83.1 | 123.26 | 123.26 | | | | |
| Transport | 94.7 | 225.03 | 225.03 | | | 87.2 | 78.09 | 78.09 | | | | |
| Services | 94.7 | 591.34 | 591.34 | | | 84.6 | 363.46 | 363.46 | | | | |
| Freight | 94.7 | 20.24 | 22.56 | 3.71 | 6.02 | 87.2 | 17.77 | 14.30 | 7.37 | 3.90 | 0.00 | 0.00 |
| QUANTITY SUM | | 212.14 | | | 242.04 | | | | 158.85 | 115.80 | 17.30 | 38.73 |
| VALUE SUM | | 204.62 | | | 234.85 | | | | 138.83 | 114.09 | 17.01 | 33.72 |

Table B-6. U.S. resource endowments increased 10 percent

SUMMARY FEATURES OF SOLUTION

| | GDP | CONSUME | INVEST | CURRENT ACCOUNT | CREDIT | EXPORT | DEBIT | IMPORT | LABOR | CAPITAL | TARIFF EQUIV |
|---|---|---|---|---|---|---|---|---|---|---|---|
| United States | 2882.0 83.5 | 2400.4 84.1 | 429.9 84.6 | 25.68 | 361.48 89.7 | 236.08 86.5 | 309.79 96.3 | 237.72 99.2 | 1874.5 81.3 | 451.0 76.6 | 9.63 |
| Japan | 1037.9 93.6 | 708.4 93.9 | 334.8 94.2 | -9.82 | 158.52 94.9 | 134.58 94.5 | 163.81 97.9 | 125.24 97.9 | 649.1 93.1 | 187.1 92.5 | 8.14 |

DETAILED FEATURES OF SOLUTION

| | United States | | | | | Japan | | | | | Bilateral | |
|---|---|---|---|---|---|---|---|---|---|---|---|---|
| | PRICES | OUTPUT | DEMAND | EXPORT | IMPORT | PRICES | OUTPUT | DEMAND | EXPORT | IMPORT | US>JPN | JPN>US |
| Agriculture | 90.6 | 493.66 | 465.16 | 50.03 | 21.26 | 119.2 | 145.48 | 163.22 | 1.85 | 19.80 | 7.51 | 0.28 |
| Resources | 110.7 | 338.96 | 420.47 | 16.76 | 98.10 | 117.0 | 117.40 | 189.44 | 2.12 | 74.24 | 3.22 | 0.46 |
| Textiles | 83.6 | 127.60 | 131.04 | 7.61 | 12.24 | 94.0 | 56.81 | 53.78 | 6.13 | 3.23 | 0.27 | 0.50 |
| Paper, wood | 83.6 | 162.90 | 162.54 | 8.54 | 8.60 | 94.1 | 72.04 | 73.62 | 1.24 | 2.83 | 1.08 | 0.13 |
| Chemicals | 84.4 | 211.05 | 194.14 | 27.84 | 11.16 | 94.5 | 94.87 | 93.62 | 9.25 | 6.03 | 3.08 | 1.22 |
| Stone, clay | 84.5 | 49.51 | 51.42 | 2.56 | 4.63 | 95.4 | 39.80 | 39.06 | 1.73 | 0.98 | 0.15 | 0.51 |
| Steel | 85.3 | 94.05 | 96.89 | 4.04 | 7.27 | 95.8 | 127.15 | 111.63 | 16.24 | 0.73 | 0.07 | 2.80 |
| Metal products | 85.0 | 126.61 | 125.29 | 5.35 | 4.10 | 94.7 | 47.24 | 43.74 | 4.02 | 0.52 | 0.24 | 1.23 |
| Machinery | 84.1 | 220.75 | 188.34 | 49.06 | 17.20 | 94.0 | 116.67 | 99.29 | 21.42 | 4.07 | 2.24 | 3.75 |
| Electrical | 84.2 | 145.55 | 138.06 | 24.77 | 17.41 | 94.3 | 95.74 | 78.41 | 20.23 | 2.90 | 1.65 | 5.14 |
| Vehicles | 84.2 | 217.06 | 211.39 | 25.93 | 20.82 | 94.1 | 118.08 | 84.10 | 36.03 | 2.05 | 1.13 | 12.70 |
| Miscel mfg | 83.1 | 107.73 | 108.68 | 7.48 | 8.74 | 93.8 | 71.93 | 67.08 | 6.10 | 1.27 | 0.43 | 1.51 |
| Construction | 83.6 | 369.91 | 369.91 | | | 94.3 | 221.23 | 221.23 | | | | |
| Utilities | 85.7 | 201.91 | 201.91 | | | 95.5 | 45.50 | 45.50 | | | | |
| Trade serv | 81.8 | 631.21 | 631.21 | | | 93.3 | 201.40 | 201.40 | | | | |
| Finance | 81.6 | 209.63 | 209.63 | | | 93.3 | 71.07 | 71.07 | | | | |
| Real estate | 80.1 | 456.16 | 456.16 | | | 93.2 | 126.22 | 126.22 | | | | |
| Transport | 82.4 | 244.10 | 244.10 | | | 94.8 | 79.65 | 79.65 | | | | |
| Services | 82.5 | 652.50 | 652.50 | | | 93.6 | 374.76 | 374.76 | | | | |
| Freight | 82.4 | 20.27 | 22.60 | 3.71 | 6.03 | 94.8 | 18.33 | 15.06 | 7.37 | 4.11 | 0.00 | 0.00 |
| QUANTITY SUM | | | | 233.69 | 237.54 | | | | 133.72 | 124.77 | 21.07 | 30.23 |
| VALUE SUM | | | | 204.26 | 235.75 | | | | 127.19 | 122.64 | 19.07 | 28.69 |

Table B-7. Japanese resource endowments increased 10 percent

## SUMMARY FEATURES OF SOLUTION

| | GDP | CONSUME | INVEST | CURRENT ACCOUNT | CREDIT | EXPORT | DEBIT | IMPORT | LABOR | CAPITAL | TARIFF EQUIV |
|---|---|---|---|---|---|---|---|---|---|---|---|
| United States | 2625.4 / 97.9 | 2206.2 / 98.0 | 395.1 / 97.9 | 23.32 | 340.46 / 98.8 | 215.06 / 98.3 | 316.37 / 99.0 | 244.30 / 99.1 | 1704.5 / 97.5 | 410.0 / 97.3 | 10.32 |
| Japan | 1141.4 / 89.9 | 774.0 / 90.8 | 365.9 / 91.2 | -10.79 | 173.54 / 92.3 | 149.60 / 91.7 | 172.10 / 99.4 | 133.53 / 100.4 | 713.8 / 89.0 | 205.8 / 86.8 | 8.63 |

## DETAILED FEATURES OF SOLUTION

| | United States | | | | | Japan | | | | | Bilateral | |
|---|---|---|---|---|---|---|---|---|---|---|---|---|
| | PRICES | OUTPUT | DEMAND | EXPORT | IMPORT | PRICES | OUTPUT | DEMAND | EXPORT | IMPORT | US>JPN | JPN>US |
| Agriculture | 98.8 | 482.09 | 454.20 | 49.47 | 21.44 | 118.1 | 152.72 | 172.69 | 1.75 | 21.91 | 8.13 | 0.27 |
| Resources | 114.7 | 327.47 | 404.85 | 17.04 | 94.49 | 117.2 | 62.42 | 203.93 | 2.10 | 80.51 | 3.51 | 0.45 |
| Textiles | 97.9 | 111.90 | 119.31 | 6.02 | 13.51 | 90.8 | 62.76 | 59.06 | 6.85 | 3.38 | 0.24 | 0.78 |
| Paper, wood | 97.9 | 150.07 | 152.62 | 7.34 | 9.92 | 91.4 | 78.25 | 79.52 | 1.32 | 2.67 | 0.89 | 0.17 |
| Chemicals | 98.1 | 197.63 | 183.26 | 25.79 | 11.44 | 92.0 | 103.55 | 101.32 | 9.95 | 7.89 | 2.74 | 1.19 |
| Stone, clay | 98.1 | 45.54 | 48.07 | 2.32 | 4.86 | 93.1 | 42.58 | 41.66 | 1.93 | 1.02 | 0.13 | 0.56 |
| Steel | 98.2 | 85.08 | 89.90 | 3.46 | 8.24 | 93.7 | 139.04 | 121.99 | 17.76 | 0.72 | 0.05 | 3.63 |
| Metal products | 98.1 | 120.01 | 119.69 | 4.48 | 4.17 | 91.8 | 51.30 | 47.23 | 4.51 | 0.46 | 0.18 | 1.22 |
| Machinery | 97.9 | 202.52 | 179.04 | 43.03 | 19.55 | 90.9 | 130.26 | 109.01 | 25.09 | 3.92 | 2.04 | 4.85 |
| Electrical | 97.9 | 132.48 | 128.57 | 20.94 | 17.04 | 91.4 | 105.48 | 85.97 | 22.39 | 2.91 | 1.56 | 5.53 |
| Vehicles | 97.8 | 194.75 | 195.64 | 22.72 | 23.61 | 91.1 | 129.23 | 91.41 | 39.70 | 1.94 | 0.94 | 15.16 |
| Miscel mfg | 97.8 | 96.85 | 100.42 | 6.29 | 9.84 | 90.4 | 79.84 | 73.00 | 8.07 | 1.28 | 0.41 | 2.24 |
| Construction | 97.9 | 339.68 | 339.68 | | | 91.3 | 241.33 | 241.33 | | | | |
| Utilities | 98.4 | 193.15 | 193.15 | | | 93.0 | 49.40 | 49.40 | | | | |
| Trade serv | 97.6 | 571.36 | 571.36 | | | 89.2 | 222.33 | 222.33 | | | | |
| Finance | 97.6 | 188.52 | 188.52 | | | 89.3 | 78.42 | 78.42 | | | | |
| Real estate | 97.6 | 401.28 | 401.28 | | | 88.6 | 139.51 | 139.51 | | | | |
| Transport | 97.7 | 225.19 | 225.19 | | | 92.0 | 86.89 | 86.89 | | | | |
| Services | 97.7 | 591.71 | 591.71 | | | 90.0 | 413.31 | 413.31 | | | | |
| Freight | 97.7 | 20.38 | 22.74 | 3.71 | 6.07 | 92.0 | 19.16 | 16.20 | 7.37 | 4.42 | 0.00 | 0.00 |
| QUANTITY SUM | | | | 212.62 | 244.17 | | | | 148.81 | 133.04 | 20.81 | 36.05 |
| VALUE SUM | | | | 211.47 | 242.16 | | | | 137.21 | 134.01 | 21.04 | 33.14 |

Table B-8. U.S. removes all formal protection

## SUMMARY FEATURES OF SOLUTION

| | GDP | CONSUME | INVEST | CURRENT ACCOUNT | CREDIT | DEBIT | EXPORT | IMPORT | LABOR | CAPITAL | TARIFF EQUIV |
|---|---|---|---|---|---|---|---|---|---|---|---|
| United States | 2624.3 / 94.9 | 2199.4 / 95.1 | 393.9 / 95.1 | 23.25 | 347.52 / 96.7 | 316.49 / 98.8 | 222.12 / 95.7 | 244.42 / 99.6 | 1704.5 / 94.5 | 410.1 / 93.7 | 0.00 |
| Japan | 1039.9 / 99.3 | 713.1 / 99.3 | 337.1 / 99.3 | -9.88 | 157.29 / 99.3 | 167.61 / 99.1 | 133.35 / 99.3 | 129.04 / 98.9 | 649.1 / 99.3 | 187.1 / 99.4 | 8.55 |

## DETAILED FEATURES OF SOLUTION

| | United States | | | | | Japan | | | | | Bilateral | |
|---|---|---|---|---|---|---|---|---|---|---|---|---|
| | PRICES | OUTPUT | DEMAND | EXPORT | IMPORT | PRICES | OUTPUT | DEMAND | EXPORT | IMPORT | US>JPN | JPN>US |
| Agriculture | 96.8 | 481.35 | 451.88 | 49.94 | 21.06 | 123.0 | 144.65 | 164.85 | 1.70 | 21.64 | 8.11 | 0.27 |
| Resources | 112.5 | 326.56 | 403.58 | 16.87 | 94.03 | 117.5 | 118.95 | 192.25 | 2.10 | 75.40 | 3.29 | 0.44 |
| Textiles | 93.8 | 109.69 | 120.50 | 6.48 | 16.66 | 99.3 | 56.82 | 54.07 | 6.19 | 3.46 | 0.24 | 0.90 |
| Paper, wood | 95.0 | 150.29 | 152.28 | 7.62 | 9.67 | 99.2 | 72.61 | 74.40 | 1.17 | 2.96 | 0.98 | 0.14 |
| Chemicals | 95.2 | 197.93 | 183.11 | 26.43 | 11.59 | 99.3 | 94.92 | 94.27 | 8.85 | 8.21 | 2.87 | 1.06 |
| Stone, clay | 95.3 | 45.53 | 48.03 | 2.42 | 4.91 | 99.4 | 41.17 | 40.41 | 1.79 | 1.03 | 0.14 | 0.54 |
| Steel | 95.4 | 85.13 | 90.41 | 3.66 | 8.81 | 99.4 | 128.81 | 113.00 | 16.60 | 0.80 | 0.06 | 3.75 |
| Metal products | 95.2 | 120.35 | 119.68 | 4.88 | 4.21 | 99.4 | 48.03 | 44.51 | 4.05 | 0.52 | 0.22 | 1.10 |
| Machinery | 95.0 | 204.94 | 178.97 | 45.18 | 19.22 | 99.3 | 117.86 | 99.80 | 22.22 | 4.14 | 2.11 | 4.31 |
| Electrical | 95.1 | 133.96 | 128.63 | 22.22 | 16.89 | 99.3 | 96.02 | 78.84 | 20.04 | 2.85 | 1.58 | 5.04 |
| Vehicles | 95.0 | 196.38 | 194.78 | 23.34 | 21.82 | 99.3 | 115.73 | 83.94 | 33.83 | 2.03 | 1.01 | 12.41 |
| Miscel mfg | 94.9 | 97.80 | 100.18 | 6.99 | 9.40 | 99.3 | 72.80 | 67.44 | 6.68 | 1.32 | 0.41 | 1.80 |
| Construction | 95.0 | 338.44 | 338.44 | | | 99.4 | 223.39 | 223.39 | | | | |
| Utilities | 95.7 | 191.94 | 191.94 | | | 99.3 | 45.99 | 45.99 | | | | |
| Trade serv | 94.7 | 570.11 | 570.11 | | | 99.3 | 200.85 | 200.85 | | | | |
| Finance | 94.6 | 188.04 | 168.04 | | | 99.3 | 70.81 | 70.81 | | | | |
| Real estate | 94.3 | 401.17 | 401.17 | | | 99.4 | 126.58 | 126.58 | | | | |
| Transport | 94.8 | 224.80 | 224.80 | | | 99.4 | 80.32 | 80.32 | | | | |
| Services | 94.8 | 589.81 | 589.81 | | | 99.3 | 376.77 | 376.77 | | | | |
| Freight | 94.8 | 20.38 | 22.75 | 3.71 | 6.07 | 99.3 | 18.64 | 15.48 | 7.37 | 4.23 | 0.00 | 0.00 |
| QUANTITY SUM | | | | 219.73 | 244.34 | | | | 132.59 | 128.59 | 21.00 | 31.78 |
| VALUE SUM | | | | 212.61 | 243.45 | | | | 132.47 | 127.67 | 20.68 | 31.71 |

Table B-9. Japan removes all formal protection

### SUMMARY FEATURES OF SOLUTION

| | GDP | CONSUME | INVEST | CURRENT ACCOUNT | CREDIT | EXPORT | DEBIT | IMPORT | LABOR | CAPITAL | TARIFF EQUIV |
|---|---|---|---|---|---|---|---|---|---|---|---|
| United States | 2626.2 | 2207.8 | 395.4 | 23.18 | 340.16 | 214.76 | 317.11 | 245.04 | 1704.6 | 410.1 | 10.38 |
| | 98.7 | 98.7 | 98.6 | | 99.2 | 98.5 | 99.1 | 99.1 | 98.5 | 98.6 | |
| Japan | 1041.0 | 707.4 | 334.4 | -9.85 | 169.57 | 145.63 | 170.36 | 131.79 | 649.0 | 187.1 | 0.00 |
| | 91.9 | 92.5 | 93.4 | | 94.0 | 93.5 | 99.4 | 99.8 | 92.9 | 92.6 | |

### DETAILED FEATURES OF SOLUTION

| | United States | | | | | Japan | | | | | Bilateral | |
|---|---|---|---|---|---|---|---|---|---|---|---|---|
| | PRICES | OUTPUT | DEMAND | EXPORT | IMPORT | PRICES | OUTPUT | DEMAND | EXPORT | IMPORT | US>JPN | JPN>US |
| Agriculture | 99.4 | 482.28 | 454.72 | 49.22 | 21.74 | 112.6 | 143.31 | 164.87 | 1.56 | 22.92 | 8.43 | 0.23 |
| Resources | 113.8 | 329.05 | 407.04 | 16.87 | 94.88 | 114.0 | 119.00 | 192.34 | 2.10 | 75.43 | 3.29 | 0.45 |
| Textiles | 98.7 | 111.79 | 119.39 | 5.99 | 13.62 | 91.7 | 55.48 | 53.34 | 6.77 | 4.74 | 0.26 | 0.78 |
| Paper, wood | 98.7 | 150.24 | 152.99 | 7.28 | 10.04 | 92.6 | 73.50 | 74.81 | 1.30 | 2.65 | 0.87 | 0.17 |
| Chemicals | 98.7 | 198.19 | 183.77 | 25.90 | 11.50 | 93.4 | 95.73 | 94.60 | 9.78 | 8.57 | 2.89 | 1.18 |
| Stone, clay | 98.7 | 45.60 | 48.16 | 2.32 | 4.89 | 94.3 | 40.41 | 39.48 | 1.91 | 0.98 | 0.13 | 0.56 |
| Steel | 98.8 | 85.35 | 90.19 | 3.45 | 8.25 | 94.6 | 131.81 | 115.02 | 17.52 | 0.74 | 0.05 | 3.58 |
| Metal products | 98.7 | 120.54 | 120.19 | 4.53 | 4.18 | 93.9 | 47.87 | 43.94 | 4.42 | 0.51 | 0.20 | 1.19 |
| Machinery | 98.6 | 203.09 | 179.53 | 43.12 | 19.57 | 93.4 | 120.90 | 100.60 | 24.42 | 4.10 | 2.05 | 4.72 |
| Electrical | 98.6 | 132.74 | 128.81 | 20.94 | 17.02 | 93.6 | 98.31 | 79.31 | 21.83 | 2.83 | 1.55 | 5.38 |
| Vehicles | 98.6 | 195.11 | 195.78 | 22.64 | 23.30 | 93.4 | 120.84 | 84.88 | 38.09 | 2.11 | 1.01 | 14.49 |
| Miscel mfg | 98.6 | 97.09 | 100.50 | 6.41 | 9.80 | 93.0 | 74.10 | 67.79 | 7.78 | 1.45 | 0.43 | 2.14 |
| Construction | 98.6 | 340.14 | 340.14 | | | 93.5 | 221.12 | 221.12 | | | | |
| Utilities | 98.9 | 194.26 | 194.26 | | | 94.3 | 45.82 | 45.82 | | | | |
| Trade serv | 98.6 | 571.19 | 571.19 | | | 93.0 | 200.60 | 200.60 | | | | |
| Finance | 98.5 | 188.50 | 188.50 | | | 93.0 | 70.91 | 70.91 | | | | |
| Real estate | 98.6 | 401.11 | 401.11 | | | 92.9 | 125.69 | 125.69 | | | | |
| Transport | 98.6 | 225.38 | 225.38 | | | 93.9 | 79.88 | 79.88 | | | | |
| Services | 98.6 | 591.89 | 591.89 | | | 92.9 | 373.89 | 373.89 | | | | |
| Freight | 98.6 | 20.44 | 22.82 | 3.71 | 6.09 | 93.9 | 18.79 | 15.70 | 7.37 | 4.28 | 0.00 | 0.00 |
| QUANTITY SUM | | | | 212.38 | 244.87 | | | | 144.86 | 131.32 | 21.15 | 34.86 |
| VALUE SUM | | | | 212.43 | 242.71 | | | | 136.17 | 131.57 | 21.43 | 32.73 |

Table B-10. Japan achieves Germany's level of openness

## SUMMARY FEATURES OF SOLUTION

| | GDP | CONSUME | INVEST | CURRENT ACCOUNT | CREDIT | EXPORT | DEBIT | IMPORT | LABOR | CAPITAL | TARIFF EQUIV |
|---|---|---|---|---|---|---|---|---|---|---|---|
| United States | 2624.2<br>101.2 | 2203.2<br>101.1 | 394.6<br>101.4 | 23.53 | 338.83<br>101.4 | 213.43<br>101.6 | 312.50<br>102.4 | 240.43<br>103.0 | 1704.4<br>101.0 | 410.0<br>100.6 | 10.13 |
| Japan | 1043.0<br>126.5 | 727.6<br>124.3 | 344.0<br>123.6 | -10.03 | 124.53<br>120.0 | 100.59<br>122.1 | 153.13<br>104.1 | 114.56<br>102.0 | 649.1<br>129.3 | 187.1<br>133.1 | 6.51 |

## DETAILED FEATURES OF SOLUTION

| | United States | | | | | Japan | | | | | Bilateral | |
|---|---|---|---|---|---|---|---|---|---|---|---|---|
| | PRICES | OUTPUT | DEMAND | EXPORT | IMPORT | PRICES | OUTPUT | DEMAND | EXPORT | IMPORT | US>JPN | JPN>US |
| Agriculture | 102.5 | 481.56 | 453.06 | 50.69 | 22.38 | 141.9 | 144.20 | 174.00 | 1.16 | 30.76 | 11.05 | 0.18 |
| Resources | 116.0 | 329.60 | 407.80 | 16.97 | 95.22 | 124.8 | 123.56 | 200.66 | 2.10 | 79.12 | 3.43 | 0.45 |
| Textiles | 101.1 | 111.59 | 119.33 | 5.77 | 13.57 | 123.3 | 60.68 | 56.44 | 4.24 | 0.00 | 0.00 | 0.37 |
| Paper, wood | 101.1 | 149.09 | 153.14 | 6.27 | 10.31 | 122.8 | 80.61 | 79.73 | 0.89 | 0.00 | 0.00 | 0.11 |
| Chemicals | 101.2 | 194.85 | 183.05 | 23.45 | 11.64 | 121.5 | 108.21 | 101.42 | 6.77 | 0.00 | 0.00 | 0.79 |
| Stone, clay | 101.1 | 45.63 | 48.15 | 2.34 | 4.87 | 119.2 | 46.59 | 45.08 | 1.51 | 0.00 | 0.00 | 0.47 |
| Steel | 101.3 | 36.80 | 90.43 | 3.64 | 7.50 | 117.6 | 123.06 | 111.10 | 11.96 | 0.00 | 0.00 | 2.01 |
| Metal products | 101.3 | 120.54 | 119.81 | 4.98 | 4.27 | 122.2 | 50.55 | 47.21 | 3.34 | 0.00 | 0.00 | 0.84 |
| Machinery | 101.3 | 203.97 | 178.38 | 43.54 | 18.16 | 124.3 | 117.52 | 100.19 | 17.33 | 0.00 | 0.00 | 3.05 |
| Electrical | 101.3 | 132.70 | 128.00 | 20.87 | 16.37 | 123.1 | 94.89 | 79.49 | 15.40 | 0.00 | 0.00 | 3.61 |
| Vehicles | 101.4 | 194.73 | 194.06 | 21.11 | 21.02 | 123.8 | 106.10 | 83.03 | 23.05 | 0.00 | 0.00 | 7.90 |
| Miscel mfg | 101.1 | 99.34 | 100.45 | 7.69 | 8.94 | 125.1 | 74.12 | 69.35 | 4.77 | 0.00 | 0.00 | 1.14 |
| Construction | 101.2 | 340.11 | 340.11 | | | 123.3 | 230.37 | 230.37 | | | | |
| Utilities | 101.2 | 194.48 | 194.48 | | | 119.2 | 47.87 | 47.87 | | | | |
| Trade serv | 101.0 | 570.90 | 570.90 | | | 128.4 | 198.95 | 198.95 | | | | |
| Finance | 101.0 | 188.29 | 188.29 | | | 128.2 | 70.39 | 70.39 | | | | |
| Real estate | 100.9 | 401.00 | 401.00 | | | 129.2 | 127.60 | 127.60 | | | | |
| Transport | 101.1 | 225.18 | 225.18 | | | 121.7 | 82.75 | 82.75 | | | | |
| Services | 101.2 | 590.72 | 590.72 | | | 126.4 | 383.56 | 383.56 | | | | |
| Freight | 101.1 | 20.28 | 22.60 | 3.71 | 6.03 | 121.7 | 18.51 | 15.31 | 7.37 | 4.18 | 0.00 | 0.00 |
| QUANTITY SUM | | | | 211.03 | 240.27 | | | | 99.91 | 114.06 | 14.48 | 20.90 |
| VALUE SUM | | | | 216.78 | 247.52 | | | | 122.75 | 116.89 | 15.30 | 25.73 |

Table B-11.  Greater bilateral balance through U.S. protection

## SUMMARY FEATURES OF SOLUTION

| | GDP | CONSUME | INVEST | CURRENT ACCOUNT | CREDIT | DEBIT | EXPORT | IMPORT | LABOR | CAPITAL | TARIFF EQUIV |
|---|---|---|---|---|---|---|---|---|---|---|---|
| United States | 2625.5<br>101.3 | 2209.3<br>101.1 | 395.7<br>101.3 | 23.42 | 335.62<br>100.7 | 315.17<br>99.8 | 210.22<br>100.9 | 243.10<br>99.5 | 1704.4<br>101.3 | 409.9<br>101.3 | 14.47 |
| Japan | 1037.3<br>95.3 | 707.7<br>95.8 | 334.6<br>95.9 | -9.87 | 157.89<br>96.4 | 162.86<br>99.5 | 133.95<br>96.1 | 124.29<br>99.9 | 649.1<br>94.8 | 187.1<br>94.0 | 8.07 |

## DETAILED FEATURES OF SOLUTION

| | United States | | | | | Japan | | | | | Bilateral | |
|---|---|---|---|---|---|---|---|---|---|---|---|---|
| | PRICES | OUTPUT | DEMAND | EXPORT | IMPORT | PRICES | OUTPUT | DEMAND | EXPORT | IMPORT | US>JPN | JPN>US |
| Agriculture | 100.4 | 483.51 | 458.20 | 47.65 | 22.18 | 121.2 | 145.10 | 162.96 | 1.80 | 19.93 | 7.27 | 0.27 |
| Resources | 114.3 | 331.44 | 410.37 | 16.83 | 95.70 | 117.1 | 117.72 | 190.01 | 2.10 | 74.49 | 3.25 | 0.45 |
| Textiles | 101.2 | 111.50 | 119.49 | 5.77 | 13.74 | 95.8 | 56.73 | 53.74 | 6.17 | 3.28 | 0.21 | 0.51 |
| Paper, wood | 101.2 | 150.31 | 153.57 | 7.11 | 10.37 | 96.0 | 72.11 | 73.55 | 1.20 | 2.67 | 0.85 | 0.12 |
| Chemicals | 101.1 | 197.87 | 184.15 | 25.42 | 11.69 | 96.3 | 95.13 | 93.48 | 9.23 | 7.65 | 2.57 | 0.92 |
| Stone, clay | 101.1 | 45.68 | 48.28 | 2.30 | 4.91 | 96.6 | 40.25 | 39.41 | 1.83 | 0.98 | 0.13 | 0.49 |
| Steel | 101.1 | 86.38 | 90.48 | 3.40 | 7.65 | 96.9 | 126.52 | 111.44 | 15.80 | 0.72 | 0.04 | 2.35 |
| Metal products | 101.2 | 120.69 | 120.49 | 4.46 | 4.25 | 96.1 | 47.66 | 43.92 | 4.19 | 0.46 | 0.18 | 0.96 |
| Machinery | 101.2 | 202.92 | 179.41 | 42.38 | 18.93 | 95.8 | 118.79 | 99.36 | 23.18 | 3.79 | 1.90 | 3.73 |
| Electrical | 101.2 | 132.55 | 128.60 | 20.48 | 16.60 | 96.0 | 96.05 | 78.35 | 20.30 | 2.69 | 1.44 | 4.26 |
| Vehicles | 101.3 | 195.75 | 195.08 | 22.00 | 21.52 | 95.8 | 113.79 | 82.82 | 32.77 | 1.84 | 0.86 | 10.12 |
| Miscel mfg | 101.2 | 97.58 | 100.50 | 6.37 | 9.34 | 95.6 | 72.84 | 66.98 | 7.08 | 1.24 | 0.38 | 1.52 |
| Construction | 101.0 | 340.49 | 340.49 | | | 95.9 | 221.37 | 221.37 | | | | |
| Utilities | 101.0 | 195.56 | 195.56 | | | 96.6 | 45.58 | 45.58 | | | | |
| Trade serv | 101.3 | 571.02 | 571.02 | | | 95.0 | 201.19 | 201.19 | | | | |
| Finance | 101.3 | 188.31 | 188.31 | | | 95.0 | 70.93 | 70.93 | | | | |
| Real estate | 101.3 | 400.14 | 400.14 | | | 94.8 | 126.15 | 126.15 | | | | |
| Transport | 101.2 | 225.42 | 225.42 | | | 96.2 | 79.74 | 79.74 | | | | |
| Services | 101.2 | 591.74 | 591.74 | | | 95.3 | 374.49 | 374.49 | | | | |
| Freight | 101.2 | 20.42 | 22.80 | 3.71 | 6.08 | 96.2 | 18.32 | 15.04 | 7.37 | 4.10 | 0.00 | 0.00 |
| QUANTITY SUM | | | | 207.86 | 242.94 | | | | 133.11 | 123.83 | 19.08 | 25.72 |
| VALUE SUM | | | | 212.19 | 241.79 | | | | 128.72 | 124.23 | 19.68 | 24.85 |

Table B-12. Greater bilateral balance through U.S. export subsidy

## SUMMARY FEATURES OF SOLUTION

|  | GDP | CONSUME | INVEST | CURRENT ACCOUNT | CREDIT | EXPORT | DEBIT | IMPORT | LABOR | CAPITAL | TARIFF EQUIV |
|---|---|---|---|---|---|---|---|---|---|---|---|
| United States | 2617.4 98.4 | 2198.6 98.4 | 393.8 98.4 | 23.45 | 339.29 99.1 | 213.89 98.8 | 314.28 99.5 | 242.21 99.8 | 1704.5 98.1 | 409.9 97.5 | 3.03 |
| Japan | 1047.0 96.9 | 715.7 97.0 | 338.3 97.6 | -9.97 | 160.20 97.9 | 136.26 97.7 | 167.13 99.8 | 128.56 100.0 | 649.2 97.9 | 187.1 98.0 | 9.25 |

## DETAILED FEATURES OF SOLUTION

|  | United States | | | | | Japan | | | | | Bilateral | |
|---|---|---|---|---|---|---|---|---|---|---|---|---|
|  | PRICES | OUTPUT | DEMAND | EXPORT | IMPORT | PRICES | OUTPUT | DEMAND | EXPORT | IMPORT | US>JPN | JPN>US |
| Agriculture | 99.6 | 481.23 | 452.54 | 50.09 | 21.63 | 115.7 | 143.18 | 167.10 | 1.43 | 25.13 | 9.24 | 0.23 |
| Resources | 113.9 | 328.79 | 406.69 | 16.87 | 94.80 | 117.6 | 118.99 | 192.32 | 2.10 | 75.43 | 3.29 | 0.45 |
| Textiles | 98.3 | 111.86 | 119.07 | 6.14 | 13.43 | 97.2 | 57.03 | 54.27 | 6.16 | 3.44 | 0.34 | 0.65 |
| Paper, wood | 98.3 | 150.81 | 152.89 | 7.87 | 9.98 | 96.6 | 73.69 | 75.78 | 1.23 | 3.35 | 1.45 | 0.15 |
| Chemicals | 98.4 | 199.32 | 183.76 | 27.02 | 11.49 | 97.4 | 95.10 | 94.98 | 9.19 | 9.11 | 3.87 | 1.10 |
| Stone, clay | 98.4 | 45.66 | 48.09 | 2.40 | 4.85 | 98.2 | 40.95 | 40.17 | 1.83 | 1.05 | 0.18 | 0.54 |
| Steel | 98.5 | 86.09 | 90.48 | 3.59 | 7.99 | 98.4 | 128.48 | 113.02 | 16.29 | 0.84 | 0.11 | 3.19 |
| Metal products | 98.4 | 120.58 | 119.90 | 4.85 | 4.17 | 98.1 | 47.94 | 44.41 | 4.21 | 0.68 | 0.39 | 1.13 |
| Machinery | 98.4 | 204.27 | 178.89 | 44.46 | 19.11 | 97.7 | 118.84 | 100.57 | 23.00 | 4.78 | 2.79 | 4.35 |
| Electrical | 98.4 | 133.35 | 128.37 | 21.76 | 16.78 | 97.7 | 96.68 | 79.36 | 20.57 | 3.25 | 1.98 | 5.02 |
| Vehicles | 98.3 | 195.80 | 194.91 | 23.19 | 22.32 | 97.6 | 117.43 | 84.81 | 35.06 | 2.47 | 1.52 | 13.04 |
| Miscel mfg | 98.3 | 97.47 | 100.23 | 6.76 | 9.52 | 97.4 | 73.66 | 67.91 | 7.13 | 1.39 | 0.50 | 1.90 |
| Construction | 98.3 | 338.93 | 338.93 | | | 97.9 | 223.66 | 223.66 | | | | |
| Utilities | 98.3 | 193.64 | 193.64 | | | 98.3 | 46.01 | 46.01 | | | | |
| Trade serv | 98.1 | 570.00 | 570.00 | | | 97.8 | 200.71 | 200.71 | | | | |
| Finance | 98.1 | 187.96 | 187.96 | | | 97.8 | 70.70 | 70.70 | | | | |
| Real estate | 97.9 | 400.40 | 400.40 | | | 97.9 | 126.65 | 126.65 | | | | |
| Transport | 98.2 | 225.02 | 225.02 | | | 98.1 | 80.40 | 80.40 | | | | |
| Services | 98.2 | 589.96 | 589.96 | | | 97.5 | 377.67 | 377.67 | | | | |
| Freight | 98.2 | 20.32 | 22.66 | 3.71 | 6.04 | 98.1 | 19.05 | 16.05 | 7.37 | 4.38 | 0.00 | 0.00 |
| QUANTITY SUM | | | | 218.71 | 242.10 | | | | 135.56 | 135.29 | 25.64 | 31.75 |
| VALUE SUM | | | | 218.35 | 241.70 | | | | 133.17 | 135.63 | 25.85 | 31.16 |

Table B-13.  Greater bilateral balance through Japanese export tax

## SUMMARY FEATURES OF SOLUTION

| | GDP | CONSUME | INVEST | CURRENT ACCOUNT | CREDIT | DEBIT | EXPORT | IMPORT | LABOR | CAPITAL | TARIFF EQUIV |
|---|---|---|---|---|---|---|---|---|---|---|---|
| United States | 2622.8 100.2 | 2205.6 100.1 | 395.0 100.4 | 23.18 | 338.77 100.1 | 316.52 99.8 | 213.37 100.1 | 244.45 99.7 | 1703.4 100.3 | 410.0 100.1 | 10.16 |
| Japan | 1042.3 98.1 | 713.1 98.3 | 337.1 98.4 | -9.80 | 157.42 98.5 | 165.41 99.7 | 133.48 98.4 | 126.84 99.8 | 648.7 98.1 | 187.2 97.7 | 11.38 |

## DETAILED FEATURES OF SOLUTION

| | United States | | | | | Japan | | | | | Bilateral | |
|---|---|---|---|---|---|---|---|---|---|---|---|---|
| | PRICES | OUTPUT | DEMAND | EXPORT | IMPORT | PRICES | OUTPUT | DEMAND | EXPORT | IMPORT | US>JPN | JPN>US |
| Agriculture | 99.9 | 482.79 | 456.54 | 48.54 | 21.87 | 122.8 | 144.92 | 164.27 | 1.72 | 21.16 | 7.77 | 0.27 |
| Resources | 114.0 | 330.40 | 408.92 | 16.84 | 95.32 | 117.6 | 118.03 | 190.58 | 2.10 | 74.71 | 3.26 | 0.45 |
| Textiles | 100.2 | 111.73 | 119.38 | 5.87 | 13.56 | 98.3 | 56.49 | 53.93 | 5.92 | 3.40 | 0.22 | 0.49 |
| Paper, wood | 100.2 | 150.50 | 153.51 | 7.22 | 10.22 | 98.4 | 72.42 | 74.06 | 1.17 | 2.83 | 0.90 | 0.12 |
| Chemicals | 100.2 | 198.09 | 184.03 | 25.67 | 11.61 | 98.5 | 94.85 | 93.80 | 8.93 | 7.93 | 2.67 | 0.92 |
| Stone, clay | 100.2 | 45.68 | 48.21 | 2.34 | 4.87 | 98.6 | 40.89 | 40.10 | 1.79 | 1.01 | 0.13 | 0.50 |
| Steel | 100.2 | 86.49 | 90.48 | 3.47 | 7.60 | 98.7 | 125.70 | 111.02 | 15.44 | 0.77 | 0.06 | 2.38 |
| Metal products | 100.3 | 120.68 | 120.33 | 4.58 | 4.24 | 98.4 | 47.95 | 44.34 | 4.09 | 0.49 | 0.19 | 0.97 |
| Machinery | 100.3 | 203.49 | 179.09 | 43.06 | 18.75 | 98.3 | 118.00 | 99.51 | 22.45 | 3.96 | 1.97 | 3.71 |
| Electrical | 100.3 | 132.81 | 128.40 | 20.89 | 16.54 | 98.4 | 95.65 | 78.57 | 19.83 | 2.75 | 1.48 | 4.26 |
| Vehicles | 100.4 | 195.91 | 194.86 | 22.21 | 21.36 | 98.3 | 113.29 | 83.16 | 32.04 | 1.92 | 0.91 | 10.27 |
| Miscel mfg | 100.2 | 97.79 | 100.41 | 6.59 | 9.27 | 98.2 | 72.82 | 67.31 | 6.79 | 1.29 | 0.39 | 1.52 |
| Construction | 100.2 | 340.20 | 340.20 | | | 98.4 | 223.31 | 223.31 | | | | |
| Utilities | 100.1 | 195.09 | 195.09 | | | 98.6 | 45.78 | 45.78 | | | | |
| Trade serv | 100.2 | 570.40 | 570.40 | | | 98.1 | 201.22 | 201.22 | | | | |
| Finance | 100.2 | 188.19 | 188.19 | | | 98.1 | 70.82 | 70.82 | | | | |
| Real estate | 100.2 | 400.57 | 400.57 | | | 98.0 | 126.75 | 126.75 | | | | |
| Transport | 100.2 | 225.32 | 225.32 | | | 98.5 | 80.14 | 80.14 | | | | |
| Services | 100.2 | 591.34 | 591.34 | | | 98.2 | 376.80 | 376.80 | | | | |
| Freight | 100.2 | 20.30 | 22.64 | 3.71 | 6.04 | 98.5 | 18.48 | 15.26 | 7.37 | 4.16 | 0.00 | 0.00 |
| QUANTITY SUM | | | | 210.98 | 241.25 | | | | 129.66 | 126.36 | 19.95 | 25.86 |
| VALUE SUM | | | | 213.66 | 240.70 | | | | 128.41 | 126.63 | 20.42 | 25.60 |

Table B-14. Greater bilateral balance through Japanese import subsidy

## SUMMARY FEATURES OF SOLUTION

| | GDP | CONSUME | INVEST | CURRENT ACCOUNT | CREDIT | EXPORT | DEBIT | IMPORT | LABOR | CAPITAL | TARIFF EQUIV |
|---|---|---|---|---|---|---|---|---|---|---|---|
| United States | 2627.2 100.6 | 2210.5 100.6 | 395.9 100.5 | 23.17 | 342.00 100.4 | 216.60 100.5 | 321.21 99.7 | 249.14 99.5 | 1704.9 100.7 | 410.0 101.1 | 10.63 |
| Japan | 1040.2 93.9 | 708.3 94.4 | 334.8 95.0 | -9.87 | 167.23 95.7 | 143.29 95.3 | 170.22 99.8 | 131.65 100.3 | 649.1 94.7 | 187.1 94.4 | 0.74 |

## DETAILED FEATURES OF SOLUTION

| | United States | | | | | Japan | | | | | Bilateral | |
|---|---|---|---|---|---|---|---|---|---|---|---|---|
| | PRICES | OUTPUT | DEMAND | EXPORT | IMPORT | PRICES | OUTPUT | DEMAND | EXPORT | IMPORT | US>JPN | JPN>US |
| Agriculture | 100.7 | 482.88 | 456.41 | 49.89 | 23.41 | 114.8 | 143.75 | 165.45 | 1.51 | 23.01 | 11.55 | 0.23 |
| Resources | 114.4 | 330.82 | 409.50 | 16.86 | 95.45 | 117.1 | 118.62 | 191.64 | 2.10 | 75.16 | 3.28 | 0.45 |
| Textiles | 100.6 | 111.48 | 119.54 | 5.88 | 13.90 | 94.6 | 57.31 | 53.99 | 6.50 | 3.28 | 0.29 | 0.75 |
| Paper, wood | 100.6 | 150.98 | 153.65 | 7.68 | 10.34 | 94.2 | 73.36 | 75.21 | 1.28 | 3.17 | 1.38 | 0.17 |
| Chemicals | 100.6 | 199.31 | 184.54 | 26.45 | 11.66 | 95.2 | 95.68 | 94.71 | 9.57 | 8.63 | 3.57 | 1.14 |
| Stone, clay | 100.6 | 45.68 | 48.29 | 2.35 | 4.96 | 96.2 | 40.30 | 39.42 | 1.90 | 1.02 | 0.17 | 0.56 |
| Steel | 100.5 | 85.63 | 90.54 | 3.47 | 8.33 | 96.5 | 130.26 | 113.99 | 17.05 | 0.79 | 0.10 | 3.51 |
| Metal products | 100.5 | 121.18 | 120.78 | 4.64 | 4.24 | 95.7 | 47.69 | 43.92 | 4.40 | 0.62 | 0.34 | 1.17 |
| Machinery | 100.5 | 203.75 | 180.48 | 43.23 | 19.92 | 95.1 | 120.42 | 100.60 | 24.29 | 4.50 | 2.61 | 4.75 |
| Electrical | 100.5 | 133.18 | 129.28 | 21.02 | 17.09 | 95.2 | 97.65 | 79.24 | 21.56 | 3.15 | 1.89 | 5.33 |
| Vehicles | 100.4 | 195.23 | 196.12 | 22.64 | 23.50 | 95.0 | 119.72 | 84.75 | 37.23 | 2.28 | 1.36 | 14.28 |
| Miscel mfg | 100.6 | 97.09 | 100.63 | 6.43 | 9.94 | 94.7 | 74.13 | 67.68 | 7.76 | 1.31 | 0.46 | 2.15 |
| Construction | 100.6 | 340.48 | 340.48 | | | 95.3 | 221.21 | 221.21 | | | | |
| Utilities | 100.6 | 195.36 | 195.36 | | | 96.3 | 45.78 | 45.78 | | | | |
| Trade serv | 100.7 | 570.98 | 570.98 | | | 94.8 | 200.67 | 200.67 | | | | |
| Finance | 100.7 | 188.46 | 188.46 | | | 94.7 | 70.90 | 70.90 | | | | |
| Real estate | 100.8 | 400.61 | 400.61 | | | 94.7 | 125.85 | 125.85 | | | | |
| Transport | 100.7 | 225.58 | 225.58 | | | 95.7 | 79.89 | 79.89 | | | | |
| Services | 100.7 | 592.22 | 592.22 | | | 94.6 | 374.42 | 374.42 | | | | |
| Freight | 100.7 | 20.58 | 23.15 | 3.71 | 6.17 | 95.7 | 18.78 | 15.67 | 7.37 | 4.28 | 0.00 | 0.00 |
| QUANTITY SUM | | | | 214.24 | 248.93 | | | | 142.51 | 131.19 | 26.99 | 34.49 |
| VALUE SUM | | | | 217.79 | 247.73 | | | | 136.54 | 132.00 | 27.61 | 32.99 |

Table B-15. Greater bilateral balance through technology transfer

SUMMARY FEATURES OF SOLUTION

| | GDP | CONSUME | INVEST | CURRENT ACCOUNT | CREDIT | EXPORT | DEBIT | IMPORT | LABOR | CAPITAL | TARIFF EQUIV |
|---|---|---|---|---|---|---|---|---|---|---|---|
| United States | 2628.0 103.1 | 2213.4 103.0 | 396.4 102.9 | 23.34 | 332.98 101.9 | 207.58 102.5 | 314.84 100.3 | 242.77 99.7 | 1704.7 103.7 | 410.0 104.4 | 10.30 |
| Japan | 1038.1 95.8 | 708.3 96.2 | 334.8 96.4 | -9.92 | 157.65 96.8 | 133.71 96.6 | 162.69 99.9 | 124.12 100.4 | 649.2 95.4 | 187.1 94.9 | 8.07 |

DETAILED FEATURES OF SOLUTION

| | United States | | | | | Japan | | | | | Bilateral | |
|---|---|---|---|---|---|---|---|---|---|---|---|---|
| | PRICES | OUTPUT | DEMAND | EXPORT | IMPORT | PRICES | OUTPUT | DEMAND | EXPORT | IMPORT | US>JPN | JPN>US |
| Agriculture | 101.7 | 484.28 | 460.18 | 46.94 | 22.59 | 121.8 | 145.11 | 163.03 | 1.75 | 19.82 | 7.16 | 0.23 |
| Resources | 115.0 | 333.55 | 413.28 | 16.77 | 96.34 | 117.5 | 117.73 | 190.05 | 1.98 | 74.40 | 3.23 | 0.13 |
| Textiles | 103.1 | 111.09 | 119.73 | 5.61 | 14.09 | 96.2 | 56.77 | 53.80 | 6.19 | 3.30 | 0.21 | 0.56 |
| Paper, wood | 103.1 | 150.48 | 154.19 | 6.98 | 10.65 | 96.5 | 72.22 | 73.67 | 1.20 | 2.68 | 0.83 | 0.12 |
| Chemicals | 103.0 | 198.77 | 185.15 | 25.19 | 11.55 | 96.7 | 95.14 | 93.58 | 9.11 | 7.65 | 2.54 | 0.81 |
| Stone, clay | 103.0 | 45.84 | 48.48 | 2.28 | 4.91 | 97.1 | 40.27 | 39.49 | 1.76 | 0.98 | 0.13 | 0.42 |
| Steel | 102.8 | 87.14 | 91.49 | 3.35 | 7.63 | 97.3 | 126.98 | 111.67 | 16.04 | 0.74 | 0.04 | 2.64 |
| Metal products | 102.8 | 122.27 | 121.89 | 4.39 | 4.01 | 96.6 | 47.65 | 43.99 | 4.12 | 0.46 | 0.18 | 0.85 |
| Machinery | 103.0 | 204.50 | 181.92 | 41.85 | 19.21 | 96.3 | 118.79 | 99.43 | 23.11 | 3.79 | 1.88 | 3.57 |
| Electrical | 103.0 | 134.35 | 130.05 | 20.13 | 15.83 | 96.4 | 95.73 | 78.33 | 20.07 | 2.68 | 1.43 | 3.90 |
| Vehicles | 102.9 | 198.47 | 196.95 | 21.69 | 20.11 | 96.3 | 114.12 | 82.98 | 32.94 | 1.83 | 0.85 | 10.46 |
| Miscel mfg | 103.3 | 97.43 | 100.76 | 6.29 | 9.59 | 96.1 | 73.18 | 67.13 | 7.27 | 1.24 | 0.38 | 1.62 |
| Construction | 103.2 | 340.69 | 340.69 | | | 96.4 | 221.67 | 221.67 | | | | |
| Utilities | 102.7 | 196.81 | 196.81 | | | 97.1 | 45.62 | 45.62 | | | | |
| Trade serv | 103.6 | 570.51 | 570.51 | | | 95.6 | 201.25 | 201.25 | | | | |
| Finance | 103.6 | 188.25 | 188.25 | | | 95.6 | 71.02 | 71.02 | | | | |
| Real estate | 103.7 | 399.54 | 399.54 | | | 95.5 | 126.25 | 126.25 | | | | |
| Transport | 103.4 | 225.76 | 225.76 | | | 96.6 | 79.81 | 79.81 | | | | |
| Services | 103.4 | 592.50 | 592.50 | | | 95.9 | 374.81 | 374.81 | | | | |
| Freight | 103.4 | 20.44 | 22.83 | 3.71 | 6.09 | 96.6 | 18.29 | 15.01 | 7.37 | 4.10 | 0.00 | 0.00 |
| QUANTITY SUM | | | | 205.19 | 242.61 | | | | 132.91 | 123.67 | 18.84 | 25.52 |
| VALUE SUM | | | | 212.75 | 241.97 | | | | 129.09 | 124.63 | 19.70 | 24.74 |

# Data Sources and Methods

## National Accounts (1960, 1970, 1980)

National income and expenditure data were imposed as controls over the model's entire accounting system. These data are primarily derived from the standard national-accounts statistics of the United States and Japan, complemented with additional balance-of-payments data. On the expenditure side, consumption includes both private and public consumption; investment (fixed investment plus additions to stocks) includes private capital formation in the United States, and both public and private capital formation in Japan. The international components of the national accounts were further disaggregated into the elements shown in Table 4.5 with balance-of-payments data, as reported in International Monetary Fund publications. This data source permitted the estimation of various categories of nonmerchandise trade, including direct trade in factor services. Special balance-of-payments data, published by both the United States and Japan, also made it possible to separate Japanese-American bilateral transactions from the overall transactions of the two economies.

On the income side, returns to labor include compensation of employees plus imputed labor earnings which are usually treated as part of business income (proprietors' and self-employed workers' income, chiefly from farm and service industry sources). The imputations were obtained by multiplying numbers of workers who were not employees by an estimated wage rate. Returns to capital consist of all other income except indi-

rect business taxes and depreciation expenses. The latter were estimated using sector-specific capital requirements (see below) and depreciation rates and are not generally equal to accounting depreciation.

Major Sources Used

Bank of Japan, Statistics Department, *Economic Statistics Annual.* Various years.

International Monetary Fund. *International Financial Statistics.* Various issues.

———— *Balance of Payments Yearbook.* Various years.

Japan Bureau of Statistics, *Japan Statistical Yearbook.* Various years.

U.S. Department of Commerce, Bureau of Economic Analysis. 1981. *The National Income and Product Accounts of the United States, 1929–1976 Statistical Tables.*

———— National Income and Product Accounts. *Survey of Current Business.* Various issues.

**International Trade (1960–1980)**

Time-series trade statistics, mainly from Organization of Economic Cooperation and Development publications, were used to disaggregate national-accounts merchandise trade totals into sectoral trade. The sector-SITC (Standard International Trade Classification) correspondence is given in Table 3.1. The OECD provides data in current dollar values on a "freight-on-board" (for exports and U.S. imports) or "cost, insurance, freight" (for Japanese imports) basis. The model requires FOB data; to convert CIF imports into FOB terms, FOB/CIF ratios were calculated for each type of import using the detailed information available in the nearest input-output table (see sources below). The trade data were converted to constant dollar terms, when required, using the price indexes described below.

For bilateral trade, the statistics of the importing country were used. Exports of the rest of the world to the rest of the world (ROW-ROW trade) were estimated in a two-step process. First, data were collected on OECD (excluding the United States and Japan) exports and imports. The larger of the two values was

used as a preliminary estimate of ROW-ROW trade. Benchmark observations, based on United Nations global trade data, then provided sector-by-sector multipliers for inflating these figures into final estimates of ROW-ROW trade.

Major Sources Used
Organization of Economic Cooperation and Development. *Trade by Commodities.* Various years.
United Nations, Statistical Office 1966. Classification of Commodities by Industrial Origin. *Statistical Papers,* series M, no. 43.
United Nations Conference on Trade and Development. Various years. *Trade and Development Statistics.* Geneva: UNCTAD.

### Output Levels (1960–1980)

Annual output data were required to calculate the market share time series. The output data were also imposed as controls over the benchmark input-output systems, as described below. Input-output compatible output series were available from unpublished Bureau of Labor Statistics data for the United States, and from unpublished Keio University data for Japan. Outputs were available in both current and constant dollars and were thus also used to derive producers' price time series.

Major Sources Used
U.S. Department of Labor, Bureau of Labor Statistics. Unpublished Input-Output Data Set.
Keio University, Economic Observatory. Unpublished Input-Output Data Set.

### Input-Output Systems (1960, 1970, 1980)

Interindustry and final transactions, excluding exports and imports, were estimated using input-output data. For the period relevant to this study, U.S. data were available for 1958, 1963, 1967, and 1972 and Japanese data for 1960, 1965, 1970, and 1975. The input-output tables were aggregated to the sectoring

plan of the study according to the correspondence schemes shown in Table 4.1. Dummy sectors (for example, office supplies) were eliminated before aggregation. The value-added rows of the tables were modified as described under factor requirements below, although total value addeds — the row sum of the separate value-added rows — were not changed.

Tables for the benchmark years of this study (1960, 1970, and 1980) were constructed by modifying a "model" transactions table as needed to meet actual controls. The RAS method used accomplishes this while minimizing the sum of the squared adjustments made to individual cells of the model table. The controls were constructed as follows. Row controls (economy-wide demands for individual products) were computed by adding net imports to output, both of which were annually estimated as described above. Column controls (total inputs by sector and total final demand by component) were obtained from output and national-account time series. The model tables used were derived as a weighted average of the tables surrounding each benchmark year. The most recent table available was used as the model in the case of the 1980 benchmark year.

Major Sources Used

Goldman, M. R., M. L. Marimont, and B. N. Vaccara. 1964. The Interindustry Structure of the United States: A Report on the 1958 Input-Output Study. *Survey of Current Business* 44 (11):10–29.

Government of Japan, Office of Statistical Standards. 1970. *Revised Input-Output Table for 1960 and Table for 1965 in 1965 Prices.* Tokyo: Government of Japan.

——— 1982. *Link Input-Output Tables for 1965–1970–1975.* Tokyo: Government of Japan.

Ritz, P. M. 1979. The Input-Output Structure of the U.S. Economy: 1972. *Survey of Current Business* 59 (2):34–72.

Ritz, P. M., E. P. Roberts, and P. C. Young. 1979. Dollar-Value Tables for the 1972 Input-Output Study. *Survey of Current Business* 59 (4):51–72.

U.S. Department of Commerce, Interindustry Economics Division. 1974. The Input-Output Structure of the U.S. Economy: 1967. *Survey of Current Business* 54 (2):24–56.

————, National Economics Division. 1969. Input-Output Structure of the U.S. Economy: 1963. *Survey of Current Business* 49 (11):16–47.

## Factor Requirements (1960, 1970, 1980)

Input-output tables provide, at best, value data on factor inputs. This information is especially difficult to use in the case of capital, since profits include scarcity rents and thus do not accurately reflect the capital stock actually employed. Labor and capital requirements were therefore added to the input-output system from alternative sources. U.S. information on employment came from the Bureau of Labor Statistics data set cited in the output description. U.S. capital stock information was pieced together from published and unpublished work by the Department of Labor and subsequently the Department of Commerce. Japanese employment and capital stock data came from the Keio Economic Observatory data already cited. Employment is given in full-time equivalent persons; capital is measured in terms of gross stocks.

The value-added rows of the input-output system were modified using this information to achieve closer conformity to theoretical concepts of labor and capital. The depreciation row was replaced by estimates derived by applying sectoral depreciation rates (the sector's capital was disaggregated into equipment, vehicles, and plant, with lifetimes of 5, 10, and 50 years assigned to the three categories) to the sector's total capital requirements. Imputed earnings of self-employed workers were transferred from capital income to labor income by multiplying a row of persons employed who were not employees by two-thirds of the wage rates of workers who were employees.

Major Sources Used

U.S. Department of Commerce, Bureau of Industrial Economics, unpublished capital stock data set.

U.S. Department of Labor, Bureau of Labor Statistics. 1979. *Capital Stock Estimates for Input-Output Industries: Methods and Data.*

## Prices (1960–1980)

Price data were required on an annual basis for the United States, Japan, and the rest of the world for estimating the market share relationships of the model. For the United States and Japan, sectoral producers' price indexes were derived from input-output-related production data; the sources included the previously cited Bureau of Labor Statistics and Keio Economic Observatory data sets. The Japanese data were extended to cover the 1979–1980 period with Bank of Japan statistics published in the Economic Statistics Annual cited above.

Rest-of-the-world producers' price data were pieced together from detailed statistics from several major exporting economies. The principal countries included France, Germany, Italy, the Netherlands, Sweden, and the United Kingdom. For light manufactures, the indexes also included data from Brazil, Korea, Pakistan, and Taiwan. The composite price indexes were built up from the most detailed information published in the country statistical yearbooks cited below and were calculated using export values as weights. Country prices were translated into dollars using the year's average market exchange rate. Since sector and year coverage are incomplete for several countries, the indexes were constructed in a chained manner; each year's price movement was calculated using export weights appropriate to that year.

Major Sources Used

Government of Pakistan, Statistics Division. 1980. *Pakistan Statistical Yearbook 1979*. Karachi: Manager of Publications.

Istituto Centrale di Statistica. 1980. *Annuario Statistico Italiano*. Rome: Government of Italy.

Lawrence, E., ed. 1980. *Annual Abstract of Statistics*. London: Her Majesty's Stationery Office.

Ministère de l'Economie, Institut National de la Statistique et des Etudes Economiques. 1980. *Annuaire Statistique de la France 1980*, vol. 85. Paris: Government of France.

National Central Bureau of Statistics. 1980. *Statistical Abstract of Sweden*. Stockholm: Norstedts Tryckeri.

Netherlands Central Bureau of Statistics. 1980. *Statistical Yearbook of the Netherlands 1980*. The Hague: Staatsuitgeverij.

Statistisches Bundesamt. 1980. *Statistisches Jahrbuch 1980 für die Bundesrepublik Deutschland*. Stuttgart: Kohlhammer.

United Nations, Economic and Social Commission for Asia and the Pacific. 1979. *Statistical Yearbook for Asia and the Pacific 1978*. Bangkok: United Nations.

Wilke, J. W., ed. 1980. *Statistical Abstract of Latin America*, vol. 20. Los Angeles: UCLA Latin American Center.

# Notes

## 1. Objectives and Methods

1. A perceptive and good-humored survey of various lines of "miracle" research is given by Johnson (1982), who himself attributes much of Japan's success to sophisticated guidance by the Ministry of International Trade and Industry.

2. For analysis up to the mid-1970s see Denison and Chung (1976) and Jorgenson and Nishimizu (1978). Data up to 1978, which are analyzed in Napier and Petri (1979), suggest that Japanese total factor productivity growth declined from 6.9 percent over the 1960–1970 period to 2.0 percent over the 1970–1977 period.

3. In the case of blouses, for example, imports grew from 48,000 to 47 million (one for each woman of blouse-wearing age) in just three years (Hunsberger, 1972).

4. Quoted by Destler and Sato (1982), p. 5, from an interview in the *Washington Post,* 2 November 1980.

## 2. Theory and Structure

1. The problem is partly conceptual and partly practical. The conceptual difficulty stems from the diverse nature of products in different economies: not only is it difficult to find truly equivalent prices, but it is also hard to derive meaningful aggregates at a sectoral level. The practical problem, of course, is the enormous data collection effort needed to develop price relatives; until the work of Kravis and Lipsey (1971) and Kravis, Heston, and Summers (1978), such information was simply not available on a systematic basis.

2. In the present model (Table 2.3) $B$ is related to income and foreign prices. This also implies full homogeneity and means that a

price-normalization equation is required for a closed-world equilibrium system.

3. The precise assumption needed is that the production functions are homogeneous and identical up to a scalar multiple. This means that all products use the same combination of inputs and vary only in terms of the efficiency with which inputs are converted to output.

4. A system with free cross-price effects, for example, requires, at a minimum, $N(N + 1)$ parameters. This can be reduced by applying symmetry and homogeneity constraints to $N(N - 1)/2$ parameters — about 190 in the present case. All of these would have to be estimated with only four observations of input-output tables in the United States, and five observations in Japan.

5. These own-price elasticities represent only the first, direct layer of price effects; in the complete input-output framework, indirect substitution effects will also occur through changes in the economy's product mix toward cheaper products.

6. The formulation implicitly assumes that the domestic transportation costs of internationally traded products are the same as the transportation costs of shipping domestic products to domestic users. Domestic transport margins are treated as purchases of transport services by the consuming sector.

7. In conventional terminology, consumers' prices include all transport and trade markups. In this context, the term refers to prices that include only markups involved in international trade — international transport costs, tariffs, and tariff equivalents — but not domestic trade and transport margins.

### 3. The Trade Share Functions

1. The problem is extensively treated in the modern econometric literature, but a classic early contribution deals specifically with the problem of import demand (Orcutt, 1950).

2. The nature of the path would be irrelevant if the demand system strictly maintained Slutsky symmetry. The double logarithmic form, however, is only symmetric at base-period prices.

3. This procedure approximately amounts to first changing the relative price 2 halfway to its final value, then changing the relative price 1 from its initial to its final value, and finally completing the change in relative price 2.

4. Strictly speaking, consumption demand also faces this problem when there is more than one consumer.

5. Large distortions could result if trend were attributed to income elasticity. When income grows at 2 percent, a plausible trend trade growth of 10 percent, for example, would yield the unlikely income elasticity of 5.

6. These statistics are very similar for the sample without priors;

the high $t$-ratios do not reflect the precision of the prior, but rather close correspondence between prior and data.

7. The agriculture and natural resource elasticities were derived by simulating the model for excess demand changes associated with particular price changes. For the determination of trade in the agriculture and natural resource sectors, see Chapters 2 and 4.

### 4. Implementing the System

1. Consistency is imposed in the following order: national accounts, trade, outputs and prices, input-output coefficients. Items low on this list are adjusted by commonsense methods (usually methods to minimize change from observed values) to meet control values from sources higher on the list.

2. Simple versions of step-modifying methods have been studied formally (Ortega and Rheinboldt, 1970).

3. It is possible to save computation time by not calculating a fresh inverse at each iteration. An option in our computer program permitted this to happen when convergence was proceeding rapidly. Alternatively, the inverse can be "refreshed" from solution data (Powell, 1970).

4. U.S.–Canadian auto trade represents shipments among different manufacturing establishments of the same firm and is governed by extensive intergovernmental agreements.

5. Factor services are valued at the factor prices of their place of employment. Exogenous goods, like other goods, are valued at the prices of the economy that produces them.

### 5. The Structure of Interdependence

1. The one-sector model of Figure 2.3 can be written as max $c(m, e)$ subject to $m = pe$; or simply as $c(pe, X - e)$, where $c =$ welfare derived from consumption, $p =$ import price/export price (terms of trade), $m =$ imports, $e =$ exports, $X =$ production. Totally differentiating this welfare function yields $\partial c / \partial p = c_1 e \cdot dp + (c_1 p - c_2) de$, where $c_1$ and $c_2$ are the derivatives of $c$ with respect to its first and second arguments. The second term vanishes because the quantity in parentheses is zero at the optimum consumption point, leaving the welfare effect: $c_1 e \cdot dp$. Assuming that the marginal utility of a good is proportional to its price, the expression is simply the value of exports times the change in terms of trade.

2. The degree of openness and the elasticity of current account transactions are not independent. The more open an economy, the harder it is to change its export prices relative to world prices because external prices also enter as input costs. For example, the export price effects of a 10-percent real depreciation (defined in terms of the GNP

deflator) of the dollar were 7.4, 6.9, and 6.3 percent, respectively, in the 1960, 1970, and 1980 benchmark systems.

3. If the system were linear, the sum of the component changes shown in Figure 5.8 would very nearly approximate the overall change in the openness of the two economies. Because of nonlinearities and omitted effects, a discrepancy remains between actual change and change accounted for by the factors shown.

### 6. Sectoral Dimensions of Trade

1. These were computed from two input-output tables which had been adjusted to 1970 relative prices using the price elasticity estimates given in Table 4.2. All remaining differences between the tables are assumed to represent technological change, and the value of these changes in each column is summed using both first and second period prices, respectively (usually, the valuations were quite close). The geometric means of these two sets of indexes are used as measures of sectoral technical progress.

2. Like Leontief's original work, this measure does not include human capital. For these and other extensions of the approach, see Baldwin (1971).

3. Another way to put this is that real devaluation is actually taking place because true (unseen) prices are falling relative to foreign prices. This is not plausible, however, because it also suggests that real GNP is also growing much faster than measured. International comparisons provide no evidence of this in cross section. Of course, they too could be fooled by quality differences!

4. Clearing world markets for agriculture and natural resources did require price changes. Product prices "pass through" the effects of these price changes in both the U.S. and Japanese economies.

### 7. Alternatives in Commercial Policy

1. The recent literature on rent seeking (Bhagwati and Srinivasan, 1980; Brock and Magee, 1978) provides a framework for rigorously exploring these issues. With some effort, the model could be extended to reflect these influences.

2. A proportional decrease in tariffs implies that larger tariffs fall by a larger absolute amount; if all commodities have the same price elasticities, those with larger tariffs will therefore expand relative to those with smaller initial shares. Thus, the average tariff will not fall as rapidly as any individual tariff.

3. Japanese plywood standards, as an example, are stated in terms of the technology of construction rather than in terms of functional requirements. Because American plywood is made of softwoods rather than hardwoods, it is constructed differently, and though functionally

equivalent, it cannot pass Japanese standards (Japan Economic Institute, 1982b).

4. The elasticities (percentage change in imports/percentage change in exports) of the offer curves facing the United States range from −0.06 to −0.16, and of those facing Japan from 0.24 to 0.31.

5. The ERP formula used was

$$\frac{t_j - \Sigma_i A_{ij} t_i}{1 - \Sigma_i A_{ij}},$$

where  $t$ = nominal tariff rate,
   $A$ = value input coefficients.

6. This question is explored in an unpublished study by the Trade Study Group, a bilateral organization of businessmen and government officials in Tokyo. The work is described in Japan Economic Institute (1982).

# References

Abegglen, J. C., and W. V. Rapp. 1972. The Competitive Impact of Japanese Growth. In *Pacific Partnership: United States – Japan Trade, Prospects and Recommendations for the Seventies,* ed. J. B. Cohen. Lexington, Mass.: D. C. Heath.

Adelman, I., and S. Robinson. 1978. *Income Distribution Policy in Developing Countries.* Stanford: Stanford University Press.

Almon, C., et al. 1974. *1985: Interindustry Forecasts of the American Economy.* Lexington: D. C. Heath.

Armington, P. S. 1969. A Theory of Products Distinguished by Place of Production. *IMF Staff Papers* 16:159–177.

———1973. A Note on the Income-Compensated Price Elasticities of Demand Used in the Multilateral Exchange Rate Model. *IMF Staff Papers* 20:612–616.

Baldwin, R. E. 1971. Determinants of the Commodity Structure of U.S. Trade. *American Economic Review* 61:126–147.

———1982. The Political Economy of Protectionism. In *Import Competition and Response,* ed. J. N. Bhagwati. Chicago: University of Chicago Press.

Baranson, J. 1981. *The Japanese Challenge to U.S. Industry.* Lexington: D. C. Heath.

Barten, A., and V. Bohm. 1982. Consumer Theory. In *Handbook of Mathematical Economics,* vol. 2, ed. K. J. Arrow and M. D. Intriligator. Amsterdam: North-Holland.

Bhagwati, J. N., and T. N. Srinivasan. 1969. Optimal Intervention to Achieve Non-economic Objectives. *Review of Economic Studies* 36:27–38.

Blitzer, C. R., P. B. Clark, and L. Taylor. 1975. *Economy-wide Models and Development Planning.* London: Oxford University Press.

Boadway, R., and J. Treddenick. 1978. A General Equilibrium Com-

putation of the Effects of the Canadian Tariff Structure. *Canadian Journal of Economics* 11:424–446.

Branson, W. H. 1972. The Trade Effects of the 1971 Currency Realignments. *Brookings Papers on Economic Activity* 1972(1):15–70.

Brock, W. A., and S. P. Magee. 1978. The Economics of Special Interest Politics: The Case of Tariffs. *American Economic Review* 68:246–250.

Bruno, M. 1966. A Programming Model for Israel. In *The Theory and Design of Economic Development,* ed. I. Adelman and E. Thorbecke. Baltimore: Johns Hopkins Press.

————1967. Optimal Patterns of Trade and Development. *Review of Economics and Statistics* 49:545–554.

Chenery, H. B., and K. Kretschmer. 1956. Resource Allocation for Economic Development. *Econometrica* 24:365–399.

Christ, C. F. 1966. *Econometric Models and Methods.* New York: Wiley.

Christensen, L. R., D. W. Jorgenson, and L. J. Lau. 1975. Transcendental Logarithmic Utility Functions. *American Economic Review* 65:367–383.

Cline, W. R., et al. 1978. *Trade Negotiations in the Tokyo Round: A Quantitative Assessment.* Washington, D.C.: The Brookings Institution.

Cochrane, D., and G. H. Orcutt. 1949. Application of Least-Square Regressions to Relationships Containing Auto-Correlated Error Terms. *Journal of the American Statistical Association* 44:32–61.

Committee on Ways and Means (U.S. House of Representatives). 1979. *Task Force Report on United States–Japan Trade with Additional Views.* Washington, D.C.: Government Printing Office.

Deardorff, A. V., and R. M. Stern. 1981. A Disaggregated Model of World Production and Trade: An Estimate of the Impact of the Tokyo Round. *Journal of Policy Modelling* 3(2):127–152.

Denison, E. F., and W. K. Chung, 1976. *How Japan's Economy Grew So Fast: The Sources of the Postwar Expansion.* Washington: Brookings Institution.

deMelo, J., and K. Dervis. 1977. Modelling the Effects of Protection in a Dynamic Framework. *Journal of Development Economics* 4:149–172.

Dervis, K., J. deMelo, and S. Robinson. 1982. *General Equilibrium Models for Development Policy.* Cambridge: Cambridge University Press.

Destler, I. M., and H. Sato. 1982. *Coping with U.S.–Japanese Economic Conflicts.* Lexington: D. C. Heath.

Dorfman, R., P. A. Samuelson, and R. Solow. 1958. *Linear Programming for Economic Analysis.* New York: McGraw-Hill.

Economic Planning Agency. 1973. *Economic Survey of Japan.* Tokyo: The Japan Times.

Evans, H. D. 1972. *A General Equilibrium Analysis of Protection.* Amsterdam: North-Holland.

Feltenstein, A. 1981. A General-Equilibrium Approach to the Analysis of Monetary and Fiscal Policies. *IMF Staff Papers* 28:749–784.

General Accounting Office. 1979. *United States–Japan Trade: Issues and Problems.* Washington, D.C.: General Accounting Office.

Geraci, V. J., and W. Prewo. 1982. An Empirical Demand and Supply Model of Trade. *Review of Economics and Statistics* 64:432–441.

Ginsburgh, V. A., and J. L. Waelbroeck. 1981. *Activity Analysis and General Equilibrium Modelling.* Amsterdam: North-Holland.

Goldstein, M., and M. S. Khan. 1976. Large versus Small Price Changes and the Demand for Imports. *IMF Staff Papers* 23:200–225.

Goldstein, M., M. S. Khan, and L. Officer. 1980. Prices of Tradable and Nontradable Goods in the Demand for Total Imports. *Review of Economics and Statistics* 62:190–199.

Gunning, J. W., et al. 1982. Growth and Trade in Developing Countries: A General Equilibrium Analysis. Discussion Paper no. 8210, Centre d'Economie Mathématique et d'Econométrie. Université Libre de Bruxelles.

Hausman, J. A. 1978. Specification Tests in Econometrics. *Econometrica* 46:1251–71.

Haynes, S. E., and J. A. Stone. 1983. Secular and Cyclical Responses of U.S. Trade to Income: An Evaluation of Traditional Models. *Review of Economics and Statistics* 65:87–95.

Heller, P. S. 1976. Factor Endowment Change and Comparative Advantage. *Review of Economics and Statistics* 58:283–292.

Hildreth, G., and J. Y. Lu. 1960. Demand Relations with Auto-Correlated Disturbances. Michigan State University Agricultural Experiment Station, Technical Bulletin no. 276.

Houthakker, H. S., and S. P. Magee. 1969. Income and Price Elasticities in World Trade. *Review of Economics and Statistics* 51:111–125.

Hudson, E. A., and D. W. Jorgenson. 1974. U.S. Energy Policy and Economic Growth, 1975–2000. *Bell Journal of Management Science* 5:461–514.

Hufbauer, G. C. 1970. The Impact of National Characteristics and Technology on the Commodity Composition of Trade in Manufactured Goods. In *The Technology Factor in International Trade*, ed. R. Vernon. New York: Columbia University Press.

Hunsberger, W. S. 1972. Japan–United States Trade — Patterns, Relationships, Problems. In *Pacific Partnership: United States–Japan Trade, Prospects and Recommendations for the Seventies*, ed. J. B. Cohen. Lexington, Mass.: D. C. Heath.

Ichikawa, H. 1981. The Liberalization of Japan's Foreign Trade and

Foreign Exchange Transactions. In *Appendix to the Report of the Japan–United States Study Group*. Washington, D.C.: Japan–United States Study Group.

Japan Economic Institute. 1982a. *Yearbook of U.S. –Japan Economic Relations*. Washington, D.C.: Japan Economic Institute.

———1982b. *Japan's Import Barriers, An Analysis of Divergent Bilateral Views*. Washington, D.C.: Japan Economic Institute.

Japan–United States Economic Relations Group. 1981a. *Report*. Washington, D.C.: Japan–United States Economic Relations Group.

———1981b. *Supplemental Report*. Washington, D.C.: Japan–United States Economic Relations Group.

———1981c. *Appendix to the Report*. Washington, D.C.: Japan–United States Economic Relations Group.

Johansen, L. 1960. *A Multi-Sectoral Study of Economic Growth*. Amsterdam: North-Holland.

———1973. *Multi-Sectoral Study of Economic Growth: Second Enlarged Edition*. Amsterdam: North-Holland.

Johnson, C. 1982. *MITI and the Japanese Miracle: The Growth of Industrial Policy, 1925–1975*. Stanford: Stanford University Press.

Jorgenson, D. W. 1983. *Econometric Methods for Applied General Equilibrium Modeling*. Cambridge, Mass.: Harvard Institute for Economic Research. Mimeo.

Jorgenson, D. W., and M. Nishimizu. 1978. U.S. and Japanese Economic Growth, 1952–1974. *Economic Journal* 88:707–726.

Joy, J., and J. D. Stolen. 1975. The Change in the U.S. Import Demand Function from the 1950's to the 1960's. *Review of Economics and Statistics* 57:109–111.

Kaplan, E. J. 1972. *Japan, The Government-Business Relationship: A Guide for the American Businessman*. Washington, D.C.: U.S. Department of Commerce, Bureau of International Commerce.

Kawanabe, N. 1978. Disaggregated Import Demand Functions for Japan. In *Trade Negotiations in the Tokyo Round: A Quantitative Assessment*, ed. W. R. Cline et al. Washington, D.C.: Brookings Institution.

Keesing, D. 1966. Labor Skills and International Trade: Evaluating Many Trade Flows with a Single Measuring Device. *Review of Economics and Statistics* 47:287–293.

Klein, L. R. 1972. Comments on Branson, 1972: The Trade Effects of the 1971 Currency Realignments. *Brookings Papers on Economic Activity* 1972 (1):59–65.

Kravis, I. B., and R. E. Lipsey. 1971. *Price Competitiveness in World Trade*. National Bureau of Economic Research Studies in International Economic Relations, no. 6. New York: Columbia University Press.

Kravis, I. B., A. Heston, and R. Summers. 1978. *International Compari-*

*sons of Real Product and Purchasing Power*. Baltimore: Johns Hopkins University Press.

———1982. *World Product and Income: International Comparisons of Real GDP*. Baltimore: Johns Hopkins University Press.

Leamer, E. E. 1980. The Leontief Paradox Reconsidered. *Journal of Political Economy* 88:495–503.

Leamer, E. E., and R. M. Stern. 1970. *Quantitative International Economics*. Boston: Allyn and Bacon.

Leontief, W. W. 1947. Introduction to the Theory of the Internal Structure of Functional Relationships. *Econometrica* 15:361–373.

———1953. Domestic Production and Foreign Trade: The American Capital Position Reexamined. Reprinted in *International Trade*, ed. J. Bhagwati. Harmondsworth: Penguin.

———1956. Factor Proportions and the Structure of American Trade: Further Theoretical and Empirical Analysis. *Review of Economics and Statistics* 38:386–407.

———1973. Explanatory Power of the Comparative Cost Theory of International Trade and Its Limits. In *Economic Structure and Development*, Lectures in Honor of Jan Tinbergen, ed. H. C. Bos. Amsterdam: North-Holland.

Manne, A. S. 1974. Multi-Sector Models for Development Planning: A Survey. *Journal of Development Economics* 1:43–69.

McKenzie, L. 1956. Specialization in Production. *Review of Economic Studies* 23(1):56–64.

Monroe, W. 1973. Technical Considerations of United States–Japan Trade and Payments. In *Perspectives on U.S.–Japan Economic Relations*, ed. A. Taylor. Cambridge, Mass.: Ballinger.

———1982. *Toward a More Viable U.S.–Japan Trade Relationship*. Washington, D.C.: Japan Economic Institute.

Murray, T., and P. J. Ginman. 1976. An Empirical Examination of the Traditional Aggregate Import Demand Model. *Review of Economics and Statistics* 58:75–80.

Nadiri, M. I. 1982. Producer's Theory. In *Handbook of Mathematical Economics*, vol. 2, ed. K. J. Arrow and M. D. Intriligator. Amsterdam: North-Holland.

Nakamura, T. 1981. *The Postwar Japanese Economy: Its Development and Structure*. Tokyo: University of Tokyo Press.

Napier, R. W., and P. A. Petri. 1979. U.S.–Japan Trade Conflict: The Prospects Ahead: A Report to the Department of State. Washington, D.C.: Department of State. Mimeo.

Nyhus, D. E. 1975. The Trade Model of a Dynamic World Input-Output Forecasting System. Ph.D. diss., University of Maryland.

Orcutt, G. H. 1950. Measurement of Price Elasticities in International Trade. *Review of Economics and Statistics* 32:117–132.

Ortega, J. M., and W. C. Rheinboldt. 1970. *Iterative Solution of Nonlinear Equations in Several Variables*. New York: Academic Press.

Ozaki, R. S. 1972. *The Control of Imports and Foreign Capital in Japan.* New York: Praeger.

Petri, P. A. 1976a. A Multilateral Model of Japanese-American Trade. In *Advances in Input-Output Analysis,* ed. K. Polenske and J. Skolka. Cambridge, Mass.: Ballinger.

———1976b. A Detailed Model of Japanese-American Trade. Ph.D. diss., Harvard University.

———1979. An Algebraic Framework for Interregional Modelling. *Journal of Regional Science* 19:449–459.

———1980. A Ricardian Model of Intra-Sectoral Market Sharing. *Journal of International Economics* 10:201–211.

Powell, M. J. D. 1970. A Hybrid Method for Nonlinear Equations. In *Numerical Methods for Nonlinear Algebraic Equations,* ed. P. Rabinowitz. New York: Gordon and Breach Science Publishers.

Quirk, P. J. 1979. Japan's Balance of Payments: Analytic Approach to the Experience of the 1970's and the Synthesis for Medium-Projections. Washington, D.C.: IMF Departmental Memoranda Series.

Rabinowitz, P., ed. 1970. *Numerical Methods for Nonlinear Algebraic Equations.* New York: Gordon and Breach Science Publishers.

Reich, R., and I. C. Magaziner. 1982. *Minding America's Business: The Decline and Rise of the American Economy.* New York: Harcourt Brace Jovanovich.

Ricardo, D. 1817. *The Principles of Political Economy and Taxation.* Reprinted, Baltimore: Penguin, 1971.

Richardson, J. D. 1976. Some Issues in the Structural Determination of International Price Responsiveness. In *Quantitative Studies of International Economic Relations,* ed. H. Glejser. Amsterdam: North-Holland.

Sawyer, J. A. 1979. *Modeling the International Transmission Mechanism.* Amsterdam: North-Holland.

Saxonhouse, G., and E. Sakakibara. 1981. Cyclical and Macro-Structural Issues in U.S.–Japanese Economic Relations. In *Appendix to the Report,* Japan–United States Economic Relations Group. Washington, D.C.: Japan–United States Economic Relations Group.

Scarf, H. (with T. Hansen). 1973. *The Computation of Economic Equilibria.* New Haven: Yale University Press.

Shoven, J. B., and J. Whalley. 1972. On the Computation of Competitive Equilibrium on International Markets with Tariffs. *Journal of International Economics* 4:341–354.

———1983. Applied General Equilibrium Models of Taxation and International Trade. Palo Alto: National Bureau of Economic Research. Mimeo.

Solow, R. M. 1956. The Production Function and the Theory of Capital. *Review of Economic Studies* 23(2):101–108.

Stone, J. A. 1979. Price Elasticities of Demand for Imports and Exports: Industry Estimates for the U.S., the E.E.C. and Japan. *Review of Economics and Statistics,* 61:306–312.

Stone, J. R. 1954. Linear Expenditure System and Demand Analysis: Application to the Pattern of British Demand. *Economic Journal* 64:511–527.

Strotz, R. H. 1957. The Empirical Implications of a Utility Tree. *Econometrica* 25:269–280.

Taylor, A., ed. 1973. *Perspectives on U.S.–Japan Economic Relations.* Cambridge, Mass.: Ballinger.

Taylor, L. 1975. Theoretical Foundations and Technical Implications. In *Economy-Wide Models and Development Planning,* ed. C. R. Blitzer, P. B. Clark, and L. Taylor. London: Oxford University Press.

Taylor, L., and S. L. Black. 1974. Practical General Equilibrium Estimation of Resource Pulls under Trade Liberalization. *Journal of International Economics* 4:37–58.

Theil, H. 1963. On the Use of Incomplete Prior Information in Regression Analysis. *Journal of the American Statistical Association* 58:401–414.

Theil, H., and A. S. Goldberger. 1961. On Pure and Mixed Statistic Estimation in Economics. *International Economic Review* 2:65–79.

Tsujimura, K., M. Kuroda, and H. Shimada. 1981. *Economic Policy and General Interdependence: A Quantitative Theory of Price and Empirical Model Building.* Tokyo: Kogakusha.

Turner, C. G. 1981. Quantitative Restrictions on the International Trade of the United States and Japan. Ph.D. diss., Harvard University.

Vanek, J. 1959. The Natural Resource Content of Foreign Trade, 1870–1955, and the Relative Abundance of Natural Resources in the United States. *Review of Economics and Statistics* 41:146–153.

Vernon, R. 1981. Alternatives to the GATT framework. In *Annual Report Program on U.S.–Japan Relations, 1980–1981.* Cambridge, Mass.: Center for International Affairs, Harvard University.

Wait, R. 1979. *The Numerical Solution of Algebraic Equations.* New York: Wiley.

Warner, D., and M. Kreinin. 1983. Determinants of International Trade Flows. *Review of Economics and Statistics* 65:96–104.

Werin, L. 1965. *A Study of Production, Trade and Allocation of Resources.* Stockholm: Almquist and Wiksell.

Whalley, J. Forthcoming. An Evaluation of the Recent Tokyo Round Trade Agreement through a General Equilibrium Model of World Trade Involving Major Trading Areas. *Journal of Policy Modelling.*

Wilson, J. F., and W. E. Takacs. 1979. Differential Responses to Price and Exchange Rate Influences in the Foreign Trade of Selected Industrial Countries. *Review of Economics and Statistics* 61:267–279.

Zellner, A. 1962. An Efficient Method of Estimating Seemingly Unrelated Regressions and Tests for Aggregation Bias. *Journal of the American Statistical Association* 57:348–368.

———1963. Estimates for Seemingly Unrelated Regression Equations: Some Exact Finite Sample Results. *Journal of the American Statistical Association* 58:977–992.

# Index

D1366626